Y0-BTD-986

Case Studies in Library Computer Systems

Bowker Series in
PROBLEM-CENTERED APPROACHES TO LIBRARIANSHIP
Thomas J. Galvin, Series Editor

CASE STUDIES IN LIBRARY COMPUTER SYSTEMS

. . . .

by Richard Phillips Palmer

R.R. BOWKER COMPANY
New York & London 1973
A Xerox Education Company

Library of Congress Cataloging in Publication Data
Palmer, Richard P
  Case studies in library computer systems.
  (Bowker series in problem-centered approaches to
librarianship)
  Includes bibliographical references.
  1. Electronic data processing—Library Science—
Case studies. I. Title.
Z678.9.P34   025'.02'02854   73-17008
ISBN 0-8352-0642-4

Published by R.R. Bowker Co. (A Xerox Education Company)
1180 Avenue of the Americas, New York, N.Y. 10036
Copyright © 1973 by Xerox Corporation.
Printed and bound in the United States of America.

Contents

Foreword

Richard P. Palmer's *Case Studies in Library Computer Systems* marks a new departure in Bowker's "Problem-Centered Approaches to Librarianship" series, as well as a novel application of the case study method to the critical examination of contemporary issues in library practice. Earlier volumes in this series have emphasized the fictionalized problem case study form, for the most part leaving to the reader the analysis and resolution of the questions under consideration. While a similar collection of problem case studies would doubtless be valuable to those preparing for library careers in a world where all must come to terms with the impact and potential of the computer in the organization, storage, and retrieval of information, Dr. Palmer has, very wisely I think, concluded that a volume of descriptive case studies, each accompanied by a critical analysis and evaluation, can at this time, be even more useful to practicing librarians and students alike. Thus, he has chosen to report in detail here the salient characteristics of 20 operational systems that utilize computers in the areas of circulation control, serial records management, or acquisitions in a wide variety of types and sizes of libraries and information centers.

This volume is presented with confidence that it will be received, especially by practicing librarians, as a unique, valuable, and welcome addition to the literature of computer applications in libraries. That literature, while abundant, has heretofore left much to be desired from the standpoint of the practitioner. Much of it is fugitive in form or so heavily technical as to prove inaccessible to all but the most rabid hardware buffs among us. Even more limiting, it seems to me, is the predominance of descriptive reports, usually prepared by those responsible for the design of particular systems, in which optimistic preoperational predictions of improved performance coupled with reduced cost are not infrequently presented as though they were operational realities. Taken in the large, the literature of libraries and computers is rendered suspect by an absence of objective appraisal, combined with a marked tendency to describe the advent of the machine as either the true path to bibliographic glory or the high road to perdition, depending on the sometimes limited personal perspective and experience of the writer.

By contrast, Dr. Palmer's book is addressed primarily to library administrators, whose need for accurate, objective description and evaluation has largely remained unmet by previous studies. Recognizing that the interests of library managers are served neither by paeans of praise long on missionary zeal but short on hard performance data, nor by colorful denunciations of the computer, Dr. Palmer offers instead an informed state-of-the-art review. He brings to this assignment the viewpoint of an experienced librarian who recognizes that the true measure of system effectiveness is the quality of service rendered to a library's clientele. He effectively exploits the value of the descriptive case study, a vehicle of investigation and reporting that enables him to present operational systems in the context of their contribution to a total program of library service in a given setting. His study is objective, analytical, and comparative in character, and above all, its conclusions are entirely accessible to the nonspecialist reader.

Case Studies in Library Computer Systems is the fifth volume to appear in Bowker's "Problem-Centered Approaches to Librarianship" series, which is designed not only to make case materials in a wide range of subfields of librarianship available for instructional use, but also to demonstrate the value of the case study as a method for the presentation and analysis of professional problems. Future volumes in this series will continue to appear at regular intervals, and will focus on such areas as the development of academic library collections, library public relations, problems of censorship and intellectual freedom, the selection and utilization of the newer media in libraries, and public library service to children and youth. As series editor, it is my privilege to present Dr. Palmer's distinguished contribution to the literature of computer utilization in libraries.

THOMAS J. GALVIN
Series Editor

Preface

In 1971, following a study of library computer systems, Ellsworth Mason, director of library services at Hofstra University, wrote:

> My observations convinced me that the computer is not for library use; that all the promises offered in its name are completely fraudulent; that not only is it extremely expensive compared to other methods at this time, but that it will become increasingly expensive in the future; that it has been wrapped so completely in an aura of unreason that fine intelligences are completely uprooted when talking about it; that its use in a library weakens the library as a whole by draining off large sums of money for a small return; and that it should be stamped out.*

At the present time little factual analysis exists to prove Mr. Mason right or wrong. The purpose of this book is to describe and document a number of operational library computer systems, including their costs, so that librarians and library school students may better determine whether computers should be stamped out or whether they are appropriate for library use.

Case Studies in Library Computer Systems does not follow the mode of the other volumes in this series because none of the persons, libraries or systems is disguised. Neither has information been withheld to force readers to explore alternative choices, as in the usual case method. Rather, all systems are identified and described as accurately as possible. Descriptive case studies are problem-oriented, however, because they analyze a situation in which a librarian had to decide if a computer could be successfully utilized to solve the problem at hand. The descriptive case method rather than the problem case method was chosen because it seemed important to describe each system in detail and to evaluate its performance in the context of a real library environment and against the background of particular institutional service objectives and goals.

Most previous reports of computer systems have been written by those who have been personally involved in their design and development. As a result, some have not been entirely objective and dispassionate. The cases in this book have been compiled by the author and individuals under his supervision, all outside observers not associated with the libraries studied. Twenty batch and on-line systems are described—circulation, serials, and acquisitions, in

*Ellsworth Mason, "Along The Academic Way," *Library Journal*, 96:10 (May 15, 1971), 1675.

school, public, college, university, and special libraries—so that librarians may better understand the present state-of-the-art of library computer use.

Each of the studies discusses (1) the environment in which the system operates, (2) the objectives of the library and the system, (3) the computer equipment and programming used, (4) what the system does and how it operates, (5) the costs of the system's products, and (6) aspects that should be considered by librarians who are wondering whether a computer system would meet their specific requirements.

While technical details are presented in sections headed "The Computer" for those who need them, librarians who find technical matters intimidating or unhelpful may bypass these sections and still discover the essential characteristics of the systems. Thus these studies are intended to provide a bridge between librarians and the technology of computers. The cases are not intended to be detailed or technical enough for computer experts or system programmers. They should, however, prove useful to a wide range of librarians, administrators, and library school students and should give computer specialists a better feel for the present quality of library computer systems. They should also give some documented indication of the extent to which Mason's conclusion is or is not valid.

The techniques that librarians use for establishing the costs of library operations are far from standardized. Most librarians would prefer not to discuss costs; they are disinclined to determine or report unit costs of manual operations and even more reluctant to discuss costs of computer operations. Cost figures in this book are therefore less uniformly based than the author would like, but they are the best that could be established at this time. Even though the figures lack some precision, they are useful in suggesting ranges of costs. It should be helpful, for example, to know that computerized circulation systems, some batch and some on-line and offering an array of services and features, vary in unit cost from about $.22 to $.76 per loan. Some of these cost figures include overhead, fringe benefits, etc., and some do not. They should therefore not be compared directly. Hopefully, librarians will develop better documented and more standardized cost figures in the future.

Many of the systems reported have merely mechanized the manual operations they replaced. Some of the systems are not innovative. Some do not exploit the capabilities of the computer. Some are inadequate because of restraints imposed on them during their development. Some, on the other hand, are responding successfully to demands on libraries that had exceeded the capacities of manual systems. One previously operational system described in this volume has been terminated because of delays in reprogramming for a new computer, increased costs, and the inconvenience and disruption of having the system down for many months.

Much of the initial gathering of information was accomplished under my direction by graduate students in the School of Library Science at Simmons College. This process was supplemented by my own knowledge and study of the systems described, including, where appropriate, additional on-site visits. Final drafts of all the cases were submitted to the librarians in charge of the computer systems described for review and comments. Having prepared and edited all the case studies in their final form myself, I assume sole responsibility for any errors of fact or opinion. Appreciation is extended to all individuals—library directors and librarians, system designers, programmers and technical personnel, as well as system operators and library science students—who have provided information and assistance.

RICHARD P. PALMER
Assistant Professor of
Library Science
Simmons College

Introduction

Twenty-eight years ago Vannevar Bush imagined totally automated libraries, equipped for computerized information retrieval, where users could make instantaneous searches of collections. Writing in the *Atlantic Monthly*, he described a machine of the future, which he called a "memex," capable of storing the contents of books, records, and communications on microfilm that could be consulted with great speed and flexibility. The machine would be about the size of a desk and have a display screen and keyboard. By pushing code buttons for a particular work, the text could be made to appear on the screen. Subject access to all stored documents would be provided by "trails," previously mapped out by the user, that would connect various papers according to their subjects.[1]

Not only are scientists and librarians far from achieving this level of electronic sophistication; they are still laboring to computerize even the purely repetitive aspects of library operations. While some citation retrieval systems are now operational, the retrieval of full text will probably be the last library application of computers that will be operationally successful.

The problem is partly that computers cannot fathom the complexities of languages, recognize ideas found in multiterm concepts, translate metaphoric speech, or cope with contextual alterations of the meanings of words. The problem is also that the quantity of textual material that would have to be controlled by librarians exceeds economically viable electronic storage capacities. Ideally, all data pertinent to a particular library operation should be contained in the memory of the computer itself. Usually, however, for economic reasons, external devices, such as magnetic tapes, must be used. While one reel of tape can store 10^7 (10,000,000) bits of information, it may take as much as five minutes to scan a tape for a specific item. It is estimated that storage of the Library of Congress *National Union Catalog* on tape would require 100,000 reels.[2] Obviously, sequential access to such a store of tapes, requiring human intervention to load the tapes on readers, would be cumbersome and complex.

Overcoming the difficulties presented by the limitations of computers is not simple. Programming and planning must be done with great precision and detail. Minor inaccuracies in computer programs or input may seriously disrupt the operation of the entire system. Programming is slow and expensive. Only careful planning and efficient programming hold down computer system costs sufficiently to permit the use of computers in libraries.

Although the electronic libraries that Vannevar Bush predicted have not yet been realized, advances in computer technology have made possible the application of computers to a large portion of the more mundane aspects of librarianship. This was of especial importance to academic librarians during the 1960s when they faced rapidly expanding student bodies and increasing numbers of faculty with a greater variety of teaching and research interests. As college and university libraries grew, their operating costs increased exponentially. In the last 15 years the cost of library services per student has doubled, but the productivity of the individual library staff member has not significantly increased.[3]

In response to the increased demands being made upon them, librarians have in recent years placed great emphasis on scientific management of libraries and a total systems approach to computerization efforts. While the total systems concept is essentially sound, attempts to computerize all library operations in a single effort often proved to be inordinately expensive and resulted in the aborting of some attempts at computer utilization.

During the late sixties, in spite of the heady promise of MARC (a communications format for the transmission of machine-readable catalog data developed at the Library of Congress), librarians began to realize the extent of the difficulties and expense involved in bibliographic control and manipulation via the computer. At the same time, larger libraries were finding that problems of scale were forcing them to attempt to use the computer to control the flood of materials they were acquiring, processing, and circulating.

Librarians have long known that libraries must be organized to permit the rapid extraction of constantly changing information. This can be achieved by having a librarian who knows every source of information in the library, a feat no longer possible in larger libraries, or by having an automated system that can free the librarian from the tedious tasks of file maintenance so that more individual service may be given to users. Frederick Kilgour, director of the Ohio College Library Center, writes:

> With the increasing growth of a college community and college library, the library becomes a monolithic arrangement of volumes and catalogs that attempts to be all things for all users, but which disregards each user as an individual having his own personal interests. Sophisticated computerization of college libraries holds out the hope of humanizing these libraries before the end of the century. At the same time, library tasks will be increasingly humanized for the staff by relieving staff of machine-like activities.[4]

Most librarians today are in a pragmatic mood about both libraries and computers. They are more skeptical about the utility or appropriateness of computers for library operations. They are more cost-conscious. They are aware that while computers have some substantial capabilities, they also have some very real limitations. They know that even though the third-generation computers being produced today are better adapted to meeting library requirements than were first and second generation ones, no computers are as well suited to handling bibliographic data as they are to dealing with fiscal data and mathematical computations.

Allen Veaner, Assistant Director for Bibliographic Services, Stanford University, has suggested three major reasons a library might consider undertaking an automated project: (1) to manage a process less expensively, more rapidly, or more accurately; (2) to do something that cannot be done manually any longer without risking breakdown of the system because of increasing volume of material, and (3) to perform a function not possible without machines—a new service to users.[5] Because demands on libraries are increasing, some of these criteria are being met more frequently and are thus increasing the likelihood that the installation of computers will prove viable and beneficial. For example, machine time is becoming cheaper and human time, more expensive. Access to more powerful computers is possible by recently developed time-sharing techniques. Also, minicomputers, fully programmed, are now available. And finally, computers do not get tired. Some are available 24 hours a day.

Unfortunately, progress in the use of computers as tools in librarianship has been hampered by the reluctance of librarians to undertake the necessary planning. Usually lacking technical training, librarians often feel ill-prepared to cope with the mechanical aspects of computer systems. Some librarians are afraid to use computers. For these and other reasons, nonlibrarians have entered the field and have adopted such terms as "computer science" and "information science" to describe their work. Since they are technologically oriented, they are seldom interested in the duties that librarians have traditionally performed, such as the preservation and provision of knowledge or the storage and retrieval of information. Librarians, in turn, may either see information scientists as "gadget happy and money-hungry opportunists with questionable academic origins . . . [using] the mystic terminology of the new information technology,"[6] or hate them because they make librarians feel inferior.

But the animosity is hardly one-sided. Documentalists believe librarians are conservative and unimaginative and see them as "filing clerks engaged in an elaborate masquerade."[7] They avoid applying the term "librarian" to themselves, fearful that this indicates a lesser status.

Oddly enough, much of the controversy is a result of *both* sides believing that the computer could solve all the library's problems and thus expose the librarian as useless and incompetent. This, of course, has not happened and will not. Machines are not going to replace librarians. However, computers can help librarians. As a matter of fact, a very substantial number of computers are serving librarians at the present time. The Library Automation, Research and Consulting Association (LARC) published a survey of automated systems in U.S. libraries in 1971. In the 506 reporting libraries, almost 1,400 computer applications were operational, and well over half of these computer systems were involved with the library housekeeping functions of acquisitions, cataloging, circulation, and serials handling.[8] Interestingly, only seven of the 20 case studies included in this volume were reported in the LARC survey, which makes it seem reasonable to assume that there are many more library computer systems in the United States than the LARC survey indicates. Whatever their actual number may be, computers are being utilized in a significant number of libraries. This book provides some documented evidence of the extent to which library computer systems are proving successful.

NOTES

1. Vannevar Bush, "As We May Think," *Atlantic Monthly*, 176 (July 1945), 101–108.

2. Herbert Coblans, *Use of Mechanized Methods in Documentation Work* (London: Aslib, 1966), p. 39.

3. Frederick G. Kilgour, "The Economic Goal of Library Automation," *College and Research Libraries*, 30 (July 1969), 307.

4. _____, "Computerization: The Advent of Humanization in the College Library," *Library Trends*, 18 (July 1969), 36.

5. Allen B. Veaner, "Major Decision Points in Library Automation," *College and Research Libraries*, 31 (September 1970), 303–304.

6. Alan M. Rees, "New Bottles for Old Wine: Retrieval and Librarianship," *Wilson Library Bulletin*, 38 (May 1964), 773.

7. Ibid.

8. Frank S. Patrinostro, *A Survey of Automated Activities in the Libraries of the United States*, vol. 1, (Tempe, Arizona: LARC Association, 1971), pp. 2–5.

Computerized Library Circulation Systems

Most libraries continue to use manual circulation systems because their collections are of moderate size, enjoy a comfortable level of circulation activity, and have a relatively low level of use per item. Usually, only libraries with very large collections or high levels of circulation activity or rapid rates of use per item are likely to use computerized circulation systems. Of the 506 libraries responding to the 1971 Library Automation, Research and Consulting Association (LARC) survey of automated activities of U.S. libraries, 197 reported automated circulation applications as follows: 158 were general batch-processing circulation systems; 16 dealt with control of overdues; 8 were on-line circulation systems; the remaining 15 dealt with such aspects of circulation as registration, statistics, reserve books, faculty charges.[1]

The library profession as yet lacks conclusive data on the relative effectiveness of manual versus computer circulation systems in different types of libraries at various levels of activity. Such figures as 100,000 annual circulations or 1,000 daily circulations have been advanced as the levels at which manual circulation systems begin to break down.[2] While the critical level may be different for different libraries, it is generally agreed that stresses, errors, and confusion increase as the volume of activity rises, that costs escalate sharply, and that there is a point beyond which manual systems will not operate successfully.

Although there are a great variety of manual circulation systems, most are single-file systems. While a single file may prove adequate for some libraries, it does not offer opportunities for easy manipulation of data to provide insights into collection use, clues as to optimal loan periods, or rapid accumula-

1

tion of statistics for operations analysis; nor, of course, does it provide instant access to information for locating every item held by the library.

In large library systems librarians and patrons frequently want to know whether an item is where it is usually stored in the collection and if not, where it is. Arguments for computer circulation systems, either batch or on-line, will often stress that such systems not only can provide automatic control of charging and discharging operations, but can also produce the "availability" status of every library item. Computerized library circulation systems have in fact been developed that will provide some or all of the following features, depending on their degree of sophistication:

1. An up-to-the-minute record of the location of all types of library material in circulation.
2. A record of the location of all materials that are not in their usual storage sites in the library, e.g.: in a reserve collection; on long-term loan to a faculty member; on interlibrary loan; at the bindery; being recataloged or reclassified in the technical services department; in closed stacks; in compact shelving or other special location; in carrels; at branch libraries; awaiting reshelving; being photocopied; being used for some special display; missing; being searched; lost forever.
3. Automatic processing of call-ins, renewals, reserves, overdues, calculation of fines, preparation of fine notices, notifications of missing items.
4. Multiple copies of printouts of the circulation record by call number, due date, borrower, or other data elements.
5. Procedures for circulating not-yet-cataloged materials.
6. Provisions for serving various types of regular patrons who enjoy various borrowing, use, loan-period privileges, and for dealing with special users and uses.
7. Programs that readily and economically compile an array of statistics and summaries to aid efficient library management, including analyzing the pattern of circulation activity.
8. Programs that present circulation records in formats to allow easy analysis for further acquisitions, duplications, or weeding of library collections.

Computerized circulation systems can readily compile records of library use so that a computer file could be easily searched for the reading activity of a patron. Not much attention has yet been paid to the development of safeguards against the invasion of patron privacy or to the prevention of the development of dossiers on patrons. Recent developments on the national scene suggest that such a possibility is not as remote as librarians might like to believe. The possibility is rare, however, and should not forestall the development of computerized circulation systems when and where they are needed. Such systems can provide the librarian with much nonsensitive data that will be extremely useful (1) in shaping acquisitions policies (i.e. duplicate or multiple copies can be ordered on the basis of book utilization by patrons, rather than on the basis of the librarian's intuition); (2) in developing intelligent weeding practices; (3) in reducing personnel needs by effectively assigning staff to circulation activities; (4) in establishing variable loan periods to deal with different levels of pressure on the library's holdings.[3]

That computer systems can collect and arrange various arrays of circulation data is not, however, sufficient argument for collecting and printing out such data in various reports. Every library circulation system, whether manual or computer, should be carefully analyzed to determine whether or not it precisely matches the library's information needs. While some adventurers may wish to climb mountains simply because they are there, librarians are well advised not to have computers collect data simply because computers can. Every additional feature offered by any system costs something. If desirable cost-effectiveness and cost-benefit ratios are to be achieved, then only data for which there is demonstrated need should be gathered and only reports for which there is valid use should be prepared. These apparently obvious truisms have been all too often ignored when computer systems were being designed and programmed. On the other hand, since computer systems usually provide increased accuracy and speed in processing, they are likely to improve the library's image and build good public relations. Since staff costs continue to rise and computer systems are able to handle higher volumes of circulation activity without increase in personnel, computerized circulation operations should help to hold the line against escalating personnel costs and at the same time increase system efficiency.

Some librarians have found computer systems to be essential, regardless of cost, because manual systems were inadequate to handle their library's volume and rate of circulation activity. Such was the case at Harvard University (see chapter 3) and at the University of British Columbia (see chapter 4). A few librarians have found that with a manual system they did not have sufficient space to meet increasing demands. This was true at the University of Michigan (see chapter 2). A number of library administrators have chosen to utilize a computer system because they believed that for a viable additional expense they could provide significantly better service. Such decisions were made at Eastern Illinois University (see chapter 5) and Northwestern University (see chapter 6). Librarians have occasionally chosen to use the computer simply because it was available. This was the case at Brockton (Massachusetts) High School (see chapter 1).

Since manual systems and computer systems provide substantially different levels of control and data, comparisons on the basis of cost-effectiveness or cost-benefit are very difficult to make. However, the continuing rise in the scale of library activities argues for more sophisticated information systems and more rapid provision of reports and summaries. An alternative that might be considered when library circulation systems approach the scale where manual systems tend to break down is to separate the library's holdings into several small collections, each with its own circulation system. Large libraries that may be exceeding optimum size for effective management or use might find this alternative reasonably satisfactory and more economical than a computer system. The possibility of breaking up massive collections into autonomous units would be worth investigation.[4]

Although Ellsworth Mason may be convinced that "the computer is not for library use ... and should be stamped out,"[5] there is substantial empirical evidence that computers are being used and will continue to be used in libraries. The situations of library organization and computer technology are in some degree of flux, however, and accurate predictions concerning the future use of computer circulation systems are difficult to make. It cannot be denied, though, that computers provide speed, accuracy, and convenience, and that they can keep track of elements involved in circulation control faster and more accurately than humans can. In addition, new computer circulation systems employing light pens for input of book and borrower information will eliminate the problems and cost of converting library records into machine-readable form.

It also appears likely that libraries will increase their utilization of computer circulation systems as manufacturers provide systems that are ready for instant use. As more librarians accept more standardization of basic elements of circulation systems and as developmental and programming costs are reduced or eliminated, costs of machine systems will come down. As this occurs, it seems reasonable to predict that computer systems will win greater acceptance in libraries and that the trend of the future is toward more widespread use of computers in library circulation systems.

NOTES

1. Frank S. Patrinostro, *A Survey of Automated Activities in the Libraries of the United States,* vol. 1 (Tempe, Arizona: LARC Association, 1971), p. 4.

2. Cecily J. Surace, "Library Circulation Systems: An Overview," *Special Libraries,* 63:4 (April 1972), 180.

3. For examples of useful insights gained from computer systems, see Michael K. Buckland,

"An Operations Research Study of a Variable Loan and Duplication Policy at the University of Lancaster," *Library Quarterly*, 42:1 (January 1972), 97–106, and Peter Simmons, *Collection Development and the Computer* (Vancouver: University of British Columbia, 1971).

4. Useful insights into the problems and potential trade-offs of decentralization of massive collections into autonomous units are provided by Philip M. Morse in "Measures of Library Effectiveness," *Library Quarterly*, 42:1 (January 1972), 15–30.

5. Ellsworth Mason, "Along The Academic Way," *Library Journal*, 96:10 (May 15, 1971), 1675.

1.
Brockton High School
Automated Circulation System

· ·

ENVIRONMENT

Brockton High School, Brockton, Massachusetts, has 350 teachers and an enrollment of about 5,300 students in grades 9–12. The school moved to a modern campus of four interconnected school "houses" in September 1970. Its own data-processing department employs two full-time programmers.

The library is staffed by the Department of Instructional Resources. In addition to the head librarian, the staff consists of six librarians, two media specialists, two audiovisual technicians, one cataloging secretary, and five teacher aides. The library is divided into four Instructional Resource Centers (IRCs) and a small core collection. For identification purposes, the IRCs are coded by color corresponding to the color code of the school "house": green, red, azure, and yellow. Some, but not all, titles are represented in more than one IRC. As an example of the distribution of resources, the bulk of the literature collection is shared between two IRCs, most of the social studies collection is located in two IRCs, the fine and applied arts collection is centralized in a single IRC, and the sports and physical education collection is shelved in one IRC. Each IRC is equipped with a union card catalog. As of March 1972, the total collection numbered 22,000 volumes.

The library circulates an average of 90 books per day for a standard loan period of two weeks. The total circulation for the 180-day school year is 16,200.

OBJECTIVES

In 1969 the library collection in the old building, as well as the plans for the new building, were evaluated and three major objectives were established: (1) the bulk of the collection, which had become out-dated, should be replaced; (2) the classification of the library's materials should be changed to the Library of Congress scheme; (3) the circulation system should be automated. Information concerning the decision to computerize the circulation system was not available.

THE COMPUTER

Along with a number of grade and high schools in the area Brockton High School uses, on a batch-mode basis, a Univac 9300 computer with 32,768 byte memory capacity that is located at South Easton Regional Technical and Vocational High School. The circulation system uses a 132-position printer, a 600-card/minute reader, and four tape drives. The programming language used is COBOL. The computer is used to handle administrative school functions, such as budgets, student grades, and student attendance, as well as the Brockton High School library's circulation system.

THE SYSTEM

After an indeterminable amount of study the library chose the Standard Register Source Record Punch (SRP), Model 1730 as the information encoder for the automated circulation system. This SRP is "a data collection machine which records data in both man-readable language (printed) and machine-readable code (punched). In one machine cycle, information from up to four sources is punched and interpreted (numeric only) on a special two-part card form which Standard Register markets under the trade name of ZIPCARD."[1]

The borrower's card, or badge—which doubles as the library card and official school ID card—is prepared under the direct supervision of the library staff using the Polaroid Land Identification System ID-2 and a separate manual card punch. The ID-2-system package consists of a Polaroid camera, a timer, a picture cutter, and a laminator. The card carries the student's picture, name, ID number, and date of graduation, and a five-digit ID number is punched on the card by the card punch. The student is issued his first card free; replacement cost to the student is $1.00. Time is allotted daily for re-photographing students who require replacement cards.

Each book on the library shelf carries a red book card to completely and uniquely identify it. An exact duplicate of this card is kept in the master file of all books for all IRCs. The data on the cards, which is encoded in human- and machine-readable form, includes the book title (up to 20 characters), book identification number, author code, title code, year of publication, volume number, month and day of acquisition, accession number, and author's name (up to 20 characters, surname first).

The SRP is set each day with the date due, the IRC, and the present date. An alternate due date for a short-loan reserve book or a special faculty loan may be manually punched into the SRP on its keyboard.

The two-part Zipcard charge card (one white, the other green) receives the record of the transaction. The two cards have a slip of carbon paper between them so that human-readable data are transferred to the green cards as data are typed onto the white card. The SRP records on the Zipcard include the date due, IRC, present date, borrower's ID number, and book identification number.

To check out a book, the student presents his ID badge and the book at the circulation desk. The attendant removes the book card from the book and inserts the book card, the ID badge, and the Zipcard set into the appropriate slots in the side of the SRP and depresses a button. The machine then produces the Zipcard record as described above.

The Zipcard set is separated, and the white charge card is kept by the librarian in a file at the desk. The master book card and the green date-due/discharge card are placed in the card pocket in the book, and the book and the student's ID badge are given to the student.

When the book is returned, the librarian simply removes the green discharge card, puts it in a file at the circulation desk, and places the book on a truck for reshelving.

Since the student carries the master book card and the green discharge card in the book throughout the book's circulation period, some lost or damaged cards are unavoidable. Should either card be lost, a slip of paper with the pertinent information is filled out by the librarian and later punched onto cards by the data-processing students. The borrower is charged $.50 for replacing a book card, but is not charged for replacement of a discharge card.

Once a week the accumulated white charge cards and green discharge cards go to Data Processing in separate packets for cross matching to determine which books remain in current circulation. The number "1" is gang punched in column 80 of each of the green discharge cards on an IBM 514 reproducing punch. White cards and green cards are sorted simultaneously by accession numbers and then by student ID numbers on an IBM 84 sorter with a special command circuit board. Then the combined file is sorted by column 80 to separate white cards from green.

Next the green and white cards are matched by student ID number on the

IBM 85 collator. The matched sets of cards are removed from the active file and are returned to the IRC office. Unmatched white cards, representing books still in circulation, are separated from the matched sets by the collator and then sorted by due date. The Instructional Resources Department does not generate overdue notices until one week after the books are due, thus saving much paperwork, since a significant number of books are returned in this one-week period. Cards dated less than three weeks earlier are replaced in the file. Cards dated three or more weeks earlier, representing books a week or more overdue, are divided again. The first group is for books taken out six weeks or more earlier. All the rest are placed in a second group.

The first group is sorted by ID number and then by school house. These cards are used to generate the "long-overdue" list, and the IBM 403 printer prints out all the information on the card in ID-number sequence. At the same time, lists are made from the complete white charge card data base, arranged by book number and accession number, so that books can be traced by these indicators. Then ID numbers from the overdue lists are manually checked against a student list for the house and homeroom of the student and then against an accession list of the respective IRC for complete book title. Overdue notices are made up by hand and sent to students at their homeroom. The same procedure is followed for the second group of overdue cards.

COSTS

Costs of the computer system and Brockton's use of computer time are shown in Tables 1 and 2, respectively.

Table 1

COSTS OF THE COMPUTER SYSTEM HOUSED AT SOUTH EASTON REGIONAL TECHNICAL AND VOCATIONAL HIGH SCHOOL[2]

Equipment	Purchase	Monthly Rental	Monthly Service
Printer, 132-position	$ 30,965	$ 139	$202
Multiplexer input/output channel	3,380	79	5
Card reader, 600/min.	6,630	152	68
Tape system	53,130	1,215	355
Computer memory, 32,768 bytes	81,145	1,853	138
Total	$175,250	$4,008	$768
Total monthly rental and service	$4,776		
Total rental and service per hour	$27.10		

Table 2
COMPUTER TIME REQUIRED BY THE
BROCKTON HIGH SCHOOL CIRCULATION
SYSTEM[3]

Weekly Operation	Est. Minutes/Week
Cards to tape	
Set up	3.0
Run 450 cards at 600/min.	1.0
Sort weekly circulation records	1.0
Update circulation file	
Set up	2.0
Read, write, merge, rewind	1.6
Print 900 circulation records	
Set up	2.0
Print at 600 lines/min.	1.3
Overdue pick-off	
Set up	3.0
Run	1.0
Sort overdues by ID number	.5
Overdue file edit	.5
Address pick-up	1.0
Print list	.5
Print overdue notices	
Set up	2.0
Print notices	.5
Total minutes/wk.	20.9

The weekly computer cost is $3.48, calculated on the basis of a discounted price of $10 per hour charged Brockton High School. Since the system handles about 450 circulations per week, the cost per circulation is $.0077.

Labor for the various procedures, such as registration (making the badge), charging, and discharging, with a 25 percent allowance for unavoidable delays is 8.5 hours per 1,000 circulations. As Brockton has 16,200 circulations per year, the time involved is about 137 hours. If the labor cost were calculated at $2.50 per hour, about the rate for a library aide, it would amount to $342.50, or $.02 per circulation. However, a professional librarian does the charging and on the basis of the librarian's annual salary of $8,000 the cost is $685.50, or $.04 per circulation.

Identification badges are distributed to 5,300 students and 350 faculty members each year. At a unit cost of $.52 the badges cost $2,938 annually, or $.18 per circulation. The cost of the Zipcard charge sets and overdue notices is about $.01 per circulation. Thus the cost of the material required averages about $.19 per circulation.

To summarize: adding the costs per circulation of computer time, $.0077; of SRP service, $.04; of labor cost, $.04; and of material, $.19, gives a total of $.28 per circulation in circulation-related costs. This figure does not, of course, reflect the cost of the computer configuration housed at South Easton Regional Technical and Vocational High School.

OBSERVATIONS

Although Brockton High School library staff achieved its objective of establishing an automated circulation system, it advanced no reasons for this objective, and thus whether the needs, if any, that triggered the decision have been met cannot be determined.

As far as is known, the library staff has not fixed the cost of operating the school's previous manual circulation system for a collection of 22,000 volumes with an annual school-year circulation of 16,200 volumes. Thus no comparison can be made between the cost of $.28 per circulation for their computer system and their manual system. However, two manual circulation systems that handle larger volumes of circulation activity than Brockton does have lower per unit circulation costs than Brockton's. In 1963, one of the systems at the University of California at Los Angeles, expended $26,000 to circulate 350,000 books, or an average cost per book circulated of $.07.[4] Even allowing for a doubling of costs during the past decade, the estimated cost in 1973 for this far larger and more complex circulation operation would be only $.14, or half that of the Brockton system. The other manual circulation system, at Wayland (Massachusetts) Public Library, circulated 169,152 books in 1972 for $35,011, or an average cost per unit circulated of $.21.[5] This figure, again for a substantially larger facility than Brockton's, is 25 percent less than the cost of the Brockton system.

It should be noted that Brockton's automated circulation system provides only weekly reporting on the library's circulation activity. Only a minimal amount of information is contained in this report. Overdue notices are not generated automatically; a program to handle overdue notices is being written, but it is not yet operational. Certainly the present mixture of computer circulation control and manual handling of overdue notices is, at best, cumbersome. Also, while the Source Record Punch has the capability of dealing with book reserve requests, i.e., that a book in circulation be held at the desk for another patron, the Brockton library staff is not planning to use this feature.

Brockton's system affords no advantages that apparently could not be provided by a manual system at a lesser cost. It is not known whether or not this automated system was established simply to make use of the South Easton Regional Technical and Vocational High School computer facility. It is known that computer use is proving expensive for this library.

A useful rule-of-thumb for a decision to computerize a library house-keeping function is to automate only when there are library needs that a manual system can no longer meet.

NOTES

1. Standard Register Source Record Punch, Model 1730, Specifications and Advertising sheet.
2. Based on a telephone conversation with Robert Byrne, Sperry Rand Univac Division, Wellesley, Massachusetts, April 6, 1972.
3. Estimated from figures provided in the American Library Association's *Library Technology Reports, Circulation Systems, Standard Register Source Record Punch Model 1730*, March 1970, p. 15.
4. James Cox, "The Cost of Data Processing in University Libraries: In Circulation Activities," *College & Research Libraries*, November 1963, 492–495.
5. Based on a conference with Marcia Lowell, Director, Wayland (Massachusetts) Public Library, June 20, 1973.

ACKNOWLEDGMENTS

The assistance of Joseph W. Scott in the preparation of this case study is acknowledged with appreciation.

2.
University of Michigan Closed Reserve System
• • • • • • • • • • • • • • • • • •

ENVIRONMENT

The Undergraduate Library at the University of Michigan is one of the busiest libraries in the country. The university has an enrollment of over 37,000 students, of whom over 21,000 are undergraduates. During fall and winter terms the undergraduate reserve collection consists of about 25,000 books, periodicals, and other materials. About 1,000 items are circulated per day.

In May 1966 the decision was made to change the open-shelf reserve system, with its very serious control problem, to a closed, or behind-the-circulation-desk reserve system. At the same time, the staff of the Undergraduate Library recognized that a satisfactory level of service could not be provided with a manual circulation system. Systems analysis and feasibility studies were conducted during 1966, and planning for an automated closed reserve circulation system was undertaken that December. The planning and design of the system were done concurrently.

During the summer of 1967, keypunchers and library staff members prepared the initial closed reserve collection. In September 1967, when the testing of the automated system was completed, the automated closed, paged (serviced by library aides) reserve circulation system became operational.

The implementation of the system provided useful experience for planning the automation of both the Undergraduate and the Graduate Library circulation systems, which became operational in January 1969. In August 1969 the IBM 357 data collection terminals were replaced by the better and faster IBM 1030 terminals.

OBJECTIVES

Better service—fast, accurate, and troublefree control of a very actively used collection—was the major objective in the design of this automated closed reserve circulation system.

The limited counter space available for circulation control made a compact data collection system imperative. Since it was essential, from a public relations standpoint, to prevent substantial queuing, the system design had to permit rapid checkout of materials. Automatic generation of overdue notices and fines was also regarded as desirable. A system that would provide information on the "availability" of each item in the collection was considered, but was quickly rejected as too expensive. While an on-line, real-time system was known to be beyond the library's budgetary resources, a batch-process system of more modest dimensions was estimated to be within budgetary limits.

THE COMPUTER

The sophisticated resources of the University of Michigan's Computer Center are available to the library on a time-sharing basis. There is no need to detail the hardware configuration of this facility. The modest needs of the Undergraduate Library's closed reserve circulation system are easily handled on Computer Center equipment.

As noted, the data collection system utilizes an IBM 1030 system. There are four 1031 terminals: one is an A4, three are B4s. There are also a 1034 card punch (shared with regular circulation) and a 1032 digital time unit clock. Very few breakdowns have been experienced; when they occur, however, a backup 1034 card punch in the Undergraduate Library may be used or manual operations may be employed until repairs are made. The processing program is written in COBOL.

THE SYSTEM

When a book is to be placed on "closed reserve," the card for the book from the office file is matched to the actual book. (The library has a book card for every circulating book in the Undergraduate Library.) This card is then used either to pull the Reserve Circulation IBM card from the file or to keypunch one. The book card (flagged with a color-coded sticker—the color depending on the term) is stamped with the term and type of reserve, then filed in the office. The permanent IBM card is replaced by a reserve computer card that is placed in the book. The permanent IBM card is used to charge out the book to reserve, and the title appears on the daily circulation fiche that way.

When the work on a list of requested reserves is complete, the list is copied, i.e., information regarding call numbers and availability is transferred from the work copy to the "master list" used by the students requesting needed books. Information regarding number of copies and availability is transferred from the work copy to the "professor's copy," which is sent to the appropriate faculty member.

The Reserve Circulation IBM card (the blue card used to initiate a transaction at the terminal) contains the transaction number, material type, library abbreviation, call number, copy number, main entry, and title. As a book is circulated, its blue computer card and the borrower's ID card are put into one of the terminals and a charge transaction card is punched by the keypunch. The charge transaction card contains all the information on the book card as well as the student's or borrower's ID number, the charge code (which indicates the loan period), and the time. The borrower is given a time due slip stamped by a time clock when the book is charged. The time clocks are not connected to the IBM terminals in any way, although students and assistants are encouraged to think that they are.

When a book is returned and discharged, the borrower's ID badge is not necessary. However, it is important for the circulation clerk to enter the appropriate discharge code; otherwise, the transaction will not be completed and will appear on an error listing.

Each evening all cards punched by the keypunch are taken to the data processing department, where they are sorted by library area and each area's particular program is run (the Undergraduate Library reserve circulation department, the Undergraduate Library regular circulation department, and the General Library circulation department use the same machines). A lead or batch card is enclosed with the cards when they are sent to central processing. It contains the information (cut-off date and cut-off time) necessary for running the program on a particular evening. The following day the reserve desk receives a printout, including fine and overdue notices.

The computer does not deal in seconds; thus the same item cannot be discharged and charged out again until a full minute has gone by. Delay can be avoided, however, by using another copy of the desired material.

The printouts from central processing consist of statistics, unresolved records, process errors, and error listing.

Statistics include the daily "circulation load," which gives the number of charges and discharges each quarter hour, and the total charges and discharges. The hourly statistics are used in determining the level of activity at the closed reserve circulation desk and for help in solving problems. The "closed reserve statistics" are broken down to give the type of material used, the type of user (e.g., student, faculty, guest), and length of use (e.g., two-hour, four-hour, three-day). These statistics are then used to make weekly compilations. The transaction charges are stored on tape at the Data Systems Center and used to compute circulation statistics.

The "unresolved records" is a list of all books in circulation as of the cut-off time (4 P.M.) the day before. It lists all charges as yet not properly matched with discharge. This printout must be carefully checked each day to determine whether the entries on the list deemed overdue are really overdue or whether some mistake has been made. The list is in call number and copy number order, with Undergraduate Library books first, followed by borrowed books, periodicals, private copies, and uncataloged material.

"Process errors" is a listing of two types of errors made in the actual charging and discharging. These transactions are unmatched and are therefore "kicked out" and placed on the error sheet. The first type is a discharge for a particular item with no previous matching charge. This may happen because a deletion (keypunched manually) was in error, the book was discharged twice, or a charge was dropped by the machine. The other type is a charge followed by other charges with no intervening discharge. This may happen because of a mispunched deletion, a dropped discharge, or a book not being discharged before being charged out again. This list provides a gauge to how smoothly the facility is operating, but it is not very useful in clearing up the unresolved records.

The "error listing" contains the transaction cards the program could not deal with. Those that are discharges may be useful in resolving certain entries in the unresolved records. The most common listing here is "Badge and Manual ID Both Zero," which indicates that while the appropriate column shows a charge, there is no ID number. This usually means that a discharge was made without using a discharge code in the appropriate column. Other errors include invalid time, blank columns, or an invalid symbol in a particular column.

Overdue notices and fine notices are automatically generated from the unresolved records printout. These are carefully checked against the process error and the error listing printouts and evaluated for possible extenuating time factors before being sent out. An example of an extenuating time factor is a four-hour book charged out at 8 P.M., returned at midnight as the desk was closing, and not discharged until 8 A.M. the following day. An overdue notice will not of course be sent in such cases. On average, over 2,300 overdue notices and over 1,200 fine notices are sent monthly.

As indicated earlier, every copy placed on reserve appears on the daily circulation microfiche as charged out to the reserve desk. At the end of each term, before any material is taken off reserve, a tape is made of all items on reserve. This tape is compared to a daily tape of all reserve circulation charges that is compiled by and kept at the Data Systems Center. The result of this comparison is a list of every call number on reserve, including the total number of copies available, the total number of circulations, and the average number of circulations per copy. This analysis of circulation activity is compared to the course reserve lists to provide circulation statistics for each course. These course statistics are used in ordering materials for future terms and in developing policies and procedures of the reserve office. These course statistics are also provided to the faculty to assist them in assessing the effectiveness of their teaching methods, the utilization of reserve materials, and the advisability of revising their reading lists.

COSTS

While specific costs for planning are not available, it is known that one systems analyst and two librarians worked together, intermittently, over a period of ten months, on planning for the Undergraduate Library closed reserve system. Programmers were involved at the time of testing and implementation, but no record was kept of their hours or cost.

Initial cost of converting the book cards for the reserve collection, excluding the rental cost of the keypunch, was $1,082 and includes purchase, keypunching, verification, editing and duplication of 37,000 plasticized book cards. The keypunching was completed in 182 hours; the verification in 92 hours.

On the basis of an average of 7,000 circulations per week, a total weekly operating cost of $1,488 (see Table 1), and an estimated cost of one cent per circulation for supplies, the cost per circulation is about $.22.

Table 1
TOTAL OPERATING COSTS—BASED ON A 107-HOUR WEEK

Salaries (Professional, nonprofessional, and hourly assistants)	$ 910
Equipment rental	158
Data processing (2.8 hours @ $150/hour)	420
Total	$1,488

OBSERVATIONS

The University of Michigan Undergraduate Library automated closed reserve system has achieved its major objectives: it is providing fast, accurate, and reasonably troublefree control of a high level of circulation activity.

This compact automated batch-processing system provides a chargeout procedure that takes only a few seconds, automatic generation of overdue and fine notices, and useful statistics on circulation activity. It operates at sufficient speed to prevent excessive queuing, achieves sufficient accuracy to preclude problems with patrons about the legitimacy of overdue notices or fines, and has reduced personnel needs to a number that can work comfortably within the very modest space available for the closed reserve operation.

Automatic generation of overdue notices and fine notices has produced a significantly larger number of such notices than were sent in the manual open reserve system. Not known is whether this indicates (*a*) that many notices that should have been sent were not sent in the manual system or (*b*) that students are less willing or less able to complete their use of library materials within circulation loan periods. What is known is that overdue notices that average over 2,300 per month and fine notices that average over 1,200 per month suggest a need for thoughtful systems analysis.

While some documentation regarding system development is missing, procedures for system operation are set out clearly in staff manuals. Errors and problems are anticipated and suggestions for dealing with them are provided.

The volume of manual work involved in checking unresolved records appears excessive. The likelihood of a discharge not being coded as a discharge and being therefore listed as a charge is great enough to recommend that some changes be made in the charge and discharge codes. Such changes should reduce the quantity of errors requiring manual intervention.

Since an acceptable level of service could not have been provided by a manual system, and since the automated system has met with a very high level of patron acceptance and satisfaction, the somewhat higher costs for the automated system seem justified, particularly since the library's paramount objective was to provide better service. In addition, the automated system permits analysis of the use of reserve materials and provides helpful insights for both library staff and faculty. This analysis of reserve circulation is a very important by-product of this excellent automated reserve circulation system.

ACKNOWLEDGMENTS

This case study is based on data collected by the author at the University of Michigan Undergraduate Library and on unpublished notes, manuals, a questionnaire, and miscellaneous papers provided by the head of the library, Rose-Grace Faucher. Ms. Faucher's helpful cooperation and that of Dr. Frederick Wagman, director of libraries, University of Michigan, and the assistance of Kay Weiner in the preparation of this case study are acknowledged with appreciation.

3.
Widener Library, Harvard Automated Circulation System

· ·

ENVIRONMENT

The Widener Library is the central and largest unit of the Harvard University library system. The size of the Widener collection is 2,652,100 volumes. Each year the library adds about 50,000 volumes to its collection. The clientele of approximately 30,000 students, faculty, library staff, and special borrowers charges out between 900 and 1,000 titles every day.

Prior to July 1963 the circulation system had consisted of a single manual file of edge-notched cards, filled out by individual borrowers and arranged in call number order. As the library's holdings and circulation figures increased, it became increasingly obvious that this single-file system could not provide the needed degree of accuracy and control. Too many operations had to be conducted at this one file, which resulted in long delays and inaccurate records.

In the spring of 1962, Foster M. Palmer, then associate librarian for reference and circulation, began planning and designing a double-file IBM punched card circulation system, and the system became operational July 22, 1963. This double-file system consisted of an information file, arranged in call number order, and a transaction file—used for discharging returned books and identifying overdue books—arranged by type of loan, then by date due, and finally by transaction number.

Utilizing IBM Data Processing equipment, records were made for each loan on two 80-column IBM punched cards, i.e., a transaction card and an information card. Two-part carbon forms were used for the first six months, but from January 1964 the information card was a machine copy of the trans-action card. The data processing equipment kept the files up-to-date by matching cards for returned books and by merging cards for books charged out into the desired files.

The two-file system was utilized in the Widener Library until 1968, when it became evident that the data processing equipment utilized in the double-file system could no longer keep up with the increasing circulation load. The deci-sion was made then to replace the information file with a computer printout.

OBJECTIVES

The library staff decided to develop a computerized circulation system in the interest of achieving more accurate circulation records and improved service. The staff also decided to improve the library's general operations and services by creating a Data Processing and Photographic Services Depart-ment, with its own staff, budget, and equipment. At that time, the computer center's IBM 1401 had been installed in the library and used in the library's shelflist conversion project and in a computer-based acquisitions system. Fi-nally, the staff concluded that substantially better control could be provided with a printout of circulating books, produced each night in a batch-processing mode and brought to the circulation desk the next morning where it could be consulted for information.

Thus, the primary objective of the library in developing an automated cir-culation system was to attain a more satisfactory level of control and service at a minimum expenditure of time and funds.

THE COMPUTER

The automated circulation system initially operated on an IBM 1401 sys-tem with an 8,000-byte memory and included four IBM 729-IV tape drives, one 1403-Model 2 printer, and one 1402 card-reader punch.

In August 1970 the 1401 was removed from the library and the library transferred its operations onto an IBM 360/30, with a 64,000-byte memory that was located in the university comptroller's office. Although the 360/30 accepts Autocoder programs written for the 1401, it would operate more effi-ciently with programs written for it.

The original programs for the automated circulation system were written and debugged by Mr. Palmer in about three months. The programs were written in Autocoder language and are on IBM cards, with the exception of the third and fourth which are recorded on magnetic tape. The first four of the following programs are used daily:

1. *Pretape Program.* Reads the information supplied by the punched transaction cards and records it on magnetic tape.
2. *Sort Program.* Sorts this tape into call number order.
3. *Tape Update Program.* Updates the master circulation file with the new information.
4. *Print Program.* Instructs the computer to print the new master file.
5. *Fines Program.* Computes fines for students. It is run to coincide with the time of issuance of term bills, to which fines are added.
6. *Officers List Program.* Produces overdue notices to faculty and staff. They are not fined. The program used to be run twice a year; now it is run once a year since the loan period was extended to one year.
7. *CUMUL Program.* Merges the cancelled transaction tapes. It is run once every ten days to two weeks. It is used to keep a historical record of books used.
8. *Bindery Program.* Prints out the call numbers of books sent to the bindery. It is run at the Binding Division's request, about two or three times a year.

The 360/30 system, which has now been moved to the Computer Center, includes an IBM 2540 card reader, four IBM 2401-Model 2 tape drives, and an IBM 1403-N1 printer that operates at a speed of 1,100 lines/minute.

While at this writing Widener's circulation system is operating on the 360/ 30, the university is planning to transfer the system onto the 370/145-370/155 computer in July 1973. All of the university's computer operations will be performed in batch-processing mode on the 370.

An emulator on the 360 computer enables it to process the 1401 Autocoder programs. However, these programs have been rewritten in PL/1 language, and are now being tested. The first four Autocoder programs described above have been combined into one. All the programs will be on disk.

The Data Processing Department presently utilizes the following data processing equipment: two 029 printing card keypunches; one 083 sorter; one 087 collator.

THE SYSTEM

The IBM 80-column cards, which are used in charging books for outside use as well as the charging procedures, have not been altered despite the various changes in computer equipment. Since Widener Library has its own classification scheme, special fields are listed on the charge card to accommodate Widener's unique call numbers. Each charge card, with the exception of bindery charges, has its own arbitrarily assigned seven-digit transaction number, which is prepunched on the card and end-printed in advance.

Building-use charge cards, which are used for holding books in stack stalls or professor's studies, consist of two 80-column cards. They are prepunched and prenumbered with transaction numbers in a 9,000,000 series. The right half of the two-card set is stamped by the attendant and placed in the book; the left half is keypunched in essentially the same way as the outside-use charge cards. A separate transaction file is maintained for building-use charges.

The following listing presents an outline of the punching fields for outside-use and reserve cards:

Columns	Data
1	X punch identifies a card replacing an original spoiled in key-punching.
2–16	Not used.
17–20	Date returned (in serial date code: each day is numbered consecutively beginning with 0001 for January 1, 1963).
21–26	Not used.
27–31	Date book can be recalled, which is ten days from date of loan (month, day, last digit of year).
32	X punch indicates completed transaction.
33–37	Call number, first element.
38–42	Call number, second element.
43–46	Call number, third element.
47–50	Call number, fourth element.
51	Series.
52–54	Volume.
55	Letter "X" indicates that punching fields were inadequate for complete rendering of call number, series, volume, part, and copy. Other letter indicates copy. Number indicates part. "&" indicates that the volume immediately following the one indicated in previous column(s) is bound with it, i.e., "17&" means 17–18.
56	Borrower's status (also, "&" indicates building-use charge, "0" indicates nonpersonal loan).
57	Type of loan.
58	Prefix to borrower's number indicates list it belongs to.
59–63	Borrower number, or departmental library or other location code. On building-use cards, column 59 is not used, column 60

is the letter part, and columns 61–63 are the number part of
the stall or study designation.

64–65 Not used.

66–69 Due date (in serial date code; cf. columns 17–20).

70–72 Not used.

73   Used for the decade position of the year for bindery charges.

74–80 Transaction number (or, for bindery charges, the units position
of the year, the three-digit schedule number within the year,
and the three-digit item number within the schedule).

When a keypuncher makes a mistake in keypunching a card, a duplicate
card, prepunched with X punch in column 1, is punched. The transaction
number of the spoiled card is duplicated, and the original is filed in a special
error file by transaction number. When cancels are sorted on column 1, the
error cards are separated and the originals are then identified by transaction
number and pulled.

Bindery charges are punched on blank 80-column IBM cards from information supplied by the bindery preparation section. The schedule and item
numbers used by that section are keypunched in the columns normally used
for the transaction number. A separate bindery transaction file is maintained
in sequence by item number within schedule numbers.

For reserve books, loans to departmental libraries, and interlibrary loans,
outside-use charge cards are used. Separate transaction files are maintained
for reserves and interlibrary loans. A "cannot be located" transaction file is
also maintained for missing books. "Being held" cards are made when books
for which another borrower is waiting are returned; the transaction cards for
these are inserted in the books waiting to be claimed.

At various intervals the university issues ID cards—embossed with name,
number, and status—to students, faculty members, and special borrowers.
For each volume intended for outside use, the borrower fills out an outside-
use charge card, stacks of which are located in trays at several locations in the
library. The borrower records on the card the book's call number, author,
title, and volume. He signs the card and records his address and status code.
The circulation attendant verifies the call number and places the borrower's
ID card and the charge card on an imprinting machine that records the ID
card's embossed information on the charge card. The attendant stamps the
slip on the back of the book (Widener books have no book pockets or book
cards) with the due date and manually records the transaction card number
under that date. The transaction cards are placed in a prefiling box with cells
for three different types of loan—ten days, one month, or one year—the loan
period is determined by the status of the borrower. A supervisor checks the

cards for incorrectly filled out call numbers and prefiling errors. All cards for a given due date are made into a batch and sent down to the Data Processing Department to be keypunched.

Returned books are placed on a conveyor belt that carries them into the book-return room. Corresponding transaction cards, which are filed by transaction number within a due date, are pulled out of the transaction file and placed in each book. A supervisor checks the call number on each card against the call number of the book to catch possible errors from either incorrectly written transaction numbers or cards wrongly pulled from the file. The cards for returned books are then sent down to the Data Processing Department. Overdue books are easily identified, as the transaction file is arranged by due date.

The charge cards are taken from the circulation area to the Data Processing Department in batches identified by due date. There they are keypunched on 029 keypunches, at a rate of 400–500 cards/hour, together with the bindery, reserve, "cannot be located," and "being held" cards. During the evening, the cards are taken to the computer where each night the master file is printed out and the cancels are removed to another tape. The cards are fed into the computer at the rate of 900/minute. When the cards are returned to the Data Processing Department the 083 sorter pulls out the cancelled transaction cards and holds them aside and arranges the regular charges in transaction number order, breaking them down into the following categories: ten-day loans, one-month loans, one-year loans, bindery charges, and CBL ("cannot be located"); these cards are later manually filed in their respective transaction files. The cancelled transaction cards are forwarded to the 087 collator, where nonoverdues are separated from overdues and discarded. The overdue cancels are again broken down on 083 sorter, this time into the following categories: library employees, officers (faculty members), students, and special borrowers. As the employees and officers are not fined, their cancels are discarded; the overdue cancels of students and special borrowers are forwarded to the billing assistant and eventually run through the fines program on the computer; the fines report is sent to the registrar's office, where the fine is added to the term bill.

COSTS

The charge for computer time for processing Widener Library's circulation system is about $50 per hour and averages between $1,500 and $2,000 per month.

The library's Circulation Department staff includes:

1 professional—head of the department (full time)

1 assistant to the head of the department (full time)
6 attendants at circulation desk (188 hrs./wk.)
2 tracers (55 hrs./wk.)
2 recall attendants (55 hrs./wk.)
3 billing assistants (99 hrs./wk.)
2 staff assistants (45 hrs./wk.)
1 secretary (part time; 22 hrs./wk.)
   students (part time; 331 hrs./wk.)

In addition to the above personnel, the circulation system uses about one-third of one systems librarian's time and the full time of two keypunchers. The keypunchers also run the sorter and collator and have other miscellaneous duties. The total personnel costs for the circulation system are approximately $150,000 per year, or $12,500 per month.

The cost for data processing equipment averages about $420 per month.

On the basis of 1,000 average circulations per day, or 26,000 per month, the average cost of one circulation is about $.56.

OBSERVATIONS

This batch-processed circulation system deals with reasonable effectiveness with a very high level of circulation activity. It provides control of circulation of outside charges, building-use charges, reserve charges, charges to the bindery, loans to departmental libraries, interlibrary loans, and cannot-be-located items. It deals with variable loan periods for students, faculty, staff, and special borrowers. Provisions are made for generation of overdue notices and fine notices. Statistics are compiled regarding levels and types of circulation activity.

These features are provided in a system dealing with holdings of over 2,652,100 items at a rate of over 1,000 circulations per day. If all charges, including reserves, bindery charges, and interlibrary loans were counted, the figure approaches 1,200 charges per day. The cost for the system is about $.56 per transaction, not including, of course, overhead and some costs carried by other departments and not charged to Widener Library.

The system does not provide up-to-the-minute reporting of the location of all types of library materials in circulation, nor does it provide reports in a format that will allow easy analysis for further acquisitions, duplications, or weeding of the collection.

Because machine-readable ID cards for borrowers have not been provided by the university and machine-readable book cards have not been provided by the library, the system requires borrowers to write out charge cards, occasioning delays, inconvenience, and some inaccuracies in the system. The system has, however, been wisely designed to be as adaptable as possible to changing computer configurations that are outside of, and beyond the control of, the library.

Although there are limitations in the Widener Library circulation system, it must be remembered that the system was designed primarily to replace an inadequate manual system. In large-scale operations, where delays, inaccuracies, and confusion threaten a total breakdown of a manual system, converting to a computerized system is justifiable, even if more expensive, especially if the system is as well designed and well implemented as the one at Widener Library.

BIBLIOGRAPHY

DeGennaro, Richard. "Automation in the Harvard College Library." *Harvard Library Bulletin*, 16 (July 1968), 217–236.

————. "The Development and Administration of Automated Systems in Academic Libraries." *Journal of Library Automation*, 1:1 (March 1968), 75–91.

Palmer, Foster M. *Punched Card Circulation System for Widener Library*. (Cambridge: Harvard University Library, 1965.)

————. *The Widener Circulation Printout System*. (mimeographed manual for employees of the Widener Data Processing Department). 1970.

ACKNOWLEDGEMENTS

The assistance of Foster M. Palmer, associate librarian, Harvard University, and of Rita Avon Spiegel in the preparation of this case study is acknowledged with appreciation.

4.
University
of British Columbia
Automated Circulation System

• •

ENVIRONMENT

With a collection of over 1,800,000 volumes and 15,000 periodical sub-scriptions, the University of British Columbia library is one of the largest academic libraries in Canada. Circulation data collection equipment is located in the Main Library, in the Reserve Book Collection, in Sedgewick Undergraduate Library, and in other branch libraries. During the 1971–72 academic year more than 19,000 enrolled students borrowed over 2 million items. Annual expenditures for books and periodicals exceed $1.25 million. These figures suggest the rapid and unprecedented growth taking place in Canadian libraries in institutions of higher education. During the decade of the 1960s, enrollment at the University of British Columbia increased 78 percent and library usage increased 320 percent.[1]

OBJECTIVES

In the fall of 1963 the library staff began considering an automated circulation system because of a rapidly increasing student body, a sharply increasing volume of circulation, and deterioration in control and service. Budgeting considerations precluded increasing the circulation staff. It was also recognized that the locating of material requested at the loan desk was unsatisfactory. The retrieval rate fluctuated between 37 percent and 67 percent, with an average rate of 54 percent. In order to increase the quality of performance of the circulation system, the specific objectives of automation were to improve

the accuracy of library records, to achieve greater time efficiency, and to simplify procedures for both users and the library. The library staff also decided
to use the computerized system to gather information on how the library operated and how its collection was used. The staff sought to relate the supply of
materials to demand by making analytical studies of the book-use statistics
collected by the automated circulation system. Data collected by the circulation system were analyzed in studies of use in relation to loan policy, in studies of borrowing by different groups, and in studies of heavily utilized library
materials.

THE COMPUTER

The library utilizes computer equipment located in the university's Data
Processing Center. The equipment consists of a Honeywell 200 with five
magnetic tapes and 32,000 characters of core, and an IBM 370/135 with
five tape drives and four disk drives. The programming language is COBOL.

The data collection equipment in the library consists of nineteen IBM
1031-B and ten IBM 1031-A data input stations. B-type stations are connected by a 32-wire cable to A-type stations, and the A-type stations are
connected by 2-wire cables to one of two PDP/11 minicomputer systems
owned by the library. Since A-type stations are more expensive than B-type
stations and only eight B stations may be connected to any A station, the
A stations are placed in the most economical manner.

THE SYSTEM

The library changed its circulation system from manual cards and slips to
edge-punched cards in 1962. Details of an automated system were worked out
between April and October 1964 by Robert Harris, now librarian of the British Columbia Institute of Technology. Arrangements were made for a daily
outstanding loans list, overdue notices, and bills, to be produced free of cost
to the library by the university's Tabulating Center. IBM 1030 data collection
equipment was ordered, and by following a timetable (drawn up in January
1965) for program development, testing, and de-bugging, the system went
into operation on an IBM 1401 with the arrival of the data collection equipment in September 1965.

The new system required that each circulating book in the collection be
provided with an 80-column punched card. Although in September 1965 only
14 percent of the books carried cards, a year later this figure had risen to 50
percent, and by early 1968, over 90 percent of the circulating books carried
cards. The cards were generated as circulating books were returned to the library. Old book cards were checked for accuracy of call number, author, and

title, and the books were held in an area of the Circulation Division while the cards were sent to the new card punching unit. When the new cards were returned, they were checked for accuracy, matched to the books and inserted in them, and the books were reshelved. In addition, process book cards are provided as part of an automated acquisition system to allow the circulation and control of new books during their processing period. The Processing Divisions have a 1031 terminal for control of these books, and the process book cards are replaced by circulation book cards when the books are ready for shelving.

Laminated, die-cut, and punch-coded ID cards are provided for most library patrons. Student card sets are issued by the university at registration each year. One of the cards provides name, registration number, date of birth, and year issued and is an insert for the library card. Faculty and staff cards are prepared in the library and include name, department, library number (based on the individual's payroll number), and year issued. Carrel cards, also prepared in the library, expire at the end of each semester. Temporary cards for visitors are not laminated, but are issued on heavy card stock and punch coded; identification and the expiration date are handwritten. The equipment for providing temporary and replacement cards is maintained in the Circulation Division. Existing name and address files, such as the registrar's student file and the accountant's payroll file, are used in establishing the ten-digit ID numbers. The first of the ten digits is a unique number representing the University of British Columbia. The next eight digits are a unique number representing the borrower. The final digit is used to distinguish the first card from subsequent cards issued as replacements for lost or stolen originals. Since two other universities in British Columbia by agreement use similar coding systems, interuniversity borrowing will be facilitated by these ID cards, when direct borrowing is allowed.

The book card contains an "accession" number of eight columns, the first number of which serves both as a transaction mode selector for the 1030 data collection equipment and as a loan category code for record processing; a Library of Congress classification field, consisting of six columns, with letters justified to the left and numbers to the right; and author-title information, which is separated from the call number by three blanks.[2]

The information coded on the borrower ID cards and the book cards comprises the input sent to the minicomputer. The 1031 data input stations have a control reset switch that will lock an ID card in place to allow multiple charges. A data cartridge reader, which is available at key chargeout locations, enables the entering of numerical data manually so that charges may be made without a borrower's ID card. Such manual charges occur frequently for faculty delivery requests.

The minicomputer inputs the time of day into each transaction record.

The minicomputer polls each input station in turn and when a connection is made, transmission begins automatically and recording begins almost instantaneously. The entire input process takes about 1.5 seconds. To control proper insertion of prepared data in punched cards and badges, a guide hole is punched off-center in the borrower's ID card and a corner cut is required in the book card.[3]

Records generated by the minicomputer include all information necessary for processing the transaction record. Abbreviated author and title are included for special printout purposes, such as overdue notices and individual book statistics.

The discharge process is the same as the charge-out, except that a return plate takes the place of the borrower's ID card. The date returned is stamped on the date slip inside the book underneath the date charged out. Renewals simply go through the charge-out process again, except telephone renewals, the information for which is manually keypunched in the form of a special transaction record.

Charge and discharge records are produced by the minicomputer. Special input cards give the library staff control for call-ins, holds, and renewals.

If an error occurs at the 1031 charge-out stations because either the ID card or the book card is faulty, a 'repeat' light is illuminated on the 1031. The mode switch can then be set on "card" or "badge" (the ID card). Set on "badge," if the transaction fails, the ID card is identified as defective. If the transaction proceeds through the "badge" setting, the book card is assumed to be at fault and is discarded and replaced.

If a 1031 terminal fails and there is no other terminal nearby, the borrower must fill out a loan card and the old manual punched card system is used. The loan card is stamped with the date charged and filed by call number in an outstanding card file. If the terminal is operable by the time the book is returned, the automated system completes the discharge transaction, but there will, of course, be no record of the charge-out. The item will therefore appear on the exceptions list printout; by means of this list, the loan card may be located by call number and discarded.

If one of the minicomputer systems fails, the alternate system is put into operation. This is a manual operation, and rarely is necessary because the systems are very reliable.

The transaction tape from the minicomputer is dismounted and taken to the Data Processing Center at the end of each day to update the active files. A loan period table, maintained at the Tabulating Center in the form of a punched card deck, is fed into the computer at the beginning of all processing to determine due dates from the transaction date, borrower type, and book loan category data.

The automated circulation system was initiated in 1965 on an IBM 1401; in July, 1966, when two Honeywell 200s were installed, the programs were changed from card to tape. The change to one Honeywell 200 and an IBM 370/135 occurred during May of 1973. The basic programs are still in use, but since 1968 some new programs have been written by the library's systems staff for analytical studies. All records are stored on magnetic tape.

Outstanding loans lists, exceptions reports, error lists, various notices, and several statistical reports are produced daily. Statistical summaries are produced monthly. The outstanding loans list, which is produced in call number order, includes not only outstanding loans, but lists materials that are at the bindery, in carrels, in the cataloging division, or at branch libraries. It also includes call-ins, overdues, holds, and missing items. In addition to the five copies produced daily, four for the main loan desk and one for the main information desk, each branch library is provided with from three to five copies of its own outstanding loans. Exception reports deal with unmatched discharges, renewals when no charge is outstanding, duplicate discharges, and returned holds and recalls. If an error is detected, the item appears on the error list, with the kind of error identified. The volume of transactions at each data collection station during two-hour periods is compiled in a traffic report. This report, together with a daily summary of circulation activity at all stations is helpful in analyzing demands on staff and the system. The daily notices include overdues, recalls, bills for fines, and reminders to faculty of the expiration of the two-week loan period.

Three major files of circulation data are maintained. A "circulation outstanding file," stored on tape, is a record of incomplete loan transactions generated by the charge action. Completed transactions also appear until they are purged, which may take up to a week. A "circulation history file" shows the once-weekly purged, completed transactions from the outstanding file, and a "circulation inventory file" is an abstracted version of the full record that is used to simplify analysis of circulation transaction statistics. The monthly reports of book use, which have revealed significant patterns of use in various libraries, have been subjected to careful analysis.[4] On the basis of these analyses, the library staff has redistributed some books between the Main Library and Sedgewick Undergraduate Library. The staff has also acquired a number of new or duplicate copies for Sedgewick and has, in certain subject areas, acquired more titles for the Main Library.

A book-use study has also been made of the Main Library's reserve book collection. The study revealed that out of a reserve collection of 9,000 volumes, 5,000 were not used enough to warrant being in the collection. The study suggested that better use could have been made of the books had they not been placed on reserve.

COSTS

From cost studies conducted for the fiscal year 1969–1970, when the circulation system controlled the circulation of about 1.3 million volumes during the year, the library automation cost was $.057 per circulation and the total personnel cost per circulation in the Main Library was $.36. This figure was calculated from annual automation costs of about $80,000 and personnel costs of about $250,000 in the Main Library Circulation Department.[5]

Basil Stuart-Stubbs, University Librarian, states that the automated system has been an economic success. He argues that it has succeeded in "leveling out spiralling staff costs while contending with a five-year (1965-1970) increase in circulation of more than 116 percent."[6]

In any transition from one system to another, there are increased costs for development and implementation. The automated system required preparing book cards, writing, testing, and rewriting programs, installing equipment, and training staff. Programming guidance from IBM and, fortuitously, free computer time from the university's Data Processing Center (though, of course, somebody paid for it), enabled the library to keep its system change-over costs to a minimum. Some initial tasks were funded with money freed by not adding any new staff positions, even though Main Library circulation during the three academic years from 1967 to 1970 increased more than 27 percent. Of course, regardless of staff size, rising salaries brought increased labor cost. Such increased costs strengthened the economic "advantage" of the computerized system that stabilized staff size.

Since the installation of the data collection equipment and inauguration of the automated circulation system, the library has absorbed the costs of its maintenance and further development. It may be noted that the fixed costs of the automated system, that is, costs excluding salaries, comprise less than 15 percent of the total cost of circulation activities. The system operates at a cost of about $.42 per circulation.

OBSERVATIONS

It is likely that the dollar cost of the total automated circulation system of the University of British Columbia library is more than the cost of the old manual system. Cost, however, was only one consideration in the development of this system; the primary thrust of the system design was to close the control loop and to achieve better levels of accuracy, speed, and simplicity. In any case, the manual system was not, and could not be equal to the demands being placed upon the automated system. The automated system is handling a very high volume of circulation activity successfully, which the manual system was not, and it is providing not only the information and control that the manual operation provided, but important additional features. It offers computer-generated overdue notices, call-in notices, fine notices, and reminders to faculty that the loan period has expired on books they hold. It prepares lists of borrowers, arranged alphabetically or by borrower card number. The system also provides statistics on heavy book use, on the use of the collection by subjects (according to Library of Congress classification), and on subject areas in which the heaviest purchasing has occurred.

Since all libraries are faced with the problem of relating library holdings to library use, analytical studies of library use are much needed, but seldom conducted.[7] The University of British Columbia Library staff went beyond the usual objectives in automation efforts—commendable as they may be—of improving accuracy in circulation records, speeding up the charging and discharging operation, and simplifying procedures for both borrowers and the library staff. They obtained and analyzed data on how patrons use the library's collection. Statistics on book use were employed to adjust loan policy, to identify heavily used items and obtain duplicate copies, and to modify acquisitions policy to conform to patterns and level of use by different groups of borrowers. The library has improved its utilization of its resources by closing its control loop.

While the system is not on-line, it generates lists, notices, statistics, and other printouts frequently enough to provide viable circulation control. It does not provide an immediate report on the location of any circulating item. However, the cost of an on-line circulation system to provide such immediate reporting in a library of this magnitude would be likely to exceed $.42 per circulation.

Also, while punched card input is a widely used procedure for mechanized circulation systems in libraries at this time, it is not without problems. It may well be that the utilization of light pens for direct input to disk packs will prove a significant system improvement.

The University of British Columbia system, one of the largest operational computerized circulation systems on this continent, has put into operation computerized systems for acquisitions, accounting, serials, backlog books, book catalogs, and document indexing. Its computerization activities deserve not only to be more widely known but to be widely emulated.

NOTES

1. Peter Simmons, *Collection Development and the Computer* (Vancouver: University of British Columbia, 1971), p. 3.

2. Ibid., p. 23.

3. Ibid., p. 20.

4. Peter Simmons, "Improving Collections Through Computer Analysis of Circulation Records

in a University Library," American Society for Information Science, 33rd Annual Meeting, Philadelphia, October 1970, *Proceedings*, 7, 59–63.

5. A more complete detailing of costs of the automated circulation system is contained in Simmons, *Collection Development and the Computer*, pp. 47–50.

6. Basil Stuart-Stubbs, in Simmons, *ibid*, p. 1.

7. A useful report of an analysis made possible by a computer-based circulation system for the purpose of identifying heavily used books for multiple-copy purchase is Robert S. Grant's "Predicting the Need for Multiple Copies of Books." *Journal of Library Automation*, 4:2 (June 1971), 64–71.

ACKNOWLEDGMENTS

The assistance of R. W. MacDonald, Coordinator of Technical Processes and Systems, University of British Columbia, and Jean L. Orne in the preparation of this case study is acknowledged with appreciation.

5.
Booth Library, Eastern Illinois University Automated Circulation System

ENVIRONMENT

Eastern Illinois University, Charleston, has over 820 faculty members and an enrollment of over 8,600 students. A state university, it provides programs in liberal arts and professional fields, including teacher training and library science. Booth Library holds about 300,000 cataloged volumes. The university has experienced a steadily increasing enrollment, and the library, in consequence, has been adding over 20,000 volumes per year to its collections in an attempt to keep pace with enrollment. The number of volumes per student (35) is about three-fourths the national average (45). The collection is being reclassified from the Dewey to the Library of Congress classification system. During 1970–71 about 115,000 volumes were circulated by the Booth Library automated circulation system.[1]

OBJECTIVES

The Booth Library on-line circulation system (BLOC) is an operational system in which on-line, real-time inquiries may be made into the computer files by use of a cathode-ray-tube (CRT) display terminal. The primary objectives of this system were to:

1. Eliminate borrower participation in the check-out process.
2. Speed and simplify circulation procedures.
3. Eliminate manual file maintenance.
4. Permit identification of the status of any book within the system.

5. Provide accurate and up-to-date statistics concerning use of library materials, including the number of times a given book is used.
6. Provide guidance from the system in case of human error in conducting a transaction.
7. Relieve professional librarians from clerical chores.[2]

THE COMPUTER

The computer system on the Eastern Illinois University campus is operated in a time-sharing mode. It serves the registrar's office and business office, as well as the Laboratory School Library and Booth Library. An IBM 360/50, with 262,000 bytes of central core, is supervised by the IBM operating system (OS).

The IBM 1030 data collection system at the circulation desk includes two 1031 card badge readers, one 1033 printer, and one 3277 display terminal that is used for on-line inquiries. The library also uses two 029 keypunches and one 059 verifier for the BLOC system. Other components, including a 1034 card punch, 2540 card read punch, a 1403 Model N1 printer, and a 2314 direct-access storage facility are located at the Computer Center. BLOC uses the 2314 disk storage facility to store the Booth master file and the patron file.

Twenty-five different application programs have been written in PL/1 (F level) for this BLOC system. Other programs have been written in Assembler language to perform some basic machine functions. These include the 1030 analyzer program (BAL), with a partition of 50,000 bytes in core memory, that monitors the 1030 data collection system, and five overlay programs that process transactions and modify files.

The 3277 analyzer program, written in PL/1, handles on-line inquiries at 13 campus terminals. Of these, only two can handle circulation inquiries. One is the master terminal at the Computer Center and the other is the terminal at the circulation desk. The 3277 analyzer, which controls 20 overlay programs, selects records required to answer inquiries. These overlays, as well as the five controlled by the 1030 analyzer program, are stored at the 2314 disk storage facility.

The systems librarian, Paladugu V. Rao, joined the library in 1968, and although he does not take credit for all 25 application programs, he found it more expedient to write or rewrite a number of the programs himself, rather than explain the requirements of the system to programmers at the Computer Center.[3]

THE SYSTEM

In 1965, the Booth Library staff launched plans for library automation. Experiments were conducted with ordering Library of Congress printed catalog cards, with controlling serials, and with monitoring acquisitions, using unit record equipment. Although none of these experimental projects became operational, they provided useful experience for the development of other automated systems.

Planning for BLOC began in 1966. At that time, the library used a call-slip circulation system that necessitated time-consuming file maintenance. Since the volume of circulation was increasing at a yearly rate of about 15 percent, the circulation staff was increased. However, the scale of circulation demands was forcing a decline in the quality of library service. The library staff believed that the anticipated growth in enrollment and the projected increase in library materials might increase the demands on the manual circulation system beyond its capacity. The library administration, therefore, undertook the development of a circulation system equal to the expanding demands.

A task force of representatives from the university administration, Data Processing Center personnel, and librarians recommended, after an investigation of various types of circulation systems, a computerized on-line circulation system, utilizing the existing computer facilities on campus. The recommendation was followed by the development of a design for the proposed system. The design for the BLOC system was revised when a decision was made in 1967 to switch from closed to open stacks in the library. The BLOC system became operational in September 1968 and continued to be evaluated and modified up to 1970.

BLOC requires two main data files for its operation: a "patron file" and a "Booth master file." The patron file contains identification data of persons eligible to borrow books from Booth Library. It is a combination of an employee master file (including faculty) and a student master file, which exist to serve business transactions of the university. Access to this file, which is arranged in an indexed-sequential method, is by the patron's Social Security Number. Each student's record consists of 408 bytes; each employee's record contains 304 bytes. The file contains about 21,000 records, and it is updated by the Computer Center under the direction of the university administrative offices. Although BLOC may borrow such information as name, address, and telephone number of the patron from this file as needed to process circulation transactions, confidential information about a patron is not accessible to the BLOC system.

The Booth master file was created by keypunching the Booth Library shelflist and then transferring the keypunched data to a disk file. The master file includes one record for every volume held by the library. The file was completed in one and a half years.

The Booth master file is also arranged in an indexed-sequential method, utilizing the first ten characters of the call number and the six characters of the accession number. Each record in this file consists of 124 bytes. The record layout appears in Table 1.

Table 1
BOOTH MASTER FILE RECORD LAYOUT[4]

Field	Byte Positions	Explanation
OS control	1	
Call number	2–11	First ten characters.
Accession number	12–17	
Call number	18–27	Remainder of call number.
Edition, year, series	28–30	
Volume number	31–34	
Part, index, supplement number	35–37	
Copy number	38–39	
Location code	40–41	
Author	42–51	
Title	52–78	
Control byte	79	
Number of checkouts	80–82	Cumulative number of checkouts.
Status of book	83	In or out.
Borrower Soc. Sec. No.	84–92	
Borrower status	93	1 = student, 3 = faculty, etc.
Due date	94–99	
Format code	100	Oversize, etc.
Save Soc. Sec. No.	101–109	Social Security Number of patron requesting save.
Save type	110	1 = student, 3 = faculty, etc.
Save status	111	Is there a save or not?
Unused bytes	112–124	For future use.

The average access time to a record in this file is 75 milliseconds. A copy of the Booth master file, which holds approximately 195,000 records, is kept separately on magnetic tape as a security measure. Its size was reduced considerably when periodicals, which were part of the Booth master file, were made noncirculating. Periodic weeding of the collection, of course, eliminates some records from the file throughout the year. Infrequently circulated books have also been removed from Booth master file to conserve space on the disk. These books are accessible to students for circulation, but they must be checked out by manual means. If more storage space were available, these books would be on the disk file, too, since the library does not wish to discard them.

Each night, records of new books acquired are input to the Booth master file in a batch operation. After a new book is cataloged, a master card is punched for it and delivered to the Computer Center, where two book cards are produced from the master card. The layout of the book card differs slightly from the master card. A "1" is punched in column 1, to be used as a transaction code. The end-of-card code is shifted to column 19 to expedite the processing of transactions. To locate a book record in the Booth master file, the accession and class numbers are sufficient. An accession number is stamped on the back of each book card to make visual verification easier.

The circulation staff compares the accession number on the book pocket with the accession number on the card to ensure that the right book card is inserted on the book pocket.

The second set of book cards is interfiled, in call number sequence, into a duplicate book card file in the circulation department. These are used to replace missing cards. When a card is removed from this duplicate file, another duplicate card is punched to be retained in the file for possible future use. Once a book has been processed by the Cataloging Department, it takes approximately 24 hours to get it on the shelf for circulation. The Booth master file is updated before new books are circulated.

A patron normally presents a badge, issued by an administrative office, whenever he or she wishes to check out books. Transactions can be processed without a badge, but rarely are. Each badge utilizes the person's Social Security Number as his or her ID number, and a one-digit code indicates the person's status as student, faculty, staff, etc. The 1031 badge reader at the circulation desk, reads the ID number, transmits it to the system, which interprets it as the address of a patron's record and takes the required information from the patron file. The loan period is determined by the status code.

After the attendant compares accession numbers on the book card and book pocket, the patron's badge is inserted into the badge slot of the 1031 terminal and the book card is fed into the card input slot. If for some reason the terminal does not accept the card, the transaction is completed by manual means on a special card that is later punched and used to update the disk files.

When the book card emerges from the exit slot of the terminal, the attendant replaces it in the book. A date-due slip, which is manually stamped, is used for a student checkout; a prestamped date-due card is used for a faculty checkout. The student checkout period is one month; the faculty checkout period is an academic year. The circulation librarian may recall a book from a faculty member after 30 days if it is needed by another patron. Consequently, the transaction date is placed on a faculty checkout record, rather than the due date. The transaction date is also used for special badge checkouts to the bindery.

When all book cards for one patron have been run through the terminal, the badge is returned to the patron. In this system the patron is relieved of the cumbersome chore of making out call slips for each book, and file maintenance is eliminated for the circulation staff.

If the transaction is not normal, the deviation is communicated to the attendant via the 1033 printer. For example, the printer may indicate that a particular book has no master record. This may occur when a book is placed in circulation before its master card is loaded onto the disk file by the Computer Center in the updating process. In such a case, the transaction would be recorded manually on a special card to be later keypunched and used to update the disk file.

When a book is to be checked in, the accession numbers on the book card and book pocket are compared to insure that they match. A special check-in badge is inserted into the badge slot. The book card is inserted in the terminal and then returned to the book pocket, completing the check-in process. If a book card does not match the book, the check-in is completed with a card from the duplicate card file.

During the check-in process, the system communicates messages via the printer regarding books that are overdue or being reserved for another patron. Overdue and reserved books are turned over to a clerk for necessary action.

On-line, real-time inquiries are made on this system through the 3277 cathode-ray-tube (CRT) display terminal. The circulation staff can readily establish the status of a book or obtain a list of books borrowed by a patron. Inquiry response time is less than a second.

A person wishing to reserve a book that is checked-out places a reserve in the on-line mode in the BLOC system. The circulation attendant simply keys identification data for the book and requester, along with the reserve code (BR), using the 3277 display terminal. When reserve information is entered, the system displays the information on the screen for visual verification by the attendant. A patron may also cancel a reserve via the 3277 display terminal. Reserves are caught immediately in the check-in process. Should a person inadvertently try to check out a reserved book, the printer alerts the attendant that the book is being saved for a particular patron. The BLOC system permits only one reserve for each book.

In addition to reserve inquiries, a variety of other on-line inquiries can be made through the 3277 display terminal. The system displays formats for various types of inquiries when the operator simply types "IN" on the screen. The "name" inquiry (NA) permits the operator to discover a patron's Social Security Number, which may then be entered into the system with code letters "SM" or "EM" to get a patron's address and phone number.

Inquiry via the "book display" (BD) reveals whether a library book is charged out, reserved, or missing. Inquiry via "book scan" permits examination of records of books in classification order. When the code letters "BS," followed by a full or partial classification number, are typed at the terminal, information about the first book in the class is displayed. Pressing the "next" button will display the next book in the class. As many records may be examined as desired. This book scan feature not only reveals which books the library holds on various subjects, but also discloses whether the book is available or checked out. Since the display terminal faces the circulation staff, it may not be viewed by a patron at the circulation desk. When students graduate or withdraw and employees leave they must be cleared by the library. The attendant types "BU" (book unclear) followed by the patron's Social Security Number. If the patron has any books checked out, their call and accession numbers will be listed on the screen.

All check-in and check-out transactions are recorded on magnetic tape. These transactions are also entered in the Booth master file on disk. The transaction tape is used to generate various lists and statistical data. A daily circulation list, generated from the transaction tape late at night, lists all books checked out up to the closing hour of 11 P.M. The circulation department gets two copies of this list. One copy, placed at the catalog, relieves the demand for display terminal inquiries during peak periods.

A cumulative overdue list, printed weekly from the transaction tape, lists books overdue on that date. It shows identification data for each book and the address of the borrower. At the same time a mail notification card, addressed to the borrower, is printed for each overdue book. These overdue notices are completely handled by the staff at the Computer Center.

The transaction tape, cumulated into weekly, monthly, and annual tapes, generates statistical data for administrative use. For example, an inventory of books by class is printed from time to time, with a tally of the total number of checkouts per class. This printout enables the library staff to see where the strengths and weaknesses of the collection lie and to locate the areas most heavily used by the patrons. By reviewing these statistical reports that show the volume of circulation in given subject fields, book budget allocations can be made on a more scientific basis. Periodic weeding, based on number of circulations, is also greatly facilitated by the study of these statistics.

Cumulative monthly circulation statistics provide management with the number of books circulated in a given class throughout the month. From these statistics peak circulation periods can be determined and staffing planned accordingly.

Booth Library may also provide subject listings, arranged in call number order, as required by various academic departments. These listings have been used by various accreditation committees. Lists of books charged out to special badges, such as binding, lost, etc., are printed periodically to facilitate follow-up by appropriate departments.

Booth Library's Circulation Department has one professional circulation librarian, who is also in charge of the reserve books. One full-time keypuncher and 270 hours of student help per month are assigned exclusively to the BLOC system. Both terminals are manned the 81 hours a week the library is open. An automation and systems librarian acts as coordinator between the library and the Computer Center. The circulation staff performs assorted other circulation tasks, such as shelving and circulating reserve books that are not connected with the BLOC system, so it is difficult to estimate how much time these staff members do spend on the BLOC system exclusively. If the 270 hours of student time per month were subtracted from the 324 hours a month that the library is open (81 × 4), the remainder of 54 hours must be covered by Civil Service personnel in order to have one terminal covered at all times. If both terminals were covered all the time, another 324 hours of Civil Service help would be charged to BLOC, for a total of 378 hours. This is a maximum figure, however, since both terminals are probably not busy at the same time and the personnel may be occupied with other tasks.

COSTS

No figures were available on planning cost, system design cost, or costs of writing and testing the programs. BLOC was developed through the combined effort of the library and the Computer Center staffs. A number of people devoted time to the planning and development effort on a part-time basis. Only two people were hired to work full time for the project, a keypunch operator and an IBM machine operator. Their combined annual salary was $9,000 in 1968 and 1969. The IBM machine operator position was terminated at the completion of the basic file conversion in 1969. Since the time of programmers and operators is spent on maintaining and operating a number of systems, it is not possible to determine how much of their time was exclusively devoted to BLOC.

Operating expenditures for BLOC may be estimated from figures given in the library annual report for 1970–71. Automation services for the university library totaled $75,492 for the year.[5] About 20 percent of this budget was allotted to the Booth Library integrated serials system (BLISS), which controlled about 3,366 serial publications as of June 30, 1971. Therefore, about 80 percent of the cost of automation services is attributed to BLOC, or $60,394 annually, $5,033 monthly.

The Circulation Department is headed by one professional librarian. The average salary of a professional librarian at Booth Library is $13,970 a year, or $1,164 monthly. The wages of one keypunch operator and 270 hours of student help required for the circulation system amount to about $745 per month. Only student help and Civil Service personnel staff the circulation desk. Since 270 hours of student time would not cover the hours the library is open, one full-time Civil Service employee, earning $357 per month, is assumed. A summary of these figures appears in Table 2.

Table 2
SUMMARY OF BLOC'S MONTHLY OPERATING COSTS

Item	Amount
Automation services	$5,033
Professional Librarian	1,164
Keypunch operator and 270 hours of student help	745
Civil Service employee	357
Total	$7,299

The number of circulations from Booth Library stacks was 115,399 a year, or 9,616 per month, at a unit cost of $.76 per circulation. The number of transactions, however, average 36,000 per month, and the unit cost per transaction is about $.20. After salaries at $511,070 per year and the book budget at $309,225 per year, automation services at $75,492 is the next highest figure in library expenditures, amounting to 8 percent of total operating expenditures. The library is also expected to subsidize free computer time for students and faculty, along with other university units, which inflates the cost of automation services to some extent.[6]

Although no library positions were eliminated because of the BLOC system, the system is handling a 20 percent increase in loans. Had the manual system been maintained, more personnel at a cost of about $15,000 per year would have had to be hired to handle the increase in circulation.

OBSERVATIONS

The Booth Library on-line circulation system (BLOC) at Eastern Illinois University, in operation since September, 1968, is one of the pioneering efforts in computerized circulation control systems. On-line, real-time inquiries are being made into the computer files by the use of a cathode-ray-tube display terminal. Utilizing the university's computer facilities in a time-sharing mode, the library has an on-line circulation system which provides control over all circulating stack books in Booth Library. Reserved books, periodicals, and nonbook materials are not included in the BLOC system.

Efforts to develop the BLOC system were aimed at designing a system that would have low cost in the long run and would allow for increases in knowledge in computer technology. While these efforts have succeeded, the success has come at a price. The director of library services writes:

It took four years of struggle and hard work for the library staff and for the computer center to develop our automation system. It is operational now and it is one of the best in the whole nation. We are pround of it, but we will never try to start research of our own in this field again. It is much cheaper for small universities to imitate automated systems which are operational at other libraries, even though it takes time to adapt a well developed system to our requirements.[7]

Although one can understand the reluctance of the director to undertake another pioneering effort, one can at the same time appreciate the importance to the library profession of such projects. The team at Eastern Illinois set out to achieve a substantial array of objectives and they succeeded. They eliminated borrower participation in the checkout process; speeded up and simplified circulation procedures; eliminated manual fine maintenance, except the duplicate book card file; achieved the capacity to identify the status of any book within the system, arranged for accurate and up-to-date statistics concerning the use of library materials, including the number of times a book is used; included guidance from the system in cases of human error in conducting a transaction, and relieved librarians of a number of clerical chores.

One of the special advantages of this on-line system is that errors may be caught immediately at the input station. With an off-line system, errors are not discovered until the next computer run, and library staff must then correct errors and re-input data.

Another advantage of this on-line system is that when a book is returned, the system immediately reports when a reserve has been made. An on-line system eliminates the separate reservations list that must be compared with returned books required by an off-line system.

Another desirable feature is that the inquiry format is displayed on the 3277 CRT terminal. This display is very useful in training new personnel.

One disadvantage of the system is that infrequently used books are not listed in the Booth Master File. Not only must such books be circulated manually, but it will cost money to put these books back into the file if the system enlarges its storage capacity.

Another disadvantage is that the display terminal at the circulation desk cannot be viewed by patrons. (A proposal to put the display terminal at the circulation desk on a swivel table met with opposition from the circulation staff.)

Since a relatively small percentage of titles are circulated by the library (about 11 percent), the duplicate book card file may be a needless duplication of effort. When book cards are stolen or mismatched, the circulation transaction could be completed manually on a special card. Labor costs are generally lower in an automated system than in a manual system. In view of the rapid growth of the student body and of Booth Library's holdings, both tending to increase circulation, the costs of the BLOC system should escalate only slightly, whereas labor costs for a manual system would doubtless climb significantly. In addition, this system has already reached the volume of activities that manual circulation systems tend to break down at. Therefore, this sophisticated on-line circulation system that provides accurate and up-to-date file maintenance, speeds patron service, and compiles useful statistics for Library management is justified not only because it provides improved service, but because it provides features that a manual system could not. It may appear cheaper to travel by bicycle than by jet aircraft, but it might not prove so in getting from Boston to Los Angeles, all things considered. Some librarians have not yet discovered that manual systems are sometimes very far removed from the best system and may not really be cheaper. The library administration at Eastern Illinois University has not only discovered this fact, but has provided in BLOC a highly effective computerized circulation system.

NOTES

1. B. Joseph Szerenyi, *Annual Report of the University Library July 1, 1970–June 30, 1971* (Charleston, Ill.: Eastern Illinois University).
2. Paladugu V. Rao and B. Joseph Szerenyi, "Booth Library On-Line Circulation System (BLOC)" *Journal of Library Automation*, 4:2 (June 1971), 86–102.
3. Interview with Paladugu V. Rao, March, 1972.
4. Rao, p. 91.
5. Szerenyi, p. 6.
6. Rao, interview, March, 1972.
7. Szerenyi, p. 8.

ACKNOWLEDGMENTS

The assistance of Paladugu V. Rao, head of the Information Systems Department, Eastern Illinois University, and of Rebecca F. Duschatko in the preparation of this case study is acknowledged with appreciation.

6.
Northwestern University Automated Circulation System
• •

Northwestern University, founded in 1851, is a privately controlled coeducational institution with a college of liberal arts and a number of graduate schools on its Evanston campus and four professional schools on its Chicago campus. The university has an undergraduate enrollment on the Evanston campus of about 4,000 men and 3,000 women, and a student-faculty ratio of 10–1. In the fall of 1971, on both campuses, over 11,000 full-time and almost 4,000 part-time students were enrolled.

The entire Northwestern library system consists of about twelve libraries in Evanston and Chicago, total holdings of over 2,300,000 volumes, and an operating budget of about $3 million. In January 1970 the university opened a new three-towered, $12,000,000, main library, capable of housing 1,700,000 volumes and seating almost 3,000 patrons. Its holdings in 1973 were about 1,000,000 volumes, of which 900,000 were in its circulating collection.

OBJECTIVES

The possibility of utilizing data processing equipment in the library was explored as early as 1961. The breaking of ground in 1966 for a new university library triggered serious planning for automated systems. John P. McGowan, appointed associate university librarian in 1966, and Velma D. Veneziano, appointed systems analyst in 1967, were given specific responsibilities for the application of computers to library operations. Following a detailed study of manual operations, they concluded that the library should develop an integrated system, covering technical services and circulation. The system was to provide for searching, ordering, check-in, fiscal control, cataloging, and physical processing in the technical services mode and for self-service charging, remote terminal inquiry and update, fine and overdue notices, and call-in and book-available notices in the circulation mode.

It was decided that only a system that would provide on-line access to computer-based files would substantially improve library operating efficiency. Since the system had to be developed within the library's budget and without outside funding, the cost of the design and operation of the system was severely limited. The major objective was to provide fast, accurate, and efficient flow of library operations at a minimal cost. Since the cost of a suitable computer for exclusive library use was prohibitive, a decision was made to share the equipment in the Administrative Data Processing Department.

The design of the library computer system was regarded as a staff function, but the operation of the system was treated as a line function. Various system modules were therefore transferred to existing library departments as soon as they were operational. As the programming staff believed the use of real-time systems in the library might stimulate other applications, they designed a general-purpose file maintenance system for the library's data processing needs. The overriding objective was to develop, at minimal cost, an integrated system that would substantially improve the central operations of technical services and circulation in the library. The library staff wanted an on-line system with no frills at minimum cost.

THE COMPUTER

The on-line, real-time computer system utilizes an IBM 370/135 computer located in the university's Administrative Data Processing Department. The IBM disk operating system (DOS) is used. The data file organization is random, with a partial call number as the key. Remote terminal input-output operations use the IBM Basic Telecommunications Access Method.

The system consists of (1) a book charge and discharge operation, (2) a general-purpose file maintenance system, which was originally developed for technical services and is more sophisticated than would be required for a circulation system alone, and (3) an off-line, batch-processing system, which is run periodically and is independent of the on-line system.

Four pairs of IBM 1031 card/badge readers and attached IBM 1033 printers are used for charging and discharging. Each of the 1031 terminals is designed to receive an 80-column punched book card, which resides in the book pocket, and a plastic punched user ID badge. The 1033 printer produces date-due slips, prints error messages requiring follow-up action, and prepares a number of special notices. The date-due slips, showing the call number of the book, the borrower's ID number, and the date due, are printed at the 1031/

1033 terminals, many of which are self-service, when valid badges and book cards are inserted in the 1031 terminal. If for any reason a self-service terminal cannot complete the charging transaction, the user must go to the main circulation desk to deal with the problem. The master charge/discharge terminal, an IBM 1030, at the main desk has "slides" with numbers and can charge books to users who may not have plastic machine-readable badges, who desire a non-standard loan period, or who wish to renew a book, pay a fine on an overdue book and recharge it, etc. The master inquiry terminal, an IBM 2740, Model 2, is also used to inquire into the circulation status of any book, to place a "save," and process mail renewals. An IBM 015 badge punch is available to produce special user and carrel holder badges.

The teleprocessing system includes a transaction file, written sequentially, which is used in processing fines, saves, and call-in notices. Each morning during the week programs are run that process the data entered into the transaction file since the previous run. The names and addresses required for printing notices are obtained from student and personnel files maintained by the Date Processing Department.

Each week another set of programs processes the entire file of outstanding books. During this run, all records in the file are transferred to a backup file as a security measure. Thus far, the backup file has not been used. This set of programs generates circulation statistics reports, information about books that have had transactions during the week, as well as books that are overdue.

Each quarter the entire file is checked, and lists are prepared of all books charged to the reserve room, lost or missing, and loaned to other libraries, to carrels, or to faculty. These lists are distributed so that verification may be made that the books are in fact located where the file indicates they are.

The circulation system has manual backup equipment consisting of a Standard Register source record punch (SRP). The SRP accepts the plastic user badge and the book card and produces a two-part form. One part serves as the date-due slip; the other part is a standard 80-column card, which is used to enter the transaction through the 1031 terminal when the computer system is again operational. If a user badge or a book card is unavailable or if the library is without electricity, circulation information may be handwritten on the two-part form.

Access to the computer is provided during library hours, 8:15 A. M. to midnight.[1]

THE SYSTEM

Programming for the integrated system started in the spring of 1968. The teleprocessing system was completed about a year later, at which time work was begun on such subsidiary programs as those for producing catalog cards, purchase orders, and other technical services records. However, the library administration, knowing that the opening of the new library was less than a year away, requested that work be suspended on the technical services part of the new system and that an effort be made to have the automated circulation system operational at the time the new library opened.

Following completion of the basic design of the circulation system early in 1969, work was undertaken during the summer to produce 80-column punched book cards, containing only the call number and location code, from the main library's shelflist that represented about 1 million volumes. The staff decided not to include author or title information, even in abbreviated form, because the data would not fit on a single 80-column card and because the use of this data would quadruple the cost. By employing part-time students, who prepared, with few exceptions, more than 400 cards per hour, over 700,000 book cards were completed well before the library opened. The students did both keypunching and error checking. Because a decision was made not to make book cards for a substantial number of noncirculating bound journal volumes and many old, mostly foreign-language, bibliographies, only 700,749 cards were initially required for the main library's circulating holdings. Cards were, in addition, prepared for the collections of the Business, Africana, Curriculum, and Technological Institute libraries. Now that both the technical services and circulation modules are operational, book cards for newly acquired books are produced, with rare exceptions, by the technical services department.

The next stage in preparation for the new system was the expensive and time-consuming task of inserting book cards in the books. This work was not completed before the new library opened in January 1970. Ten percent (70,000 cards) remained to be inserted. As a matter of fact, the computer circulation system itself was not ready for testing until December 1969, and the system received only a three-week test in the Technological Institute Library before being placed in service in the main library.

In addition to book cards, the system utilizes a machine-readable borrower ID badge. The punched plastic badge for students includes a picture, Social Security Number, user code, and expiration date. These badges are ordered by the Student Finance Division of the university from an outside contractor. Badges are ready for returning students at registration. For new students, temporary badges are issued until the plastic badges have been prepared by the contractor. Student badges are valid for one year. The user code is changed each year to prevent the use of an expired badge. Faculty and staff badges, which are issued by the university's Personnel Department, are good for three years and do not carry a picture. For special users, the library assigns a five-digit number from a list of sequential numbers and produces the badges on an IBM 015 badge punch. Since carrel holders, mostly graduate students and faculty, charge out large numbers of books to their carrels, plastic badges containing the carrel number, carrel code, and expiration date are provided for them. These badges may be used at the self-service terminals in the stacks. If a borrower loses his badge, he is issued a special user badge and the computer system "blocks" his regular user number. If the lost badge is used, the terminal will produce an "unprocessed" message instead of a valid date due slip. However, since "blocking" is done only once a day, some lost badges are used improperly before the blocking is done.

As with most new buildings and systems, there were break-in problems. The new building was not quite finished; some of the books had not been moved; some of the circulation terminals had not been installed; and backlogs of work had developed during the weeks the library was being moved. An initial decision to run the new computer system in parallel with the old manual system was abandoned in two weeks when it was found that the new system was working well and that the staff could not cope with the double work load of the dual system operation.

The automated system, which has been fully operational for more than three years, circulates between 1,000 and 1,200 books per day during the regular school year, or between 260,000 and 300,000 during the calendar year. Interestingly enough, about 560,000 volumes are returned by the library staff to the shelves each year, indicating that about as many books are used in the library building as circulate. About 60 percent of the charging transactions take place at self-service terminals.

The 1033 printers, which are used for self-service charges, originally produced a date-due slip which had to be torn off. For proper tearing, the slip had to be pulled forward or down. Many students pulled up, causing the paper to skew and eventually jam. The library staff had the printer modified so that the paper could be cut manually by a knife installed on the printer. Even this device is not fully satisfactory. A ticket-ejector system, under consideration during the summer of 1973, may eliminate this problem.

The main circulation desk is equipped to deal with any circulation or charging problems. Borrowers, with or without badges, and books, with or without cards, can be circulated under various special options available in the system. The date-due slip, which is checked by the exit guard, serves as a pass to permit the removal of a book from the library. The library has a standard loan period of four weeks.

Inquiries about the status of a book may be made at the main circulation desk via the 2740 terminal. All books not in their normal location on the shelves should be listed in the computer circulation file. Books in the reserve room, returned to the catalog department, loaned to library departments, on interlibrary loan, at the bindery, or lost or missing and not yet withdrawn from the catalog, are included in the file. Out of a circulating collection of about 900,000 volumes, from 50,000 to 60,000 records will be in the file at any one time. Access to each record is provided by a search key consisting of the Dewey classification number, the Cutter number, and up to four work letters. A key extension, which includes the edition, volume, or copy number, is also provided. Although the individual records for books in the file consist of only 67 characters, the cost of maintaining in the file records of all books in the library would be excessive. As a result, the file is limited to books not in their usual places as represented in the card catalog.

If a patron wishes to have a book saved, the operator of the 2740 terminal at the circulation desk adds the patron's identification number to the book's loan record. This "save" request causes the batch-processing mode of the system to produce a call-in or book-needed notice. When the called-in book has been returned and discharged, a book-available notice is prepared by the computer system.

All renewals are processed at the main circulation desk. The printer will produce a date-due slip containing the words "renew to" and the new due date. No telephone renewals are accepted; mail renewals, which require the return of the date-due slip, are processed on the IBM 2740. The same date-due slip, updated, is mailed to the borrower.

Borrowers returning books may leave them in book bins; one is inside, the other is outside the library building. The books are picked up by the circulation staff, placed on trucks, and examined to separate regular discharges from books without punched book cards, with incorrect book cards, or without date-due slips, all of which require some special processing. One operator can process books with proper date-due slips and book cards very quickly—at the rate of about five books per minute. When discharging books, the operator sets slides on the 1031 terminal to deal with fine status (paid or not paid), date of return (today, yesterday, or before yesterday), and then the book card is inserted in the terminal. After the card runs through the terminal, it is replaced in the book and the book is ready for shelving. The date-due slip, which the borrower returned with the book, is discarded. Printed messages are generated in the discharge operation only when a book has been saved for a patron, when a book has been reported as lost, or when the terminal misreads a card. Misreading may be caused by the folding of a card or the mispunching of cards or badges. Procedures have been established to deal with these problems.

Faculty and staff are exempt from fines. Students are fined for books more than three days overdue and for failure to return called-in books. For students who do not pay fines as they return overdue books, four-part fine notices are prepared by the computer each weekday. One part is mailed; the remaining three are filed by borrower's name. Copies of the fine notices may be used for follow-up notices if needed. Overdue notices for books more than four days overdue are produced by computer once a week. If needed, two weeks later a second notice is prepared; a third and final notice is sent two weeks after that. If the borrower does not respond to the final notice within two weeks, he is billed for a "lost" book.

Quarterly notices are prepared to advise faculty of books charged to them. In addition, quarterly listings are run of books charged to carrels, and to departments, such as bindery, cataloging, and the reserve room.

Although the reserve room books are carried in the computer circulation file to indicate their location, they are circulated manually. A quarterly computer listing in call number order of all books charged to the reserve room serves as the reserve room's shelflist.

Books beyond repair are charged and set aside for bibliographers' consideration until they are replaced, withdrawn, or tied and returned to the stacks. For all periodicals or other materials requiring binding, an extra bindery ticket is used to prepare a punched book card, which, in turn, is used to charge such materials to the bindery. When library materials are returned from the bindery, they are discharged before they are sent to the stacks.

If a book charged out to a patron is lost, the circulation record is changed from a charge to the patron to a charge to a "lost" category. A duplicate book card is prepared, on which the name and address of the borrower, as well as the history of the loss, is entered. This card is manually filed in a "lost/missing" file in call number order.

If a patron is unable to find a desired book in the stacks, he may ask the operator at the main circulation desk to search for the "missing" book on the 2740 master terminal. If the book is not listed in the computer circulation file, a "locate" form is completed and the book is searched for nightly in the stacks and repeatedly on the 2740. If the book is found, it is placed on the "save" shelf, and the patron is sent a notice that it is available. If the book is not located after a two-week search, it is charged to a "missing" category in the computer file because such a charge will block any transaction record. A duplicate book card is prepared and manually filed.

The library staff is interested, of course, in holding down the percentage of lost or missing items. For example, *a study of the Africana collection revealed that 5 percent of the collection was missing.* To facilitate the search for lost or missing items, each department is assigned different "missing" numbers. Quarterly lists are prepared, by department, of missing materials to encourage continued searching or replacement. In addition to these efforts to maintain the integrity of the library's holdings, the staff is conducting ongoing studies to develop profiles of collection use.

The computer circulation system has enabled the staff to conduct an inventory. The main library collection was established in the 1880s and no substantial inventory had ever been taken. The effort to match book cards prepared from the shelflist to physical volumes in the collection uncovered discrepancies in the catalog and the shelflist. All cards without books were examined for possible replacement of the books or withdrawal of the cards. All books without cards were compared with the catalog and cards were prepared or appropriate corrections were made. These original discrepancies have been corrected. All data listed on the book cards have been placed on magnetic tapes to serve as an inventory of the circulating collection. The tapes are periodically updated and printouts are produced as needed. An on-going inventory is therefore possible.

An important advantage of the computer system is that the integrity of the computer file is never violated, as was the case with the manual file. In the manual system, charge cards were pulled to send overdue notices, to search for missing items, and to withdraw records of items that had been missing for two years. It was seldom possible to keep up with the refiling and many cards were out of the main file for long periods of time. In the computer system, records are not, and need not be removed from the file for such purposes.

About 37,500 patrons enter the library each week. Part of the reason for this heavy library use is the existence of a noncirculating undergraduate Core Collection of 50,000 volumes in a study area with 400 seats. As indicated earlier, the circulating system handles 900,000 of the 1,200,000 books housed in this library. Since, however, many books are consulted in non-circulating collections, e.g., Government Publications, Reference, Special Collections, Art, etc., the circulation figures are only a partial measure of the library's service to those who use the main building.[2]

COSTS

In 64 days during the summer of 1969, students produced 700,749 machine-readable book cards from the shelf list of the main library's collection for $7,740, or an average cost per card of $.011.

During the fall of 1969 and the early weeks of 1970, an average of 113 book cards per hour were placed in books in the main library. The cost of matching cards and books and the accompanying inventory was less than $20,000. About 70,000 cards were processed at the time the library opened. About 20,000 errors were found, mostly in serials.

In other words, for less than $30,000, or about $.04 per book, book cards were punched, proofread, and inserted in books, and the main library book collection was inventoried.

Annual costs for operating the circulation system are listed in Table 1.

Table 1
OPERATING COSTS

Circulation System	Annual Expenditure
Professional staff	$ 23,500
Clerical staff	53,900
Student staff	56,000
Computer use	33,000
Terminal rental	9,450
Supplies	12,000
Total	$187,850

Since about 560,000 books are used annually, of which about 280,000 volumes are charged out through the computerized circulation system and an equal number used within the library, the average cost to the library to provide access to 560,000 volumes is about $.34 per volume. If the books used within the library are excluded from consideration, the average cost for circulating 280,000 volumes is about $.67. It should be noted that this figure includes staff time for administering 600 study spaces, 18 seminar rooms, inventory, collection management, lost and found, etc. Were it possible to identify and exclude the cost of rendering these services, the unit cost would be lower. In any case, for $.67 or less per circulation, this automated system records circulation, provides self-service charging, offers on-line inquiry regarding book availability, produces fine, overdue, call-in, and book available notices, prepares quarterly charge lists, compiles statistics, and permits effective inventory control.

OBSERVATIONS

This on-line, real-time computer circulation system has substantially improved the quality of service provided by the library. Library materials are no longer in limbo. Volumes that are not where they are usually stored are carried in the circulation file. Patrons have only to check the stacks or consult the circulation record to learn where books are located. However, the on-line inquiry capability of the system would be enhanced if patrons as well as staff were able to use the inquiry terminal. If a cathode-ray-tube (CRT) display terminal is acquired, as contemplated by the library staff, the inquiry capability should be significantly improved.

The library staff wisely did not choose to use a batch-processing computer circulation system (where the existence of a problem might not surface until the patron or the information were no longer readily at hand), but chose instead an on-line system, where problems are immediately visible and can be dealt with as they occur.

Another wise decision of the staff—to use only the full call number and exclude the author and title for identification of circulating items—has brought significant savings in the preparation of book cards and is continuing to bring savings in operating costs, since far less computer memory is required. There have been very few requests that more information be made available on the book cards. An examination of the library's circulation records revealed that fewer than 5 percent of the books circulated required any attention beyond the regular discharge.

The experience at Northwestern suggests that some librarians may be recording more data in their circulation systems than patrons or the systems really need. It is certainly true that there are far more data in library card catalogs than patrons actually use.[3] Real cost savings and better distribution of library resources will occur when librarians pare their records to genuinely needed and useful information, as the librarians at Northwestern have done with their circulation system.

The Northwestern library staff also decided that it was not necessary to provide for multiple saves on the same book. The number of such requests did not justify the increased system complexity and costs that multiple saves would cause. The staff concluded that if there were multiple requests for a title, the library would be well advised to obtain additional copies, place the book in the reserve room, or both.

When the library had a two-week standard loan period, 16 percent of the book loans were renewed. In order to improve service as well as to reduce the quantity of renewals, the library staff decided to increase the standard loan period to four weeks. Requests for renewals have dropped sharply.

The decision to use a manual circulation system to handle the reserve room's circulation is worthy of special commendation. Good library administrators use systems that are appropriate for the task to be performed. There can be little doubt that a manual system is fully adequate to meet the needs of patrons of the reserve room.

In this system a very low priority has been assigned to the gathering of management information. The reason given is that reports that would be most useful to the library's management staff have not yet been identified. Monthly and yearly summary reports of circulation by major Dewey classification areas and by type of user are prepared, however.

Most mechanized systems have problem areas. In this system, a problem with the tearing or cutting of the date-due slips has been particularly stubborn. If the new ticket-ejector system proves as trouble-free as expected, the problem should be nearing a permanent solution. Of course, problems at the self-service terminals can be remedied at the main circulation desk, but good public relations require that patrons be spared frustrating experiences with faulty equipment.

Another possible problem area is the discharging of books. For example, if a book is returned without a date-due slip and is discharged, it must not be returned to the shelves before the due date has passed, or someone who may have intentionally withheld the slip may insert it in the book and walk out of the library with an uncharged book. It is also necessary during discharging to check carefully to see that books and book cards do, in fact, match. Fortunately, the computer relieves the operator of the task of checking manual files for "saved" books or "lost/missing" books. Overall, the system significantly reduces the volume of clerical work, especially the maintenance of files, that is required in manual systems.

The Standard Register source record punch, used as the machine backup system when the computer system is down, has occasionally dropped punches from badges that have a slight defect, resulting in faulty charges. The error rate is, however, lower with the punch than with manually prepared and key-punched charges. When the computer system is down, queuing is likely to develop at the main circulation desk because only one punch is available, but the library staff reports that the computer has seldom been down. If the library should experience a total power failure, manual charges may be made. Experience indicates that such manual charges are often illegible, miscopied, or wrongly keypunched. The reports from Northwestern suggest that machine systems are definitely less error-prone than manual ones.

While the library staff still has a few remaining problems with badges, book cards, equipment, records, and machine and human errors, they have been successfully reducing the number of difficulties in the system.

A major impact of the new system on other library departments has been to promote tighter control of and consistency in cataloging, even though the circulation system itself is flexible enough to circulate books using Dewey or Library of Congress call numbers, or documents numbers.

While the system has not reduced personnel in the circulation department, the same number of staff members are not only handling a much larger volume of circulation, but are performing a number of additional tasks, such as the on-going inventory and updating of records, which they did not have time to do before.

The library staff has considered adding system improvements, such as on-line validation of users or automatic regulation of loan privileges, but has concluded that these improvements would require more time and money than the improvements would be worth. It is apparent that the goal of this system has been to achieve maximum efficiency, accuracy, and service at a minimum cost. The fact that this system is able to handle the circulation requirements at Northwestern University's main library with a relatively inexpensive time-shared computer, and still include such features as on-line inquiry and self-service charging, should encourage other librarians to emulate this excellent system.

NOTES

1. James S. Aagaard, "An Interactive Computer-Based Circulation System: Design and Development," *Jounal of Library Automation*, 5:1 (March 1972), 3-11.
2. Velma D. Veneziano, Joseph T. Paulukonis, and Rolf H. Erickson, "On-Line, Real-Time Circulation; A Report on the Northwestern University Library System," *The LARC Reports*, 3:4 (Winter 1970-71), 1-52.
3. Richard Phillips Palmer, *Computerizing the Card Catalog in the University Library: A Survey of User Requirements* (Littleton, Colorado: Libraries Unlimited, 1972).

ACKNOWLEDGMENTS

Thanks are extended to John P. McGowan, director of libraries, Velma D. Veneziano, systems analyst, and Rolf H. Erickson of the Circulation Services Department, Northwestern University, for providing information and assistance during the author's on-site visit in May 1973. A grant from the Emily Hollowell Research Fund, Simmons College, made this case study possible.

Computerized
Library Serials Systems

Experienced librarians know that serials are among the most difficult library materials to control. At the present time, most libraries have not attempted automated serials systems. Only 216 serial and periodical computer applications were reported by the 506 libraries responding to the 1971 LARC survey. Of those that are applying computers to serials control, 94 have automated title listings, 71 have complete serial systems, 16 have subscription control, 12 have bindery control, and the remainder deal with other serials applications. Interesting to note, however, is that of all library automation efforts, only cataloging applications surpass serials applications.[1]

The technical core of the serials operation in large libraries parallels the acquisition and cataloging operation for books, but is more complex. Among the technical activities carried out in order to handle serials are: placing and renewing subscriptions, either directly or through subscription agents; checking in individual serial items; posting to the master serials holdings record, claiming issues not received; maintaining bindery records, departmental cost records, fiscal records, routing records, location and disposition records, vendor activity records, and title, subject and language indexes.

In many large libraries the records maintained by the serials department are generally not suitable for or not available to the library's users. The automation of lists of serial titles, or of lists of serial titles including the library's holdings of these serials, which can be duplicated and distributed throughout the library's environment, sometimes is a relatively simple process and may significantly improve the library's serials service. Such lists, by title and by subject, are proving very useful at Swarthmore College (see chapter 7). Peri-

59

odic union lists are being prepared by the Southeastern Massachusetts Cooperating Libraries (chapter 8) and at Tufts University (see chapter 13). If a library has a particularly important collection of serials, title and subject lists may be compiled in book form and distributed to a number of branches or other libraries. San Francisco Public Library has significantly improved its service with such book catalogs (chapter 9). Serials lists are also useful in expediting interlibrary loans and in facilitating cooperative serials acquisition programs.

In some libraries prepunched arrival cards are automatically generated for serials check-in. Other libraries have computer-produced cards for bindery control. Still others, based on the arrival cards, have arrangements for claiming, including the necessary notification of nonreceipt to be sent to publishers. Features of this type are included in the serials control systems at M.I.T.'s Lincoln Laboratory (chapter 10), and at Harvard Business School's Baker Library (chapter 11).

Some serials systems prepare routing lists or address labels for routing. The Arthur D. Little Company uses a computerized routing slip system that does more and costs less than the old manual procedures (chapter 12).

In addition to producing a variety of lists by title, subject, language, or place of publication, a few systems compile daily, weekly, monthly, or other time-period statistical reports, some of which are cumulative. Holdings lists that reveal missing items facilitate placing orders for back files. While few, if any, library serials systems include all these features, a handful of large libraries are bringing most of their serials operations under computer control.

Serials systems also include those that expedite the subject searching of periodical literature. The Tufts University Medical and Dental Library system, which is linked to the national medical literature computer system (MEDLINE), permits on-line searches of vast files of current periodical articles (chapter 14).

The increasing size of libraries and the mounting user demands for service are putting heavy pressure on libraries to provide greater accuracy and speed in all their processing operations. In order to maintain or improve the library's image, to build good public relations, and improve serials service to users, librarians should consider automated systems. Such systems can provide the library with levels of detail and precision of timing for claiming, ordering, reordering, payments, and binding that manual systems cannot equal.

Unfortunately some of the problems in manual serials handling will not disappear in computer systems. Among them are: the unannounced birth and unexpected demise of a periodical; the frequent name changes; changes in frequency of issue; changes in editor, format, indexing, etc; nonappearance or nonreceipt of individual issues; faulty numbering òf volumes and issues. An automated system may, however, simplify dealing with some of these problems, but the simplification could prove costly. On the other hand, it may prove costly not to automate. Because labor costs are rising faster than computer costs, automated serials operations are more cost-beneficial today than they were a few years ago.

In any case, since manual serials systems and computer serials systems provide significantly different levels of service and control, it is difficult to make direct cost comparisons. This, however, does not eliminate the need to be cost-conscious when considering computer applications. Rather, it suggests that consideration be given to whether more accuracy, more speed, a more sophisticated information system for more effective management of a library are needed. In some libraries, more accuracy, more speed, more of the right kind of statistics, and more of the right type of control data are becoming increasingly essential for accountability and informed decision making. If, for example, librarians accept the view that the Bradford distribution [2] holds true for periodicals (at the risk of oversimplification, the inference may be loosely drawn from Bradford's work that about 20 percent of the periodicals in a given field will meet about 80 percent of user requests), then many libraries may be subscribing to far more periodicals than most of their users require. A computerized serials system that would monitor the use of serials, which no known presently operational systems do, would enable the library to pattern its holdings to user requirements. Certainly, such a computerized serials system would offer the library an opportunity to close its management information control loop and, in turn, enable the library to make the most effective use of its always limited resources. Such a control system would require an advance in perception and design beyond that required for the automated serials housekeeping systems that are presently being developed in libraries. Many of the operational systems merely relieve librarians of tedious clerical chores. While such relief may be welcome, someday librarians may regret that they have given more attention to escape from housekeeping chores than they have to optimal utilization of their resources.

NOTES

1. Frank S. Patrinostro, *A Survey of Automated Activities in the Libraries of the United States* vol. 1 (Tempe, Arizona: LARC Association, 1971), p. 4.
2. Bradford's distribution or "law of scattering" deals with the phenomena he observed when he grouped the source periodicals on a given subject into three zones, in order of decreasing yield, with each zone yielding the same number of articles on the subject. He found that the number of periodicals in each zone increased in an essentially geometric fashion. For a more complete discussion, see S. C. Bradford, *Documentation*, (London: Crosby Lockwood, 1948).

7.
Swarthmore College
Automated Serials System
· · · · · · · · · · · · · · · · · · · ·

ENVIRONMENT

Located about 14 miles southwest of Philadelphia, Swarthmore College is a coeducational institution offering courses in liberal arts and engineering. A two-year independent study program is available to juniors and seniors. The college has an enrollment of some 1,200 students. The library has approximately 415,000 volumes, including bound periodicals, and about 2,000 current subscriptions, of which about 500 subscriptions are in three science libraries, located in separate buildings on campus—Dupont Science (mathematics, physics, chemistry, and engineering), Martin Biology (biology and psychology), and the Observatory Library.

OBJECTIVES

The Swarthmore Library automated serials system was first set up as an answer to several needs of both the library and the faculty:

1. Although complete bibliographical information on periodicals was available in the library's public catalog, there was no complete and up-to-date list of periodicals subscribed to by the library other than the periodical check-in file, a visible card file maintained in the serials section of the catalog department.
2. The single, typewritten, occasionally revised, list of currently received periodicals that was available was unable to meet the needs of all patrons of the three science libraries—Du Pont Science,

Martin Biology, and the Observatory Library—because of the libraries' separate campus locations.

3. Many of the periodical subscriptions were probably no longer needed or wanted as a result of faculty and curricular changes over the years; they were being continued either because academic departments were unaware of the costs involved or because no simple procedure had been established for terminating them.

Another, less direct objective underlying the development of this simple computer system was a "consciousness-raising" for all library workers involved in the project, so that if the library hooked up to regional or national networks in the future, much more vital library operations, such as cataloging and acquisitions for the whole library system, would not be hampered by "computer shock."

THE COMPUTER

An IBM 1130, located in the Swarthmore Computing Center, is used for this library serials operation. The programs employed are simple FORTRAN character-manipulating routines, some of which are subroutines already set up by the Computer Center on disk storage. The most sophisticated subroutine is a rapid alphabetic-numeric (alpha-numeric) sort that sorts successively on any column of an 80-column punched card. To sort the entire periodical file of 2,200 records in alphabetical order requires approximately five minutes.

Whatever programming was necessary was done by Dr. Eleanor A. Maass, the science librarian, with the help of the director of the Computer Center. The program is usually run by Dr. Maass, but two of the library's clerical staff have been trained to assemble the program and data decks and operate the computer. A clerical or student library assistant does the necessary keypunching for all library computerized operations, which include certain phases of reserve book handling and special acquisitions, as well as the periodicals program.

THE SYSTEM

Flexibility was the underlying principle in the design and modification of this periodicals handling system. While new programs and capabilities were being constantly added to it, whatever planning went into it had as the primary requirement that no operation would be initiated that couldn't be abandoned if it proved to be too complex or to take too much of either programming or of clerical time.

Each of the separate operations that has evolved into this system was first tried out with the science periodicals. This provided enough records to test a procedure without wasting too much time or money.

A basic step in the system was to keypunch periodicals data: title (no more than 60 characters), subject (a two-digit code), fund (also a two-digit code), and library location. The "fund" code is important because in this library's accounting methods each academic department is annually allotted a share of the total library budget for books and periodicals. Several space-saving short-cuts were used that depart from usual library practice. The titles selected were "working" titles familiar to the readers of the periodicals, but not necessarily conforming to library standards of corporate entry; thus "Institute of Electrical and Electronics Engineers. Systems, Man and Cybernetics Group. Transactions" became "I E E E Transactions on Systems, Man and Cybernatics." However, abbreviations were kept to a minimum to make the computer sorting process conform more nearly to library filing order. No cross-references were included.

As soon as printouts by subject and by fund were available on demand to science departments and library users, and had been received with at least a moderate amount of enthusiasm, the project was extended to *all* library periodicals. Since the factor of cost was important to academic departments considering cancelling periodical subscriptions, the system undertook to indicate to departments whether they were still subscribing to a journal and how much the subscription was costing.

The basic title, fund, subject, and library location data were converted to punched card form for all periodicals. The library's visible check-in file was the source of input. Other useful data were added directly to each keypunched card with a felt-tip pen, including:

1. the annual cost of the subscription;
2. an indicator for a "group subscription," that is, a group of periodicals arriving as part of a single membership fee if subscribed to as a unit;
3. a code letter "F" if the periodical is retained in microform;
4. a code letter "B" if the periodical is bound;
5. the number of physical volumes bound per year;
6. a decimal fraction if the cost of a subscription is shared by two or more funds; for example, the library's subscription to *Annals of Mathematical Logic* is shared by the Philosophy and Mathmetics departments;
7. a second two-digit subject code to provide an interdisciplinary feature for sorting.

The additional keypunching that was necessary to enter this data was done from the inked corrections on the cards. An interdisciplinary subject sort has been added to the system, so that all periodicals dealing with Africa, for example, whether they are primarily art, anthropology, political science, economics, or music journals, may be selected as a separate list.

The data bank consists of a deck of cards arranged alphabetically by periodical title, for each library location. When periodical subcriptions are shared by two or more departments, a separate card is prepared for each "fund" to simplify programming. In the few cases where periodicals are in more than one library, a record is kept for each location. Thus, the deck consists of 2,200 records, although the actual number of periodical subscriptions is approximately 2,000.

One of the categories included and coded in the fund listing was "gift" subscriptions. These had been painstakingly processed for many years by periodical assistants. This list made it possible to weed out, and subsequently discard, unwanted newsletters, propaganda handouts, house organs, and other peripheral material.

The system makes more periodical statistics readily available. A simple counting device in the system totals the number of periodicals in any category. A list of new periodical subscriptions initiated during the year is also prepared for the reference librarian.

A very simple bindery preparation operation was developed to eliminate at least two typings of lists by clerks. A program was written to punch a title card for every periodical volume bound; this deck is printed annually. When periodicals are to go to the binder—once a month—a card is pulled from the deck, the volume number, part, months, year (as needed) are added to it, keypunched, and from these cards a list is printed that goes to the binder for his records. The operation also totals the numbers of volumes in each of several categories. The punched cards are retained as the library's record of materials at the bindery and, when the bindery lot is returned, as a record for adding holdings to the shelflist.

Updating is the responsibility of the periodicals cataloger, who fills in a work slip for cancelled subscriptions, new subscriptions, cost changes (supplied by the periodicals assistant), and title changes. These are keypunched periodically (about once a month) by a student, after which the punched card file is manually updated.

Early in the history of this project the possibility of developing a check-in and claiming procedure for periodicals was investigated. Although this has been tried at a number of fairly small institutions, the library concluded that such a system was not feasible for Swarthmore. The visible file, when well maintained, was found to be economical and adequate for 2,000 periodicals;

batch processing by computer, on the other hand, was felt to be inconvenient and costly because of the relatively small number of subcriptions.

The library staff has considered adding precise information about the library's holdings to its system, but has not done so, believing that a network may soon take over. An experimental grant-supported project at Bryn Mawr and Haverford, sister colleges of Swarthmore, and the University of Pennsylvania seeks to convert periodical holdings to the Library of Congress Machine-Readable Cataloging (MARC) serials format. If the project is successful, Swarthmore will not need to develop its own system. It will add its holdings to the network. However, even if the union list of serials contemplated by Philadelphia area colleges and universities becomes a reality, Swarthmore will probably maintain its local system since it provides users, at their convenience, with information precisely suited to their needs.

COSTS

This system provides each department with a list of its periodicals, their individual cost, and for the benefit of future budget estimates, the cost of each department's periodical subscriptions, as well as the total cost for the whole library. With the list goes a covering letter from the librarian asking each department to consider its list carefully with a view to cancelling unnecessary subscriptions. As a result of this procedure, 67 titles have been cancelled at a saving to the library of $2,816 annually. This may be compared to the overall cost of the project itemized in Table 1.

OBSERVATIONS

The computerized serials system at Swarthmore provides convenient access, at as many contact points as are desired on the campus, to a current list of periodicals arranged by department or by one or two subjects. Academic departments and the library are given up-to-date, precise information on periodical subscription costs. Bindery preparation has been made simpler and more economical.

Some librarians believe that periodical lists must include precise information about a library's holdings in order to be useful to patrons. The decision not to include holdings information has not occasioned sufficient inconvenience for patrons at Swarthmore to justify the substantial additional expense of entering this information into the system. However, larger libraries with considerably greater periodical holdings than the 2,000 subscriptions handled in Swarthmore's system, may find holdings information essential for satisfactory service to patrons since searching substantially more extensive periodical stacks is difficult and consequently more time-consuming.

Table 1
OVERALL CONVERSION COSTS AND
MONTHLY UPDATING CHARGES

Original File Conversion	
25 hr. keypunching at $1.80 per hr.	$ 45
Supplies (punchcards, paper, etc.)	5
Computer time	50
Clerical time to add additional data to cards	30
Subtotal	$ 130
Plus 10% of the time of professional librarian for 11 months	1100
Total cost of the conversion	$1230.00
Updating	
Keypunching and computer operation 3 hr./mo.	6
Computer time for printing revised lists	10
Subtotal	$ 16
Plus programming, debugging time for professional, averaging 1/2 day per month @ $48/day	24
Total charges for updating/month	$40.00

While there is nothing technically unique about Swarthmore's system, it has avoided some of the pitfalls of library computerization: (1) it has avoided a "total system" concept, which often gets libraries into situations they can no longer control; (2) it has kept careful track of costs and has not required special funds for inputting, for programming, or file maintenance; (3) it has utilized computer personnel, but has not allowed them to change the system simply to fit the computer; it has not computerized for the sake of computerization, and has avoided performing any operation by computer that was more easily and economically done manually.

The Swarthmore system clearly indicates that, with knowledgable caution, even small institutions can make the computer a time-and-money-saving tool.

ACKNOWLEDGMENTS

The assistance of Dr. Eleanor A. Maass in providing information and assistance in the preparation of this case study is acknowledged with appreciation.

8.
Southeastern Massachusetts Cooperating Libraries Union Serials List System
• •

ENVIRONMENT

Southeastern Massachusetts Cooperating Libraries (SMCL), formed in 1968, is an unincorporated service organization representing the libraries of four collegiate institutions in an area that is approximately 35 miles south of Boston. The colleges are Massachusetts State College at Bridgewater, Stonehill College at Easton, Southeastern Massachusetts University at North Dartmouth, and Wheaton College at Norton.

The four colleges have a combined enrollment of about 10,250 students. The member libraries have a combined collection of about 480,000 volumes.

Because of the colleges proximity to one another and the relative scarcity of funds, the librarians at the four colleges have developed various cooperative programs over the years. Students at each college, for example, have interlibrary loan and direct circulation privileges at all libraries. An open telephone line connects the libraries for inquiries as to holdings and availability of materials, and a truck delivery service transports requested material.

A Data Processing Center at Wheaton College is used by all four colleges, chiefly for financial, personnel, and administrative matters. In 1969 Ruth A. Fletcher, reference librarian at Wheaton, obtained the approval of Colette E. Powers, data processing manager at Wheaton, for having the Data Processing Center print a union list of the serials titles and holdings at the libraries. Following a series of meetings the member librarians decided: (1) to organize a system for collecting the data necessary for the list; (2) to identify what the list should contain; (3) to set up guidelines regarding title entry, notations for holdings, abbreviations, etc.

The *Union List of Serials* was used for choice of entry when listing the periodicals. The most time-consuming part of the development stage was standardizing the title entry, since many periodicals were listed in different ways in the member libraries. This was particularly true of journals or proceedings of various societies and also of periodicals known commonly by initials.

Meanwhile, Mrs. Powers wrote a program that would fulfill the librarians' requests. She insisted on standardization of title entry. One of her key tasks was to prepare a numbering sequence to be used to keep the serials in alphabetical order. At first she tried an alpha-numeric system, using five alpha characters. This did not work well for two reasons: (1) it was difficult to choose five characters that would immediately identify a particular serial to the exclusion of all others; (2) it was difficult to interfile new titles that began with similar words. She then chose a six-digit number, leaving about 300 blank digits between each six-digit title number for future interfiling.

Following the gathering of serial lists, the standardizing of entries, and the writing of the program, the first list was printed in November 1969 using unit record 80-column cards and an IBM 407. Throughout the following year, further meetings were held by the librarians to work out problems and expand the list to cover such items as newspapers, indexes, series, and annuals.

OBJECTIVES

The participating libraries had as their objective the production three times a year of 17 copies of a single alphabetical merged list of standardized serial titles and holdings of the participating libraries. The list was to include a unique serial number for alphabetizing purposes, a standardized (among the six libraries) title, holdings, identification as to type of serial, and location.

It was hoped that the list would expedite interlibrary loans and facilitate cooperative serials acquisition programs and thus bring about efficiency and economy in handling serials in the libraries.

THE COMPUTER

In early 1971, the Wheaton College Data Processing Center acquired an IBM System/3-Model 10 computer and its components. All programs then in use at the center, including the library serials titles and holdings list, were converted to the new system. All data were repunched on the new square, 96-column IBM cards, and the program was rewritten in RPG II programming language.

At the center of the System/3 is an IBM 5410 processing unit. Wheaton has Model A14, with a core storage capacity of 24,576 bytes. Two 5444 disk storage drives are used, each with a capacity of 4,915,200 bytes. The 5424 multifunction card unit (MFCU), not only reads cards (at the rate of 500/ second), but punches, interprets, sorts and collates. Data are printed out on a 5203-Model 2 printer at 200 lines/minute. It has 120 print positions and uses a chain set of 60 characters. Cards are keypunched on a 5496 data recorder that has a "memory" device that allows the data to be typed at the top of the card and then verified before being keypunched.

The IBM System/3 uses a nearly square 96-column card. The top of each card provides for four print lines, each having 32 positions for printing. The bottom provides three tiers of 32 positions each for hole punching. The data on the cards for the SMCL serials list are arranged as follows:

Columns	Data
1–2	Card code.
3–5	Location in library (e.g., REF, RES, PER).
6–28	Library of Congress call number. The call number is divided into the following six units:
	6–8 Class (Alpha).
	9–12 Period (Numeric). This is the only element which is right justified.
	13–16 Period Subdivisor (Numeric).
	17–21 Author (Alpha-Numeric).
	22–24 Topic (Alpha-Numeric).
	25–28 Year (Numeric). This is optional and used for works having several editions.
29–33	Subscription data. Designed for Wheaton College Library budget analysis. The Alpha designation represents the code for the teaching department originating the request for the subscription.
34	Blank.
35–40	Sequence numbering.
41–88	Title—one or more cards (first card). Holdings—(following title card or cards).
89	Type of serial:
	D = Document (especially for the two depository libraries)
	I = Abstract or Index
	N = Newspaper

P = Periodical

S = Serial (annual, semi-annual, parts of series, etc.)

90–94 Library designations:

BRI = Massachusetts State College at Bridgewater

SMU = Southeastern Massachusetts University

STO = Stonehill College

WH-M = Wheaton College–Main Library

WH-F =   –Fine Arts Library

WH-S =   –Science Library

95 Continuation code.

96 Title code (letter T). Columns 95 and 96 represent "housekeeping" tags which do not appear in the printouts except for the edit copies of the Union List.

THE SYSTEM

As serials are received in the libraries they are checked in and sent to their proper locations in the usual manner. In addition, for each subscription special cards are made out providing the information needed for the union list of serials and sent to the Data Processing Center at Wheaton to be kept in a separate file. One or more IBM 96-column cards are used for title, depending on the length of the title, and separate holdings cards of individual libraries, including location, designations and call numbers are filed behind the title card. During 1972 and 1973 one edition per year has been published. A month before a new printing, all cards are taken from the file and checked, especially for accuracy and standardization of entry. All additions and changes are keypunched on new cards. The new cards are interfiled with the cards already forming the data base, and then all the cards are fed into the multifunction card unit. The data they contain is transferred to a disk and run through the central processing unit in accord with the instructions in the program. The resulting list is printed out three copies at a time. Nine such runs are made, since the libraries want a total of 27 copies. After the runs are made, it takes about 15 minutes to remove the carbon and burst each list.

COSTS

Since the participating librarians kept no records of the time they spent setting up the system, the costs involved for planning and development must be estimated. If one assumes they spent approximately 100 hours each in planning sessions, planning costs would amount to about $3,300. About eight hours were used for the program, (planning, card design, redesigning, etc.), at a cost of about $100.

Keypunching of the original set of cards for the IBM 407 took 80 hours (two weeks, full time), which at $5 per hour amounts to $400. Transferring the data from the original cards to the System/3 cards in 1971 involved one hour to transfer the information from the old cards to the disk in the new machine, and two hours to keypunch the new cards from the disk. At $.25 per minute of computer time, this operation cost about $45.

No record has been kept of the time spent collecting and verifying the material to be sent to the Data Processing Center for each new serials list. Consequently, costs cannot be established for this step.

The Data Processing Center bills individual libraries for producing the list. Table 1 shows the manner in which costs are broken down.

OBSERVATIONS

SMCL's regional union serials list gives titles and holdings, and nothing more. The only point of entry is the title. The list provides no control over such aspects as missing volumes, publishers, vendors, etc. Since it is updated only once a year, it can be as much as eleven months behind in supplying data.

Even if more items of information were included on the data cards, these additional data would not correct two major drawbacks of the list:

1. Since the SMCL system uses its own numbering system for arranging the serials, instead of a standard system, such as ISSN or CODEN, it will be difficult in the future to integrate the SMCL system with a wider regional, state, or national system.
2. Since the title is the only point of entry, there is no provision for control over other serials operations. To obtain bindery information, publisher, vendor, etc., one must look in the card file or call the particular library on the open line telephone.

About the most than can be said for the SMCL system is that it produces a single-purpose union list much faster than would be possible without computerization. While the objectives of this computerized serials system were reached, an inadequately conceived system such as this, even with computer-midwife, bears a product of limited usefulness.

Table 1
COMPUTER COST DATA — SMCL UNION LIST OF SERIALS

Item or Activity	Time/Rate 1972	Cost 1972	Time/Rate 1973	Cost 1973
Key punch serials data (corrections, new titles, edit corrections)	117.61 hrs. @$5/hr.	$588.05	143 hrs. @$5/hr.	$715.00[a]
Computer time on IBM Systems/3 (edit & final print-out runs)	865 min. @$.25/min.	216.25	1,791 min. @$.25/min	447.75
Time Analysis				
Edit runs	210 min.		420 min.	
Load to disk	—		192	
Merge data file	120		106	
Sequence check	—		123	
Misc. tests, etc.	—		40	
Print out 27 copies	535		910	
Total	865 min.		1,791 min.	
Paper (4½ cartons, 20-lb. stock)	$17 ea.	76.50	$17 ea.	76.50
Decollate and burst	4 hrs. @$4/hr.	16.00	4 hrs. @$4/hr.	16.00
Programs	2@ $10	20.00	2@ $10	20.00
Total cost		$916.80		$1,275.25
Per copy cost[b]		$ 36.67		$ 51.00

General Statistics: SMCL Union List	*1972*	*1973*
Total serial titles, including cross-references	4,367	4,640
Total new serial titles	457	349
Total cards key punched, including corrections, updating	3,136[c]	1,121[d]
Total deletions of titles and holdings	—	76
Total pages per copy	278	425

[a] Entire data file repunched.
[b] Computer Center retains two additional copies: one regular, one edit. Total copies produced in 1972 and in 1973: 27.   [c] Computer count.   [d] Editor's count.

ACKNOWLEDGMENTS

The assistance of Hugh Montgomery, editor of SMCL Serials project, Ruth Fletcher, Reference Librarian, Wheaton College, Colette Powers, Wheaton College EDP Center, and Joseph A. Horn in the preparation of this case study is acknowledged with appreciation.

9.
San Francisco Public Library
Automated Serials System

● ● ● ● ● ● ● ● ● ● ● ● ● ● ● ● ●

ENVIRONMENT

The San Francisco Public Library, comprised of a main library and 27 branches, serves the Bay Area population of about 700,000. With an annual expenditure of about $5 million, the library and its branches circulate about 3,250,000 items from a total collection of 1,356,000 volumes. The annual periodical budget of $75,000 provides the library with about 10,000 subscriptions.

OBJECTIVES

The San Francisco Public Library, like many other libraries across the country, was faced with increasing operating costs and potential decreases in budget. Seeking to provide more and better service, the library staff decided to introduce automation into the Serials Division. The reasons for beginning in this division were the shortage of clerical help in the Serials Division, the growth of clerical records to insure control over the serials collection, and the need to provide quicker access to periodical holdings. Other reasons for choosing the Serials Division were that while it was large enough to provide a good experimental foundation for further automation, its automation would be less costly than that of any other department. Also automation of this division would change internal processes, but would not directly involve the public. The three major objectives of the automation effort were (1) to produce book catalogs of the complete periodical holdings of the library, (2) to automate the check-in process, and (3) to automate the binding procedures.

THE COMPUTER

The San Francisco Public Library makes use of the computer facilities at the city's Electronic Data Processing Center. During the time the library was developing the book catalogs of periodical holdings, it used an IBM 360/50 in a time-sharing mode. Data were fed into this computer from an IBM 2741 Datatext computer terminal, which was rented for this initial input and then returned. The Stromberg Datagraphics system was used to transfer the data from magnetic tape to microfilm and then to printing plates to produce the book catalogs.

San Francisco's Electronic Data Processing Center now has two IBM 370/ 100 computers. Large printing jobs are done on an IBM 360/20. All new input into the library's periodical file is done by optical scanning, using an IBM 1288 page reader. IBM keypunches are used only to add or correct arrival cards.

THE SYSTEM

Planning for the system began in 1967 with a $30,000 grant to the library through the Public Library Service Act of the State of California. The library, with Linda F. Crismond as its electronic data processing coordinator, in conjunction with San Francisco's Electronic Data Processing Center and the Computer Usage Development Corporation, designed the system. In February 1967 surveys to determine the needs of the library were begun, and a $20,000 contract with the Computer Usage Development Corporation was granted for the purpose of writing the 22 programs that were necessary. A systems analyst was also assigned on a part-time basis by the city. From October 1967 to February 1968 final decisions were made concerning size and format of the catalogs, method of input, and information to be included.

In December 1967 the preparation of the serial records for input was begun. Data for input were gathered from four files. The first, the title card catalog, gave a holding statement indicating individually bound volumes, the call number, the department location, medium of publication, place of publication, language, and the subject headings. The second, the bindery "rub" file of information to appear on the spine of the bound volume and related information, was used to determine which titles were bound and the number of issues found in one volume or binding unit. The third, the check-in file, gave the frequency of publication, the latest issue received, the number of issues per volume, and either the date of publication or the issue number for the latest issue received. This file also provided the order source, the publishers' names and addresses, and the number of subscriptions per title. A fourth file, to show lacunae in the library's holdings, the expected date of an issue, the expected issue number, and the expected date of arrival, was created by having one clerk and one part-time page survey past issues of each title. Three years' holdings were checked for titles published six times a year or less; two years for titles published monthly; and the past year for titles published more frequently than once a month.

Between February and April 1968 the data from the four files were fed into the computer using an IBM 2741 Datatext computer terminal, which allowed for immediate proofreading of the input and immediate correction. For three months the data for 9,470 subscriptions, representing 6,622 titles, at an average of 152 subscriptions per day were input for 11 hours a day, five days a week at a cost of $.308 per subscription (excluding salaries of the terminal operators).[1]

From this initial computer base, three serial catalogs were produced. Unlike many title listings, the title catalog includes descriptive notes as well as cross-references. The subject catalog has place of publication notes and cross-references. The foreign language catalog indicates the languages used in multilingual publications in addition to place of publication details. The catalogs also indicate the locations of multiple copies of a title and identify those that circulate.

The data for these catalogs were transferred from magnetic tape to microfilm and then to printing plates to produce the catalogs. The Bay Area Reference Center financed the initial printing of 200 copies of the catalogs in book form, which were then distributed to Bay Area libraries.

Once the production of the book catalogs was completed, work was begun on the production of arrival cards to be used in the check-in process. The arrival cards, which were produced monthly, included one arrival card for each issue expected to be received during the month. The arrival card is a blank card except for a prepunched six-digit number in the upper left corner. Because the card is blank, no codes or abbreviations are used, and it can accommodate 2,200 characters. The information on the card includes full title, frequency of publication, month in which issue is due, expected date of issue, volume number, issue number, or part, department to which it is sent, serial number in upper right corner—a unique number for each title that is a key to the master file—a one-digit order source code, and publisher's name and address.[2]

To produce these cards, 16 additional data elements were added to the computer base. Between May and June 1968 two librarians coded titles from A to M to produce the first set of arrival cards in August. The entire alphabet was completed by November 1968. The delay in completing the coding— caused by the unexpected amount of time needed to do it—proved to be valuable, because examination of the first set of arrival cards in August revealed that refinements were needed in the coding of the expected arrival date and the expected date of the issue. Some difficulty was experienced in coding the arrival of periodicals received semiannually, since the gap between issues was not necessarily six months. A more refined coding system was designed to deal with the problem.

The coding performed by the librarians onto keypunch worksheets depended on several basic elements: (1) coordination of frequency control with date control to produce a correct issue date on the arrival card; (2) coordination of issue control with date control to produce a correct issue date; (3) correlation between issue date and issue number, and (4) correct estimation of the possibility of issue delay or early issue in order to produce the arrival card in the month when issue is received.[3]

If a periodical is to be bound, the librarian must select the correct binding code, correlate the binding count with latest issue number and date to produce a binding card, and code the expected binding delay so that a card will be produced in the month desired.

Arrival cards are used daily in the check-in procedure for serials. As a periodical is received, the arrival card is pulled and checked. When the card is correctly updated, the card is put in a bundle that will eventually be arranged according to the prepunched numbers. If any information is incorrect, a correction form is filled out and sent to be keypunched at the Electronic Data Processing Center. New cards are prepared and processed with the rest of the daily receipts. Any information punched on new cards overrides whatever was previously assigned to the prepunched number on an incorrect card. If no arrival card is found, two cards are punched as follows: the "A" card contains issue date, volume and issue number, serial number, and the first line of the title; the "B" card contains receiving code, department location, serial number, frequency code, and the second line of the title. The arrival cards are then batched together with a control card, giving the date of arrival, and are sent daily to the Electronic Data Processing Center. The Periodical Department and all subject departments receive daily, weekly, and monthly cumulated lists of periodicals received. This eliminates all check-in procedures in all departments. At the present time with approximately 10,000 subscriptions, 86 percent have arrival cards that are accurate, 8 percent have cards needing correction, and 6 percent have no arrival cards.[4] All arrival cards unused at the end of the month are checked for possible claiming and are then reprinted in alphabetic sequence with the new cards being prepared for the coming month.

Because the library orders most of its periodicals from two vendors, the automated system is not designed to provide for automatic claiming or subscription renewal. However, since the unprocessed arrival cards that remain at the end of each month suggest issues that may need to be claimed, the system provides more control than was available with the manual system. Under the manual system, the library conducted about one complete review of the check-in file per year.

The system is designed to provide binding notification. When the correct number of issues has been received, the computer produces a binding notification card. The card shows the issues that are ready to be bound and is used as a guide to pull issues from shelves. The card then becomes a record of what is at the bindery. The bindery card is blank and can accommodate 2,000 characters. The information on it includes title, inclusive dates and numbers of binding units, code for department location, call number, textual statement for binding (such as bind JA/JL), or other instructions (such as index bound separately, and issues missing from binding unit).[5]

Among the statistics generated are:

> Subscriptions currently received,
> Titles currently received,
> Titles held,
> Titles currently bound,
> Titles with lacking materials (missing issues),
> Titles by order source,
> Titles by foreign language,
> Titles by state of publication,
> Titles by main library department and branches,
> Titles by publication medium (microfilm, microfiche, etc.),
> Number of arrival cards produced,
> Number of arrival cards reprinted from previous month,
> Number of titles with predictable issue dates,
> Number of binding slips produced,
> Number of records read from and written on arrival index,
> Daily arrival card count.[6]

The daily arrival card count is useful in helping to ensure that no records are lost.

All phases of this system have been operational for over three years. The master file is updated once a month showing accumulation of titles, frequency changes, additions to holdings, and newly added bound volumes. All new input into the file is done by optical scanning, using an IBM 1288 page reader. Keypunching is used only to produce corrected or missing arrival cards. After each update of the master file, new arrival cards are calculated and printed. With each printing an arrival card index also is created that associates the information printed on the card with the prepunched six-digit number on the card. This provides a check against loss of records. During the first nine months when defects in the automated system, equipment down time and debugging delays caused problems, a manual check-in system was maintained to ensure against the loss of records.

The title catalog is produced twice a year, the subject catalog once a year. Editions of the foreign language catalog are issued only when they are deemed necessary.

COSTS

Only generalized and estimated costs of this system, as listed in Table 1, are available:

Table 1

COSTS (EST.) OF SAN FRANCISCO PUBLIC'S SERIALS SYSTEM

Computer, annual	$27,000
Staff, annual (1/3 time on this project)	16,500
Data processing staff, annual	16,500
Total	$60,000

The cost of launching this system included an initial grant of $30,000, input costs of $2,900, and the salaries of the terminal operators.

During the three years that the system has been operational, the generalized annual cost for maintaining a subscription in the system is about $6. Assuming a daily input of about 480 issues, the estimated average annual cost per issue is $.41.

OBSERVATIONS

By means of its automated serials system, the San Francisco Public Library has maintained control over an ever-increasing number of periodicals and has made information regarding its holdings available to a wider circle of users. The 200 copies of the book catalog are used extensively both inside and outside the library. The library has also acquired statistics about the periodical collection that reveal its strengths and weaknesses. These statistics are helpful in improving holdings in certain subject areas, in acquiring useful foreign-language items, and in ascertaining whether an appropriate geographical distribution of titles is being held by the library.

This system has brought about the elimination or reduction of files in all serial-related departments. The subject departments no longer maintain separate title files; the main dictionary catalog no longer lists periodical cards; the bound-volume serials file, formerly maintained in the Catalog Department, has been eliminated, and the check-in files that were formerly necessary in all departments have been replaced by the cumulative arrival lists. The file recording materials at the bindery has been simplified because the computer-produced cards indicate the volumes that are at the bindery.

The system, as intended, furnishes book catalogs of periodical holdings in the library by title, subject, place of publication, and foreign language; provides an orderly system for check-in, and regularizes binding procedures. It produces annual order lists and a lacking-materials list used to facilitate purchasing of back files. It generates a daily cumulative arrivals list and monthly statistical reports. The book catalogs not only afford an accessibility not provided in the manual system, but facilitate interlibrary use and loans. The check-in and binding features have reduced clerical chores, contributed to staff morale, and provided statistics for improved library management.

While the inception of the system was not without developmental problems and delays, it has been functioning successfully for several years. It has given the library and electronic data processing staff experience and insights into the problems and benefits of a computerized system. It appears more than likely that the automated serials system has improved the library's serials service to patrons in the Bay Area.

NOTES

1. Linda F. Crismond, "A Computer System for Periodicals: A Report on the Experience of the San Francisco Public Library," *Library Journal*, 94 (October 15, 1969), 3620.
2. Ibid.
3. Linda F. Crismond and Sylvia B. Fatzer, "Automated Serials Check-in and Binding Procedures at the San Francisco Public Library," in American Society for Information Science, 32nd Annual Meeting, San Francisco, October 1969, *Proceedings*, 6:15.
4. *Library Automation-Computerized Serials Control* (White Plains, New York: IBM, 1971), p. 72.
5. Crismond, "A Computer System for Periodicals," 3620.
6. *Library Automation-Computerized Serials Control*, pp. 97–98.

ACKNOWLEDGMENT

The assistance of Jana M. Jevnikar in the preparation of this case study is acknowledged with appreciation.

10.
Lincoln Laboratory, M.I.T.
Government Documents
Computerized Serials System

· ·

ENVIRONMENT

Lincoln Laboratory, begun in 1951, is a Massachusetts Institute of Technology facility under contract to the United States Air Force and several other federal agencies. While all personnel at the laboratory are employed by M.I.T., the physical plant is not located in Cambridge, Massachusetts, with other M.I.T. facilities, but in Lexington, Massachusetts, about 12 miles northwest of Boston, on Hanscom Field property owned by the Air Force. Laboratory personnel are predominantly involved in applied research, the contracts for which are renewed on a yearly basis. The laboratory has now expanded into nondefense areas, such as air traffic control.

Engineers and scientists working on various projects in the laboratory need information fundamental to their research. Besides the more common reference tools, such as abstracts, indexes, books, and periodicals, lab personnel need technical reports, manuals, and documents. When a government contract is issued to the laboratory, a specific sum of money is allotted to fulfill that contract. The money pays for equipment, salaries, and any services needed by the personnel. Since the scientists need the services of an information center, such a service—the Lincoln Laboratory Library—has been set up.

The book collection of about 40,000 volumes, exclusive of bound periodicals, includes about 700 periodical titles. The library expends annually about $27,000 for books, $50,000 for periodicals. Such voluminous works as *Chemical Abstracts* are on microfilm and, for space saving, hard copy of many journals is being replaced by microfilm as soon as it becomes available. There is free photocopy service for library clientele. Because of the need for specialized materials to suit the requirements of the scientists, the library has a separate government documents room. This room was designed to meet government security requirements for storing classified materials. While the general library on the first floor is open, during regular laboratory hours and after hours by arrangement, the documents room is not for browsing and is open only from 8:30 A.M. to 5:00 P.M., when the library staff is on duty. The documents room door is locked when the staff leaves for the day.

OBJECTIVES

The objectives of the M.I.T. Lincoln Laboratory computerized government documents system were (1) to provide scientists and engineers in a large research laboratory with improved access to documents and technical reports necessary to their work; (2) to provide laboratory personnel with a useful circulation system; (3) to provide the library with control of classified documents, and (4) to reduce manual operations and speed up processing.

THE COMPUTER

The laboratory's Computer Center houses an IBM 360/67 that can economically and efficiently handle large arrays of data, operate under a variety of programming support systems, handle a variety of routines that enable the user to stack jobs for continuous processing, and operate under TSS, a time-sharing mode. While operating under TSS, it is capable of concurrently processing two or more independent programs and doing conversational interactive computing together with batch processing on a time-sharing basis.[1] The computer has four storage units and is capable of storing 1,024 million bytes of information.[2]

Peripheral devices relevant to library use (in addition to the magnetic tape drives) are an IBM Model 1403/N1 printer and a card reader. Input cards are keypunched on an IBM 029 keypunch machine.

The scientists at Lincoln Laboratory use the 360 system in time-sharing mode from terminals in the Computer Center during the day, and the library uses it in batch-processing mode at night.

The library does not store its information in the central core storage memory, but utilizes magnetic tapes. The magnetic tape drives process 11,200 bytes of information/second.

While the 360/67 has cut costs and time for the library, the library's use of the computer was not a consideration in installing a computer center at Lincoln Laboratory. The work done for the library by the computer is a miniscule amount compared with that done for scientists involved in research. The computer processing for the documents department* could be accomplished equally well on a smaller, less expensive machine, but the large system required for Lincoln Lab is convenient, accessible, and more than adequate for the library's requirements.

The 360/67 has the ability to use several languages, such as FORTRAN, PL-1, and COBOL. Most of the scientific work is executed in FORTRAN. The library uses COBOL exclusively.

The input of the documents system depends upon the frequency of use of certain items in different programs. There are four computer programs for the documents system, levels one through four. The level 1 program, which produces a document addenda report, is run three or four times a week and takes 0.01 hours of computer time. The level 2 program, which produces a current accessions list and a new and added list of documents by accession number, is run twice a month, and takes on the average 0.06 hours of computer time. The level 3 program, which is an update of the fourth program, is issued occasionally, and takes 0.15 hours of computer time. The level 4 program, which updates a number of listings from the master tape, is computed once every three months, and uses 1.0 hours of computer time.

THE SYSTEM

The Lincoln Laboratory Library personnel decided to initiate a computer system when a librarian at the Raytheon company, in Wayland, Massachusetts, became one of the first to successfully use IBM cards in her system. The first phase began in 1960. Document information was keypunched onto IBM cards, the librarians alphabetized and sorted the cards in the proper order using electronic data processing (EDP) equipment, and the cards were then listed on a printout.

In January 1961 library personnel realized that they had too many card trays holding too many cards, so they transferred all the information to magnetic tape, using an IBM 1401-C3 computer, available at the laboratory. At this time the library used some time on an IBM 7094, the main computer for laboratory scientists for speeding up their sorting processes, but the 1401 served most needs of the library.

The IBM 360 family was introduced in March 1965. The laboratory replaced its 7094 in June 1965 with an IBM 360/40, which was installed until the Model 67 was made operational. The library had to wait six months for a COBOL compiler to be delivered for the system. Since then, a number of scientists have made use of the COBOL compiler in the 360 system. In addition, the library requested a print chain with upper and lower case

*The library refers to the Documents Department as the documents section. Text correction was noted too late for inclusion.

letters for its programs; upper and lower case are now also used by other divisions at the laboratory.

The staff worked with a systems analyst who advised very careful planning so that redesign would not be necessary. By December 1968 the library system was completely debugged and fully operational. Although new versions of programming languages used in the 360 computer have been brought out to improve processing, no major changes have been made in the library's programs since then.

Documents, including government reports, technical reports, journals, serials, etc., some of which are classified documents, come to the laboratory in a variety of ways. The primary means of receiving documents is by automatic distribution. That is, either the library initially writes to a company, such as General Electric, to request reports in certain subject areas or on specific projects, or people who know individuals working on projects at the lab send material on a regular basis. A secondary means of receiving documents is by ordering materials, as they are needed, directly from the Defense Documentation Center (DDC), National Technical Information Service (NTIS), National Aeronautics and Space Administration (NASA), Atomic Energy Commission (AEC), other government agencies, or universities. Most documents the library acquires are free. Recently, however, NTIS has put a $.95 charge on microfiche, and a $3 charge on standard size DDC documents, and an $8 charge for larger sized documents.

In 1971 the library's Documents Department ordered about 300 documents per month. Since about 300 documents per month came in by automatic distribution, a total of about 600 documents is processed each month. As of January 1972 the library had 76,000 technical reports and documents on tape, representing 52,000 titles—that is, 24,000 documents are duplicates and are indicated as such and added to the master tape as copy numbers.

No acquisitions work is performed by the computer. One library employee by telephone or through government channels, orders all the reports that need to be ordered. Any lab employee may request documents. The documents department provides a "rush" service on requests so indicated. The library keeps a Document Request Form on file until the document arrives, and then reports its receipt to the person who requested it.

Document information for computer input and recording on magnetic tape is filled in on a coding sheet that indicates all the information to be transferred to the IBM cards by a keypunch operator. An identifying number for each document includes its classification (unclassified, confidential, secret), accession number, copy number (if more than one copy), and an article number which refers to in-house abstracting of articles. The title entry may include 150 characters; if the maximum number of characters were used, they would be divided onto three cards. Since most documents come to the laboratory with the instruction that in a certain number of years the classification will be reduced (for instance, from secret to confidential), a card is prepared for the regrading code, which indicates the change in classification. A source card indicates where the document came from, the date it was received, the Post Office Registered Mail number of the package in which the document arrived, if applicable, and whether the document is earmarked for circulation, reference, or interlibrary loan. A maximum of 16 subject terms may be allocated. Depending upon the length of information necessary to identify each document, the number of cards prepared varies between 10 and 30. The maximum record length of a single document is about 900 characters. Usually, under 80 characters are used per IBM card—the average is 60-70 characters. When duplicated documents arrive, the duplication information is indicated on the appropriate card, but a whole set of cards for a duplicate document is not prepared.

When documents arrive at the lab, they are sent directly to the documents department. An accession number and the date are immediately added, and the coding sheets are filled out as described above. The keypunch operator fills out all the information on the form, except for the subject headings. The professional documents librarian fills in the subject headings, and checks the sheets. The keypunch operator can punch coding sheets in a little over a minute for each sheet (14 sheets in 15 minutes).

All the information punched onto the IBM cards is fed into the computer and put on magnetic tape storage. Each group at the lab using magnetic tape storage has its own bins in a special room where the magnetic tapes are stored. As of 1972 the library had about a dozen tapes in its bins. While the library has a dozen full tapes, only a few are used in performing the various levels of programs. The grandfather-father-son system is used as a backup protection if any tapes should be destroyed.[3]

Part of the circulation process is handled by the computer. Two circulation cards, white and yellow, are assigned to each document. If a document that arrives has not been ordered for or requested by anyone, it is assigned its accession number, coding sheets are prepared, and the document is placed on a shelf by accession number in a special room in the documents area. If the document has been requested, the requesting person's badge number is punched out on the white card along with the document's accession number and its classification. The card goes to the circulation clerk who in turn routes the document to the requester. If a document is classified, the recipient's signature must also appear on the white card.

Every time program level 1 is performed, the white circulation cards are sent down to the computer (when a document is loaned and returned) with the set of cards for each document. In the meantime, the yellow card is kept in a file in the documents room by document accession number. When a document circulates there are two records of its whereabouts: (1) the yellow card, which is filled out by hand, indicating the recipient, his badge number, and the dates on which the document goes out and comes in, is kept in the documents room; (2) the white card, keypunched to indicate the appropriate information, is sent to the computer room so that a second record may be kept. It also serves as the basis of the circulation statistics derived from the output of the system.

Thus two cards, handled manually and by computer, enable the librarian to know where documents are at all times. Individuals who want documents can quickly be told who has them. When a lab employee's employment is terminated, the librarian can check whether this person has not returned any documents. In this system, there is no strict circulation period; in fact, the documents department often does not require personnel to return some materials, such as NASA and DDC reports obtained on microfiche. If these reports are unclassified, there is no strict control. Classified documents are, of course, very carefully controlled.

When the computerized documents system was planned, the designers attempted to anticipate all possible needs. Consequently, there are a variety of outputs from the four levels of programs, despite the small amount of computer time used. Level 1, the most frequently used report list, is a document addenda report prepared about three or four times a week. It produces a printout by report numbers. Level 2 output reports, issued bimonthly, include a circulation report, a current accessions list by subject, and a new and added Master List of documents by accession number. Level 4 reports are issued quarterly. The library staff helped the systems analyst plan the computer programs to cover all contingencies, thus 14 reports are output at level 4. The 14 titles are self-explanatory: Master List (shelflist by accession number), NATO list, Location code, Subject index, Documents Not Used, Circulation Statistics, Post Office Registry list, Contract Number list, Author list, Subject list, DDC Number list, Source list, Issuing Agency list, and Title list. The reports provide many avenues to reach any document in the collection. Of course, some lists are used often, others seldom. For instance, the Post Office Registry list, an aid to locating mishandled documents, is infrequently used; there are few problems in this area. The Level 3 program is issued at unspecified intervals to prepare updated addenda reports to any of the above quarterly lists.

The reports are housed in the government documents room. The room is divided into four main areas: document storage room; work space including offices and keypunch room; storage area for microfiche, including viewers, and a separate room where the lists are kept, with tables and chairs for the convenience of lab personnel. The documents for 1960–69 are printed out in one long accessions list. The printout sheets are bound in manipulatable volumes and are stacked vertically on one set of shelves. Reports providing other approaches to the collection are arranged around the room. The latest accession lists and frequently used report lists are kept on a separate shelf near the entrance to the room.

COSTS

The laboratory computer center estimates that the monthly cost for the computer time used by the government documents department is $175. This figure includes service, computer personnel salaries, computer time, supplies, and some overhead.

Although the Computer Center's processing of government documents department programs could be performed effectively and efficiently on a smaller and less expensive computer, a less expensive computer facility that the library would have to finance would prove far more costly to it that sharing the IBM 360/67.

The Government Documents Department employs one keypunch operator, one acquisitions clerk, one circulation clerk, and one professional librarian who also serves as a part-time subject specialist. The library staff has calculated that it would require at least three more people to accomplish by manual procedures what the computer system provides for the library. If it were necessary for the Government Documents Department to hire three nonprofessionals to supplant the computer's services, it would cost the department at least $1,000 more per month than it is spending for its present system.

Costs for many of the supplies used by the Government Documents Department have not been established: they are produced in-house and the library is not billed for them. The coding sheets, for example, are produced in the laboratory's print shop as an overhead or service activity. The IBM cards used by the Government Documents Department are purchased by the Computer Center and supplied as needed without charge. A special card is required for circulation. The library expended $45 for a permanent cut of this card and orders copies from an outside agent as they are needed. The cost for these cards is nominal.

The major expense of the computerized government documents system, excluding salaries of the department's personnel, is the inclusive computer rental charge of $2,100 per year. For this figure the computer center processes about 7,200 documents per year and maintains control over the access to more than 76,000 reports and documents. Were the $2,100 computer rental charge to apply exclusively to the processing of 7,200 documents per year, the cost of processing would be $.29 per document. Since circulation processing is included in the charge, the per-unit cost is lower than this amount.

OBSERVATIONS

The computerized government documents system at M.I.T.'s Lincoln Laboratory operates more quickly and more accurately than a manual system would. Library personnel have calculated that it would require three additional employees to accomplish the tedious processing that the computer does with ease and without complaint. The system eliminates many filing and typing operations. The system saves the library a great deal of money. Those who have looked into computer operating costs know that the amount of computer time one can purchase for $175 per month is a very small fraction of a large computer's capabilities and, therefore, a very small fraction of a large computer's real costs. The Lincoln Laboratory Library is, of course, operating in an environment where most of the demands on the computer center are made by, and most of its costs are charged to, other departments. Many other computer systems operating within scientific or industrial complexes offer significant opportunities for other libraries to improve their operations and services. The small amount of computer time required to perform necessary operations in a special library may often be obtained in a time-sharing or batch-process mode from a large computer center for far less than it would cost to own and operate a library's own independent computer system, even if the system were much smaller. It is unlikely that a special library's requirements would ever interfere with the major demands on the Computer Center's time and personnel. Also, since Computer Center facilities are practically never used to their fullest capacity, it is unlikely that a library would be denied access to the computer for the running of its programs. However, experience suggests that a library should obtain firm commitments for computer time before embarking on a new computer system.

Since many of the operations performed in libraries are regarded by non-librarians as menial tasks, librarians are sometimes regarded as unworthy of professional status and esteem. One of the advantages of establishing a computerized government documents system at Lincoln Laboratory was the prestige it won for librarians among the laboratory's scientific personnel. The scientists were impressed with the fact that the library was using the computer effectively. In addition, the Air Force was impressed and satisfied with the library's use of the computer, since the circulation of classified documents is as carefully controlled as it was in a manual system, and since Air Force personnel may obtain information regarding the status of both classified and unclassified documents immediately.

This computerized system has achieved its objectives of providing improved access to government documents, establishing an effective circulation control system for classified documents, reducing of manual operations, and speeding up document processing. It has achieved these objectives at a very nominal cost to the library.

(The description of this system is as of April 1972 and may not reflect the system at the time of publication since the system is a dynamic one.)

NOTES

1. International Business Machines Corporation Reference Library, *IBM System/360 System Summary.* GA22-6810-10. (New York: IBM Publications), pp. 6–14.
2. GML Corporation, *Computer Characteristics Review,* 11:3, (Lexington, Mass.: GML Corporation, 1971) pp. 34–35.
3. In the grandfather-father-son system, information is put on tape 1. When new information is added, the information on tape 1 and the new information are put on tape 2. When further new material is recorded, the information on tape 2 and the new material are placed on tape 3, and so on. Thus every newly created tape contains all information accumulated to date.

ACKNOWLEDGMENTS

The assistance of Mary A. Granese, Documents Librarian, and Susan R. Panoff in the preparation of this case study is acknowledged with appreciation.

11.
Baker Library, Harvard
Automated Serials System

· · · · · · · · · · · · · · · · · ·

ENVIRONMENT

The Baker Library of the Harvard Graduate School of Business Administration has holdings of 461,000 volumes and serves about 1,600 masters' students and 165 doctoral students in business administration. It also serves over 300 students taking 13-week programs in middle and advanced management. The faculty of the business school numbers slightly under 200. The library's average circulation is 32,000 volumes each year. It subscribes to 6,500 journals, periodicals, and other serial publications. Of these, 2,600 are "periodical" titles, i.e., those received oftener than twice a year, and only these 2,600 are included in the automated serials check-in system. Its annual expenditure for books and periodicals is about $72,000. It disburses $14,000 yearly to bind periodicals. The 1973–74 budget for operation of the serials department is $18,465, exclusive of salaries.

OBJECTIVES

Baker Library's automated serials systems, initiated in 1962, had four project objectives and four systems goals.

The objectives were: (1) to explore the potentialities of the computer as a tool in library operations; (2) to make serial publications more easily accessible to faculty, staff, and students; (3) to save staff costs by utilizing a computer and other equipment; (4) to write a final report to include all details and technical descriptions of the system.

The goals were: (1) to replace manual methods with a system that automates key phases in serials record-keeping, eliminates duplication, improves accuracy, and speeds processing; (2) to produce at regular intervals printed lists of the library's serial holdings that, when supplemented by daily cumulative lists of periodical arrivals, would become the basic source of information for the user; (3) to provide faster claiming of missing issues of periodicals and thus maintain more complete files; (4) to provide a more detailed subject approach to all serials titles than was possible in a card catalog.[1]

THE COMPUTER

At the time of this study the system used an IBM 370/155 computer that is located at MIT's Information Processing Center and an IBM 370/145 located at the Harvard Computer Center. Since Baker Library no longer has an on-line terminal, the processing is done in batch mode. Every night a shuttle takes the library's cards to the Harvard terminal for the IBM 370/145, where the card reading, line printing, and card punching are done. Cards are read at the rate of 1,200/minute; lines are printed at 2,000 lines/minute, and cards are punched at 300/minute. The system programs are processed on M.I.T.'s 370/155.

In-house, Baker Library has an IBM 029 keypunch that is used to punch cards for new acquisitions or for corrections in the daily procedures. It is generally used about two hours per day.

Also in-house is an IBM 557 interpreter that the library shares with other Harvard Business School departments. It is used to print on a computer-produced special format card, whatever information has been punched onto the monthly expect card. Another shared machine is an IBM electronic accounting machine that is used at various times in the routine to sort punched cards.

On an average night, the library utilizes one-half of a minute of actual computer-run time. Total system residence time may be as much as two to three hours. This, of course, does not include the printing and card-punching time. Each morning the shuttle returns the output and input to the library.

Before the data from the IBM punched cards are processed they are read onto a magnetic disk reserved for Baker Library. Also stored on that disk are the master bibliographic files, the current working information file, and most programs. Because of limited space on the disk, near the end of each month the superseded files are transferred to a magnetic tape. Baker Library has about 30 magnetic tapes in storage, which not only hold backup information, but also other bibliographic files.

Baker Library's serial programs were written in COBOL by the Harvard Business School Computer Services Division, supervised and proofread by

Bill Turk, head of the Catalog and Data Processing Department, and his predecessors. At present 16 programs are involved in the serials check-in system.

THE SYSTEM

In the fall of 1962 the library staff began studying the feasibility of mechanizing serial acquisition procedures. The staff examined a feasibility study that had been conducted at the Chicago campus of the University of Illinois and an actual application of a computer to serial procedures at the University of California at San Diego. In May 1963 the staff visited the M.I.T. libraries in order to learn as much as possible about M.I.T.'s serials program, which closely resembled Baker's proposed project.

The first phase in the system design was a study of each step in the manual procedures, a consideration of any useful alternatives that a computer might offer, and an exploration of how patrons sought and used information in serials. Examination of the checklist file and visible index revealed that the serials records had to be corrected, standardized, and current receipts noted, before the manual system could be converted to an automated system. By the end of June 1963 over 900 sets of cards had been corrected in anticipation of conversion to a computerized system.

In October 1963 an IBM systems engineer presented a "Proposal for the Installation of Data Processing Equipment" that contained outlines of mechanized procedures patterned on Baker's manual procedures. The proposal was deemed inadequate for the probable demands on the system.

In December 1963 source documents and codes for information to be converted to punched cards were designed and existing records were transferred to documents for keypunching. A feasibility study was completed in February 1964.

A pilot project was run that resulted in sample printouts of a list of 500 periodicals. Thereafter work on converting the 1,500 titles remaining continued and was completed early in the summer of 1964. The documents were keypunched by an outside service bureau.

In July 1964 an IBM 1401 was installed in the Harvard Business School's Computer Services Division to be shared by several departments at the school and the library.

During the summer of 1964, subject headings were coded and assigned to converted titles. Six-digit publisher code numbers were assigned to all entries in the master list and publisher source documents were completed. In late summer 1964 the master file was recorded on magnetic tape and programs to print subject and student lists were written. In the fall of 1964 the master list was revised with respect to holdings.

Early in December 1964 the final copy for the printed catalog was sent to the printers, and in February 1965 the subject list was ready for printing. The subject catalog contained only author-title and call number entries under appropriate subject headings.[2] In March 1965 computer-produced holdings lists were in use at the public catalog, the circulation desk, and in the reading room, and the visible index was removed from the reading room at that time.

During the spring of 1965 conversion of the remaining serial records proceeded, using xerographically reproduced catalog cards as work sheets. On the work sheets, information for the master list was corrected and standardized, extraneous information eliminated, and appropriate subject and geographical headings assigned. Cards were keypunched, not by experienced keypunchers, but by a person trained especially for this job.

A geographic list was produced in June 1965, after a major revision of geographic headings, their assignment, and the insertion into the master file of a new card created to hold country codes.

It was then found that the records as originally set up would not facilitate updating by computer, so all holdings statements were rewritten and coded during the summer of 1965 to enable machine updating. This new information was added, in September 1965, as the master list was revised. A translation program was written to decode the coded holdings information. Since then, a program that updates holdings lists mechanically has been written.

In the spring of 1966 full bibliographic information, including place of publication and noncommercial publisher, was added to the master file. In the summer of 1966 a program to punch the "expect file" was worked out and tested on 200 titles. Coding of all titles for the expect file was begun in the fall and finished in May 1967. Also in the fall of 1966, routing lists were transferred to punched cards and a program was written to produce routing slips.

To facilitate routing and deletions from the routing lists, code numbers were assigned to all faculty and staff and were included in the master routing file in April 1967.

Between May 1969 and June 1971 all programs were converted from AUTOCODER programming language to COBOL. This was necessitated by a change in computers in August 1970, when Baker Library switched from the IBM 1401 at the business school to an IBM 360/65 located at the Harvard Computer Center. At the same time, a remote-job-entry terminal was installed at the Harvard Business School, but not in the library.

In November 1971 another change was made as the Harvard Computer Center converted to an IBM 370/145 and became, in essence, an on-line terminal for the IBM 370/155 at the M.I.T. Information Processing Center. When this change occurred, all that needed altering was the format of the job control cards.

All input in the Baker Library automated serials check-in system originates with the Data Processing Department and all output is returned to it. All special format cards are supplied by the library.

A deck of punched cards, representing the dates in the following year on which Sundays fall, is used by the program LDWKNØ, which is run annually, to create what is known as the "week end file"—a list of weeks in the following year. This file is stored on the disk.

Correction cards are accumulated over a month with the changes and deletions to be made in the working information file. The change cards are punched in any of four formats in order to delete an entire record, delete a single field in a specified record, change a single field, or add a single field in a specfied record. Information from these cards is transferred to the disk by the program WICHGIN.

The correction card information is joined by the "current working information" file (produced by a later part of the system and stored on disk). Both are input to the program WICHANGE(C) that is run monthly and updates the working information file as data from the correction cards indicate and prints a list of errors (usually errors on the punched cards, since the programs are considered debugged) on standard (15 inches wide) 1-ply computer printout paper.

Correction cards may also add a new record to the master file. This information is also run through WICHGIN to be stored on the disk. Program WICHANGE(A), also run monthly, takes the additions and the updated working information file (from WICHANGE(C)) to further update and revise the working information file. It also prints an error listing on standard 1-ply computer printout paper.

The updated working information file is used by the program WEXPECT, run near the twenty-second of each month, to punch, on the basis of a "header card" supplied by the library and the week end file, the weekly expect cards and to print a list of cards punched. The header card is a standard, 80-column IBM card punched with the month of the first Sunday, the day of the first Sunday, the month of the last Sunday, and the day of the last Sunday for which these weekly expect cards are to be punched. The expect cards, standard IBM card in size, are punched by the computer with the following data: grid code, time frame, seven-digit sequence number, status, routing code, copy number, location code, binding symbol, format code, abbreviated title, volume and issue numbers, date (day, month, and year), supplement, part, and abbreviated frequency. They are, however, punched in a way that necessitates the use of the IBM 557 interpreter to make them readable for the manual subsystem. The output expect cards become the input "receipt cards."

WEXPECT also updates the working information file, which is in turn used by MEXPECT, another program that is run monthly. MEXPECT generates the monthly expect cards in the same format as above (except that the header contains the year), lists them, and updates the working information file. The updated working information file is used once again as data for LISTWORK, a program run monthly or as needed, to print, besides an error listing, a spaced listing of the current working information file to be used by the Data Processing Department as a worksheet for adjustments and corrections. The error listing is in the same format as those produced above, but the spaced listing is printed on 2-ply printout paper.

Each title in the current working information file is alloted 250 characters (four punched cards when originally keypunched) and includes: sequence number, copy number, abbreviated title, volume number, issue number, date (month—one-digit code—day, and year), routing symbol, binding code, supplement code, date (month and year) of annual issue, frequency (up to 52 characters, one for each possible issue), publisher's and subscription agent's codes, claims decision code, abbreviated frequency (as on expect card), number of issues per year, issue of volume change, number of issues per volume, etc. There are spaces between these codes and some room has been left for adjustments in bibliographic requirements.

Everything that is output by the computer is returned to Baker Library. The expect cards are kept on file in the library's Acquisitions Department. As an issue of a magazine is received, its expect card is pulled. A code indicates whether or not the magazine is routed. If it is, the issue is laid aside until the next day when the computer will have printed the necessary routing slip. Whether the issue is routed or not, the pulled expect card becomes the receipt card for that issue.

The daily current "receipt cards," under the program CUMLISTIN, are run onto the disk. The header card this time contains only the date of processing (month/day/year). Also run onto the disk (monthly) is the routing file, consisting of punched cards bearing coded information covering which serials are routed and the persons to whom they are sent, by means of the program RTSCRACH/RTCREATE. These two files plus the "cumulative current receipts" file, also on disk, are the data for the CUMLIST 1 program, which is run daily.

CUMLIST 1 is the work horse of this system. It produces an error listing (in the same format as the others), prints routing slips on 3-ply, 8 1/2-inch-wide paper, and punches and prints binding cards. The binding cards are standard IBM punched cards that include an abbreviated title, issue information and a 1-digit coded location in the library of the issues to be bound. Some of the information on these cards varies slightly according to a code in the working information file.

CUMLIST 1 also produces a "processing dates file" and updates the cumulative current receipts, both of which are stored on disk to be used in CUMLIST 2.

CUMLIST 2, also run daily, produces an error listing (same format again) and the all-important cumulative daily list of receipts. This list, cumulated from the beginning of each month, includes for each title, the sequence number, title, issue information, library's receipts during that time, the location of those issues in the library or routing (though no names are given), and the date of processing. Any card that contains a routing symbol will cause the location "Routing" to be printed until otherwise notified. Two copies of the list are made on standard 2-ply printout paper. One copy is returned to the Acquisitions Department, but the other is placed in a binder, along with the cumulative lists of previous months, for public use in the reading room. For added convenience, the monthly lists are cumulated quarterly. Also in the reading room is a copy of the monthly "descriptive bibliography," or master file, that indicates the call number and the complete bound and microfilm holdings. (This master file is updated and listed by other programs.) In addition, CUMLIST 2 updates the working information file. CUMLIST 2 is also able, on request, to delete old records from the cumulative receipts file.

Periodical routing procedures in Baker Library start with the daily current receipts file of cards, used by CUMLIST 1, which have been returned to the library. These cards are sorted by the EAM (electronic accounting machine) according to the code in column 11—"Routing." Any cards that indicate that the issue is routed become the "routing receipts card" file. They remain stored as such until the issue is returned to the Acquisitions Department, at which time the card is pulled and the routing symbol removed by the data processing assistant who uses the keypunch to change the symbol in column 11 of the card. These cards are added to the daily current receipts file that is input into CUMLIST 1. When the CUMLIST 2 printout is next produced, the location "Routing" for these titles will be replaced by a specific library location.

Monthly, or as needed, the routing file subsystem is run for Baker Library. The routing file, on cards, is run onto disk. Then ROUTTITL prints a listing on standard 2-ply paper, by title and by person, of all serials that are routed, for easier access by the Acquisitions Department. Semiannually, the routing file is sorted to produce two decks of cards: a routing file of title cards, and a routing file of people cards. The former are used by CREATFIL, a program to generate and store an indexed sequential file of titles that is used along with the "people cards" in ROUTNAME. Program ROUTNAME produces a listing by person and by title printed on 1-ply computer printout paper for use by the routing clerk and the Reference Department.

There is one additional subsystem involved, the claiming subsystem, that became fully operational in April 1972. In it, expect cards that are two months old are sorted according to sequence number. They are run, together with the current working information file in the DOLLLIST program that pulls and prints, for each title there, the order information, the decision (whether or not to claim) information, and the publisher's code number. Then selected expect cards, along with the current working information file, the publishers' file in numerical order, and the master bibliographic file are input into the VICLAIMS program, which prints out claims forms that can be inserted into window envelopes and sent directly to the publisher.

Personnel involved in the development of this system included the various heads of the Data Processing Department, a programmer, an IBM systems engineer, and a keypuncher who was trained especially for this job.

The present personnel needed to debug, maintain, and run the automated serials check-in system includes the head of the Catalog and Data Processing Department, a full-time nonprofessional assistant, a part-time student assistant, two keypunchers, each of whom punch an hour per day, and a full-time Acquisitions Department employee who checks in new receipts.

COSTS

Developmental costs are not available. The 1973–74 budget of the Serials Department at Baker Library is about $18,465, exclusive of salaries. The budget is distributed approximately as listed in Table 1.

Table 1
BAKER LIBRARY SERIALS DEPARTMENT BUDGET

Item	Amount
Machine costs	$15,000
Outside keypunching	500
Programming (redesign)	2,500
Supplies (special format cards)	465
	$18,465
Salaries: (1/4 of $18,000)	$4,500
Total	$22,965

This system handles about 2,600 serial titles. Each day the system handles an incoming load of between 100 and 150 issues. If this is averaged to 125 titles, about 31,200 issues are processed in a year. It is estimated that about one-fourth of the staff's time is devoted to this system, or a cost of about $4,500 (based on total salaries of $18,000). The average cost, is, therefore, about $.74 per issue.

OBSERVATIONS

The first objective of the computerized serials system project was "to explore the potentialities of the computer as a tool in library operations." The fact that the library devoted more than ten years to developing this system indicates that the library was, and is, interested in utilizing the computer in its serials control process. Of course, the fact that the system operates in a batch mode suggests that the full potential of the computer is not being exploited. However, an on-line operation is not available to Harvard Business School administrative users.

The second objective was "to make serial publications more easily accessible to faculty, staff, and students." While it is true that the use of a computer system has standardized the procedures and the bibliographic control of all serial titles, it might still be argued that a Kardex or visible file is easier to consult to locate holdings of a single title than multiple lists—monthly, quarterly, master, etc. It might not be as easy to consult the Kardex when searching for a number of titles, since multiple titles are seen at a glance on the printout, but only a single title card is seen in a Kardex file. In any case, in the computer system the updating is done automatically and daily, so the computer printout can be "guaranteed" to be uniformly up to date, whereas the Kardex did not give that assurance.

Whether the project's third objective, "to save staff costs by using a computer and other equipment," has been reached is difficult to evaluate since there are no "before" costs available to compare with "after" costs. There apparently have been no changes in the number of personnel involved with serials.

The fourth objective was to "write a final report to include all details and technical descriptions of the system." Such a report has not yet appeared.

The first goal of the automated serials system was "to replace manual methods with a system that automates key phases of serials record-keeping, eliminates duplication, improves accuracy, and speeds processing." The automated system has reached these goals. It has replaced, rather than imitated, manual procedures. It has automated the holdings reports, binding decisions, routing slip, and claims form production. It has also produced the multiuse "expect cards" that, to eliminate duplication, become "receipt cards." The elimination of duplication increases accuracy, and in addition, the numerous computer-produced error listings assist the staff in locating whatever mistakes may occur. Increased speed is probably achieved by this system, since the expect-receipt cards are ready with all necessary information, both punched and printed, before an issue arrives. However, it should be taken into consideration that, since all cards are processed in the batch mode, the bibliographic control of an issue is not available until about 24 hours after it arrives at Baker Library. It is likely that this delay is less than that experienced in the manual system, when posting of holdings information was often delayed.

The second goal was to regularly produce printed lists of the library's holdings and daily cumulative lists of arrivals to serve as basic sources of information for the user. This goal has been reached. The Baker Library staff has recently produced, with relative ease because of its control of holdings information, an annual successor to the first printed catalog, the *Current Periodical Publications in Baker Library*.[3] Besides being for sale, this publication is used at the circulation desk, the reference desk, the public catalog, and, along with the daily cumulative printouts, in the reading room.

The third goal was to "provide faster claiming of missing issues and thus maintain more complete files." Although the periodical claiming subsystem has been in full operation for over a year, this is still too brief a period to permit evaluation of its utility in maintaining more complete files. However, the claiming subsystem became operational ten years after the automated serials system was launched. This fact alone suggests the kind of commitment in time, manpower, and money that must be made if a reasonably sophisticated custom-made computer system is to be established.

The fourth goal was "to provide a more detailed subject approach to all serial titles than is possible in a card catalog." The published *Subject List of Current Journals*[4] was a computer-produced companion to the *Printed Catalog*. However, since September 1971 both have been replaced by *Current Periodical Publications in Baker Library*, which includes main entry, subject, and geographical access to Baker's serial holdings.

A cumulative, monthly listing of title changes and new aquisitions is made available, in-house, as a supplement to *Current Periodical Publications*.

This system's estimated cost is about $.74 per issue. For this sum, all major functions of the Serials Department have been brought under speedy and accurate control. In addition, machine-manipulatable data are available for the production of printed catalogs. In the opinion of the library staff, the system is an effective, efficient, and successful application of computer capabilities to library procedures.

NOTES

1. Carol A. Laucus and Susan J. Russell; *Preliminary Report on the Serial Automation Project at Baker Library* (Cambridge: Harvard University Press, 1966), p. 1.
2. Harvard University Graduate School of Business Administration, Baker Library, *Printed Catalog of Current Journals*, 1st ed. (Cambridge: Harvard University Press, 1965).
3. Harvard University Graduate School of Business Administration, Baker Library, *Current Periodical Publications in Baker Library* (Cambridge: Harvard University Press, 1971— annual).

4. Harvard University Graduate School of Business Administration; Baker Library, *Subject List of Current Journals* (Cambridge: Harvard University Press, 1960).

ACKNOWLEDGMENTS

The assistance of Wilbur Turk, head of the Catalog and Data Processing Department, Baker Library, and of Janet P. Johnson in the preparation of this case study is acknowledged with appreciation.

12.
Arthur D. Little, Inc.
Serials Routing Slip System

· ·

ENVIRONMENT

Arthur D. Little, Inc. (ADL), a research and development, engineering, management consulting, and economic services organization, is one of the oldest, largest, and most diversified firms of its kind in the world. ADL advises clients on planning, implementing, financing, organizing, and managing the use of capital and human resources. These professional services are provided to business, industry, government, professional and trade associations, nonprofit institutions, and individuals in the United States and abroad. In recent years, ADL has been increasingly called upon to provide assistance in the public sector to the U.S. federal government, state and local governments, and foreign governments.

ADL has a staff of about 1,500 employees, more than half of whom are professionally trained management specialists, scientists, engineers, and economists. In addition, ADL has contract relationships with over 350 consultants, drawn primarily from universities, to provide specific skilled advice.

ADL's Management Sciences Division (MSD) and Public Affairs Center (PAC) apply mathematical and scientific methods to problems of industry and government. They specialize in quantitative techniques for use in management decision-making, operations, and process control, planning and forecasting, and economic planning. The Management Sciences Division/ Public Affairs Center Library provides materials for employees of these divisions. The library has a staff of five and holds about 3,000 books and 450 serial titles.

OBJECTIVES

The manual routing of serials (periodicals or journals) became more time consuming, more difficult, more tedious for the library staff, and more costly as the number of employees and the numbers of subscriptions rose. The primary objective in developing a computerized periodical routing system was to reduce the time, tedium, difficulty, and cost of routing periodicals to employees in these divisions.

THE COMPUTER

The equipment used by the MSD/PAC Library for its routing system is the same equipment used by ADL for its various automated programs. The keypunching is done on an IBM 029 card punch. The computer used is an IBM 360/40, with 256,000 core memory running under IBM's disk operating system (DOS). The keypunched cards are fed into an IBM 2540 card reader. An IBM 1403 printer produces the printout sheets. These are placed in an IBM forms decollator to be burst and unfolded. The operation does not require a collator or sorter.

The program for the periodicals routing system is written in COBOL. It utilizes three tape drives and one disk. A user's guide has been prepared by ADL giving details of the program.[1] The program, which is on the disk, is kept in the computer library. A new master file tape is produced each time the program is run.

THE SYSTEM

This project was launched in February 1970 in the Management Sciences Division. Since the project was not regarded as urgent and there was no deadline set for completion, it was advanced during the librarian's spare time. She had the part-time assistance of a staff member who was not a computer programmer.

The manual system of routing was analyzed and decisions were made as to which data elements would be essential to the program. The manual system had worked as follows:

1. A numbered list of all titles received by the MSD Library was prepared.
2. This list was routed to all staff members.
3. Each staff member indicated the titles he or she needed to receive and returned the list to the library.
4. An index card for each journal title was prepared.
5. Staff selections of each journal title were recorded on title cards.

6. Routing lists were typed.
7. Routing lists were reproduced.

This manual system required 18–20 hours of staff time per week to route 150 titles to about 100 employees.

The first computer program went into effect in May 1970. It was on magnetic tape and could only handle 150 serials and 200 names, and it proved to be too limited in scope. The librarian decided to rewrite and enlarge the program's capabilities, this time with the aid of Gerald Kramer, an ADL computer programmer. The rewriting project was undertaken in August 1970 and became operational in October. The system presently handles 300 periodicals and well over 150 names and serves PAC personnel as well as MSD employees.

The new program is on a disk operating system, thereby providing for random access, and it was completely debugged in ten runs. The disk system has a capacity for data far beyond that required by this routing system. It has the following capabilities:

1. New slips may be printed as new subscriptions are placed.
2. A cancelled serial may be deleted from the system.
3. A serial title may be changed.
4. Old or new employees may be added to the routing slips for any items they want to receive.
5. The name of an employee whose interest changes may be deleted from any of the slips or added to any of the slips. The employee's name may be removed when he or she leaves the company.
6. To accommodate (*a*) female employees who marry and (*b*) management's frequent need to rearrange office space, the name or room number of an employee may be changed.
7. Employee priority codes may be established or changed on slips to ensure that project leaders or key personnel are at the top of the list.

The first step in this automated system is the creation of a list of titles to be routed and distributed to staff members. Each employee indicates his or her choices and returns the list to the MSD/PAC Library. Three lists, to be made by the librarian with the information she has acquired, are necessary for operating the automated system: (1) a list of all employees in the MSD/PAC divisions, each with his employee number; (2) a list of all journals to be routed, each with an identifying number; (3) a list of choices of periodicals to be routed to each employee.

Only new data or corrections are fed into the program, which is run biweekly, on a batch basis. To enter a new serial into the system, the title (abbreviated according to *American Standard for Periodical Title Abbreviations*), its number, and the coded instructions are entered on the coding form. The deletion of a serial from the system, changing the title of an existing journal, entering an employee and his or her choices for routing, deleting an employee, changing an employee's name or room number, adding or deleting an employee's name on a periodical list, and adding, changing, or deleting priority status of an employee are all accomplished by established transaction codes, plus whatever information is pertinent, such as new names, new room number, or new journal titles.

All necessary input data are listed on a coding form by member of the library's clerical staff, and the coding forms are then taken to the in-house keypunch facility, where the information is entered on punched cards and verified. The keypunched cards, together with program and job control decks are fed into the computer for each run. Through the coded keypunched cards the computer is instructed (*a*) to make copies of all slips, (*b*) to prepare only copies of slips involved in change transaction, (*c*) to furnish copies of slips involved in a change transaction, plus special requests for particular slips, or (*d*) to print copies of only particular slips that are needed.

The computer prints on $9\frac{7}{8}$ by 11-inch printout paper with one carbon leaf. Since four slips are printed on each sheet, each printing yields eight slips. Each routing slip lists the journal title, the names and room numbers of all employees requesting the periodical, and a note at the bottom indicating that the serial should be returned to the MSD/PAC Library. One slip is attached to the issue; one is filed in the library. Each routing slip lists names in room number order to facilitate interoffice delivery. The system is capable of listing names on a slip in priority code if desired.

With each run, this system generates a list of periodical titles in an assigned periodical number order. It also generates a listing of all employees, their room numbers and employee numbers, and the titles of serials currently routed to them, with assigned periodical numbers, and priority codes for each journal. These lists enable the librarian to keep track of the journals a staff member receives without the need to maintain manual records. Once a year the staff members are sent a list of their current choices for revision. Statistics available in this automated system include the average number of serials received by each employee and the number of requests for each title. These totals influence the ordering of extra copies of a title or the cancellation of a subscription.

COSTS

The librarian's, the programmer's, and the computer time in the development of this system are estimated to have cost about $3,000. Since the debugging was accomplished in ten runs, the computer costs for testing were minimal.

The present monthly operating costs to route journals (i.e., maintain and update slips, attach to journals, and keep circulation records) are less than $50 for computer usage, about $24 for staff time, and about $6 for supplies. Since about 300 issues per month are routed to employees, the system's operational cost is about $.25 per issue.

At the library's current level of service, namely, 300 issues distributed during the month to over 150 employees, a manual routing system would require 25 percent of the time of a library clerk or aide and cost about $125 per month for staff time alone. The present system therefore not only relieves the library of a tedious task, but has a potential savings of about $50 per month. Most important at Arthur D. Little, however, is that eight hours of a clerk's time is now available for other library needs.

OBSERVATIONS

The Arthur D. Little, Inc. computer-produced serials routing slip system is a simple, efficient, and cost-beneficial system. It is flexible, and its capacity to handle names and journals far exceeds its present requirements. The system can easily make corrections, additions, or deletions. The eight routing slips provided for each title by each computer run are proving to be a convenient number; backlogs are prevented by having some extra slips on hand, but obsolete slips do not accumulate. The routing slips are always neat and up-to-date. Substantial amounts of clerical time spent on tedious chores have been eliminated at a significant cost reduction. The fact that all details of the system have been delineated in a user's manual makes training new library staff quick and simple. In spite of the frequent changes in personnel, room assignments, periodical subscriptions, titles, requests, etc., which were very difficult for the manual system to handle, the computerized system has been kept up-to-date and operational without stress or difficulty.

One minor procedural difficulty with the present system is that most employees are listed on the routing slips in room number order; thus employees who happen to be assigned to upper floors are always the last to receive routed materials. Originally considered a random-order process, this inequity is now recognized and some corrective action is contemplated.

The efficiency of this system has greatly enhanced the library's services to ADL's Management Sciences Division and Public Affair Center and, correspondingly, has enhanced the library's reputation.

The ADL system is excellent proof that a library operating in an environment where a computer facility is available can achieve genuine system improvement and provide better service to its users at a reduction in cost. This very commendable goal was reached because users' needs were clearly perceived, the system was tautly designed, the provisions for maintenance and updating were kept tidy, and the magnitude of demands on the system were sufficient to justify utilizing the computer's vast capabilities. Even as it is often hazardous to one's fingers to try to drive a tack with a sledgehammer, it is hazardous to one's budget if manual operations being considered for computerization do not involve complexities or ranges or repetitive activity that put genuine stress on manual processing. Such stress was obvious in the MSD/PAC Library's manual system for routing periodicals.

The computer has proved, for this library, such an effective and viable solution that ADL plans to use this system to route over 2,500 journal titles to all professional staff members. The enlarged system will be implemented in 1974.

NOTE

1. *User's Guide for Journal Routing Slip System* (Cambridge: Arthur D. Little, Inc., 1971).

ACKNOWLEDGMENTS

This case study is based on information obtained in interviews with Joan Blair, librarian of the MSD/PAC Library, and her article, "Routing Slips from the Computer," *Special Libraries*, 63:2 (February 1972), 82–84, as well as on ADL's *User's Guide* (see Note, above). The assistance of Ms. Blair and of Sheri Davis in the preparation of this case study is acknowledged with appreciation.

13.
Tufts University
Automated Serials System

• • • • • • • • • • • • • • • • • • •

ENVIRONMENT

Tufts University, Medford, Massachusetts, is a small school when compared with its giant neighbors Harvard and the Massachusetts Institute of Technology, but it enjoys an excellent academic reputation nationally. In addition to men's and women's undergraduate colleges, it has several graduate schools serving such areas as child study, law and diplomacy, dentistry, and medicine. The holdings of the university's libraries totaled some 459,447 volumes as of June 30, 1973, and are increasing at the rate of 18,000 volumes annually, not including materials obtained in microtext form. The libraries also have almost 100,000 documents and technical reports. Over 4,500 periodicals are currently received.[1]

Wessell Library, the university's main library, holds 294,200 volumes. The acquisitions, cataloging, and interlibrary loan operations for all components of the University Library are centralized in it. The main card catalog in Wessell Library serves as a union catalog for the libraries. The Library of Congress classification scheme is used throughout the libraries. The Tufts University libraries consist of ten libraries: Wessell, Engineering, Chemistry, Physics, Child Study, Barnum (biology), Lane (geology), Afro-American, Medical and Dental, and Fletcher (law and diplomacy). The holdings of all libraries except Wessell number 165,247 volumes.

OBJECTIVES

The automated serials system was undertaken in 1969 to provide "a record of all types of serial publications held by the libraries, including closed as well as current files, and not just periodicals currently received."[2] Twice previously, the staff of the libraries had attempted to produce such a union list by hand, but "it took forever," in the words of Joseph S. Komidar, university librarian. The benefits of an automated list of serials holdings, produced with the cooperation of the university's Data Processing Department, were clear; many articles in library literature have enumerated them.[3,4]

> The main purpose of almost every mechanized serials program is to produce holdings lists or catalogs of periodical holdings. These lists, since they can be distributed throughout the library, to branches, other libraries, departments, schools, and individuals, are extremely valuable for telling the library patrons and the library staff exactly what journals are available. One university library reports that, when its periodicals catalog was issued, the use of its journal holdings jumped 20%. Also, with a periodicals list available, the number of inquiries for titles and issues that are not in the collection usually drops.[5]

In addition, the compiling of a union list of serials is a relatively simple data processing operation:

> A union list of periodical holdings is probably one of the most elementary projects one can initiate by data processing. The arrangement of the list is not difficult, and basic IBM billing machines offer sufficient speed and versatility to cope with its length and dimension.[6]

Furthermore, the compiling of such a list does not disrupt other library operations:

> The processing of serials and the maintenance of serial records are sufficiently independent areas of library activity to make a system feasible which is not necessarily tied to other aspects of library operation. Also, the repetitive nature of much of serials work lends itself to mechanization.[7]

With these advantages in mind, and with the knowledge that the libraries would not be charged by the Data Processing Department for use of its personnel and equipment, the decision was made at Tufts to develop and implement an automated serials system.

THE COMPUTER

The hardware involved in the production of Tufts's union list of serials is located in the basement of East Hall in the Data Processing Department. The computer used is a second-generation Honeywell 200, equipped with a central processor, a memory capacity of 32,000 bytes, a control panel, a card/reader punch, random access drums, five tape drives, and a high-speed printer. Data processing devices used to produce the union list include a collocator to separate carbons and copies, and a burster to split the printout into pages.

The object programs for the system are on a binary run tape (BRT) named "Wessell." The source programs are on a master source program and library tape (MSPLT). The programs involved in the production of the union list of serials are written in COBOL-D. Twenty-nine programs were written to handle the various operations, such as updating and editing, which must be performed on the list. The major program is entitled SERNUM:

> Input is serials-master. Program lists one line of title of each record with its unique number and subject code. Program also tabulates periodical count by type and location, tabulates count of titles in multiple locations, and lists summary totals.[8]

LISTUP is another important program in the system:

> Input is new-serials-update tape and serials-master tape. Output is cumulative update list to standard serials lists and serials-master tape. List includes new periodical titles acquired, changes of title, new locations for titles already held and changes of holdings locations. Program also outputs old-serials-update tape which is identical to input tape except for labels. During next cycle old-serials-update is merged with new-serials-transaction from program "FORMUP" in program "MERGUP" to create current new-serials update.[9]

From these two programs alone, it is obvious that the serials list may be manipulated in a variety of ways to produce a number of different sub-lists.

THE SYSTEM

The responsibility for the initial development of the system was given to William C. Horner, a member of the library staff who had some training in data processing and computer programming. By June 1970 a manual had been written codifying the programs and the operational procedures necessary for the project. Meanwhile, Mr. Horner had left Tufts for a position as systems librarian at North Carolina State University at Raleigh. The responsibility for the project was given to Stanford Terhune, a member of the technical services department at Wessell.

Mr. Horner defines the purpose of the automated serials system as follows:

The main purpose of the Serials-Master file is to produce lists of the University's periodical holdings. Normally, a comprehensive list, seven location lists, and four subject lists are printed each year. However, an almost infinite variety of lists can be produced using the several sort parameters. For example, a comprehensive list of a particular subject (e.g., physical chemistry), or just the current periodicals in that subject, or a more general list (e.g., chemistry), or a list of a particular or general subject in a particular location, or a list of periodicals held in one or several locations, or a list encompassing several particular subjects, or a combination of all these parameters. In addition, a list association of each title with its unique number is printed each month along with a statistical analysis of the number of titles held in each location by periodical type, titles held in multiple locations, and summary totals. A cumulative supplement to the comprehensive serials catalog is also printed each month.[10]

It should be noted that the cumulative supplement that Mr. Horner mentions actually appears semiannually, not monthly as originally planned, since the volume of data accumulated each month is not sufficient to warrant a separate publication. The list is published once a year, around October 31.

An infinite variety of lists was to be produced by SPESER, a special listing program that could work any combination of location, subject, or type codes (current periodical, closed periodical, etc.) and produce special lists on demand. It has not worked properly, and the Data Processing Department programmers have declared the program to be unworkable. They have suggested starting to write a new program from scratch.

The file structure of the system includes not only the master serials file but also subject thesauri files and the subject-index file to the master serials file. The master serials file, which has a tape label of SERIALSMAS, contains main entry records and "see" references. Each record is 1,020 characters in length. The three subject thesauri files, which have a tape label of THESAR-MAS, also consist of main entry records and "see" entries. Each record contains 225 characters. The files are maintained in alphabetic order by subject, by subject code, and in classified order, that is, in alphabetic order by specific subject within each main subject.

The master index file, which has a tape label of INDEX-MAST, is used once each year to generate a printed subject index to the comprehensive serials catalog. Each record contains 224 characters. The index is created by combining parts of the master serials file and the subject thesauri files.

Editing and updating the serials list are performed by use of keypunch worksheets. When the worksheets are completed, they are delivered to the Data Processing Center, where the information is keypunched and prepared for the computer.

As a finished product, the union serials list is printed and bound in a spiral binding. Copies are distributed to many departments within the university, as well as to major libraries in the Boston area that wish to use it for location and interlibrary loan purposes. Copies are also distributed among the campus libraries.

COSTS

Based on the Tufts library salary scales in the Technical Services Department and on a rough estimate of three-fourths of a year's time to develop and debug the system, developmental costs were about $8,000. Of this figure, about $6,000 was expended for time and labor, and about $2,000 for data processing expenses.

Labor costs for updating and editing the serials list, at a processing rate of about ten titles per hour, either for new titles or for corrections, run to about $.58 per record. Typing the forms for keypunching costs $.17 per record. Thus library cost for input is $.75 per record. As approximately 500 of these entries are made each year, the annual cost to the library is about $375 for staff time and labor.

Costs at the Data Processing Center for the serials operation are presently absorbed by the university. However, the Data Processing Department is contemplating and, indeed, would like to begin charging the libraries for the project in the near future. The serials list requires about five hours of processing time semiannually. At an approximate rate of $100 per hour, the cost of the data processing for two lists per year is about $1,000. This figure includes the operator's salary, computer time, supplies, and overhead.

The published list reaches its final form through a photo-offset process. The computer prints one copy of the list on white, 8½-by-11-inch paper; the list takes up most of the sheet. The body of the printing is reduced to 6⅜ by 8 inches to give good margins. An average of 150 copies are printed each year by the Tufts University printer. The cost per copy is $5.63, including printing and binding in a spiral-binder format, or printing costs per year of about $844.

The cost of the production of the Tufts University union list of serials, excluding developmental costs, but including staff costs, data processing costs, and printing costs, is about $2,200 per year. Since about 5,900 titles are listed, the annual cost is about $.37 per title.

OBSERVATIONS

The automated serials system at Tufts University has greatly enhanced access to the libraries' serial holdings. It has eliminated a great deal of the clerical time and effort that were required in the manual system. The present system can be taken care of by one staff member, part-time. The union list is helpful to the acquisitions department. It is used to determine guidelines for budgeting and costs. It provides a useful reference tool for academic departments, faculty, students, and even other libraries. As expected, the number of requests for purchase or interlibrary loan of serial titles already in the libraries' collections has decreased.

The system has not, however, been without developmental or operational difficulties. A substantial problem was encountered with the program SPESER, which selects and lists serial holdings from the serials master tape, according to type of periodical, subject, and location. In the fall of 1970 it was discovered that the program did not work as it was written. It was believed that the wrong compiler had been used in writing it and the program was recompiled in November 1971. When even after this effort the program failed to work, the Data Processing Department scrapped the original and recompiled SPESER programs as unworkable in December 1971. Although the programmers have suggested that a new SPESER program be written from scratch, this has not yet been done.

There is an operational difficulty in the editing and updating of the serials list. The first time the list is updated, changes are checked against the master file. Thereafter, updating is checked against the amended file. The records do not show which data are on the master file and which are on the updated tape. If the data are in fact on the updated tape, then the input has to be treated as though it were a brand-new record. The only record of this operation is held on the updated tape. The program directs the computer to check input against the master file, however, thus the computer will find no record of the amended data and will register the transaction as an error. Fortunately, this problem occurs only rarely.

A minor inconvenience to the editor and users of the list is caused by the fact that to save space the dates for closed serials include only the last two digits of the opening and closing dates. A closed serial may have the dates "36–50" beside it, and one is unable to tell whether the dates are, in fact, 1836–1850, 1836–1950, or 1936–1950. For the journal *Astronautics*, the abbreviated dates are not a problem, since the title indicates what the dates are. However, for some of the more obscure, defunct medical journals, the ambiguity in date presents some difficulty.

As an initial library automation project, the union list of serials was a simple and relatively inexpensive choice for the Tufts University libraries.

The system does not interfere with other library processes. The project has provided some insights into automation problems. The library staff realizes that it is still all too easy to hit quicksand in the often swampy world of library automation. After evaluating the serials project, the Tufts libraries concluded that the acquisitions operation should be the next system to be automated. However, as do almost all libraries, the Tufts libraries face financial restrictions. Any funds for automation must be taken from the book budget. Unless this financial obstacle can be removed, and this appears unlikely, the road to further automation at the Tufts University libraries is probably going to remain closed.

NOTES

1. *Faculty Guide to the Tufts University Library* (Medford, Mass.: Tufts University Libraries, 1970), p. 3.
2. *Serials Holdings* (Medford, Mass.: Tufts University Libraries, 1970), p 1.
3. Kenneth D. Olson, "Union Lists and the Public Record of Serials," *Special Libraries*, 61 (1970), 15–20.
4. Peter H. Wolters and R. Arthur Green, "Union List of Scientific Serials in Canadian Libraries, 1967: Edition Design Conversion, Computer Operations," *Canadian Library*, 24 (1968), 327–332.
5. *Library Automation: Computerized Serials Control* (White Plains, N.Y.: IBM Corporation, Technical Publications Dept., 1971), p. 42.
6. J. T. Michna, "Automation at the U.W. Libraries: Computerized Union List of Serials Project," *Wisconsin Library Bulletin*, 62 (July–August 1966), 224.
7. Melvin J. Voigt, "The Costs of Data Processing in University Libraries: in Serials Handling," *College and Research Libraries*, 24 (January 1968), 489.
8. *Tufts University Libraries Automated Serials System Operating Procedures and System Programming* (Medford, Mass.: Tufts University Libraries, 1970), p. IV–47.
9. Ibid., p. IV–84.
10. Ibid., p. I–1.

ACKNOWLEDGMENTS

The assistance of Stanford Terhune, serials cataloger, Tufts University, and of Paulena P. Hollenbach in the preparation of this case study is acknowledged with appreciation.

14.
Tufts University
Medical and Dental Library
Medline System
· · · · · · · · · · · ·

ENVIRONMENT

In October 1971 the National Library of Medicine established MEDLINE (MEDLARS-on-line), an on-line bibliographic searching service, as part of the Biomedical Communications Network (BCN). MEDLARS is the acronym for *Medical Literature Analysis and Retrieval System*. It was felt that MEDLINE would meet with acceptance due to the success of the pilot project, AIM-TWX (*Abridged Index Medicus* via the Teletypewriter Exchange Network), which was established in June 1970.[1]

In January 1973 the Francis A. Countway Library of Medicine *Newsletter* stated that the computer file of the MEDLINE data base contained "over 400,000 citations from 1,200 major journals indexed in *Index Medicus* from January, 1970, to date."[2]

The MEDLINE services are coordinated by the 11 Regional Medical Libraries that are part of the national Regional Medical Library System. The medical libraries in Massachusetts are part of the New England Regional Medical Library System for which The Francis A. Countway Library of Medicine is the Regional Medical Library.

The National Library of Medicine (hereafter called NLM) has prescribed definite steps that a library must go through to subscribe to MEDLINE service. These steps are clearly outlined in the NLM publication, *MEDLINE Network Participation Procedure Manual.*[3]

First, a form entitled, "Notice of Intent of Interest in MEDLINE," has to be completed and filed with NLM and a copy sent to the director of the Regional Medical Library. (The "Notice of Intent" for the Tufts Medical and

Dental Library was completed February 1, 1972.) Upon receipt of the "Notice of Intent," the NLM sends the subject institution copies of the "Memorandum of Understanding" with instructions for completion. The application must be supported by "Exhibit A," which gives the following information:

1. Description of the library's present resources,
2. Identification of the user groups that will be provided with MEDLINE service,
3. Type and volume of service now rendered (i.e. document delivery.)
4. Charges to users of MEDLINE service, if any are contemplated,
5. Type and number of terminals.[4]

Tufts Medical and Dental Library's application for MEDLINE service was submitted in March 1972, accompanied by its "Exhibit A" which provided the pertinent information concerning the library's holdings, staff, and persons served. An excerpt from this document follows:

Tufts will have holdings of 60,000 volumes in its medical-dental library before the end of this year (bound journals and books). . . . We are revising our count of serial holdings and using the publication *Periodicals in the Countway Library* as our guide since we catalog continuations as books rather than periodicals. Our final count will be somewhere over 1,800 for serials currently received.[5]

The full-time equivalent of the library's present staff is $13^1/_2$ persons, five of whom are full-time professionals with the graduate library degree.

Tufts Medical and Dental Library serves a rapidly expanding medical and dental complex in the Boston's downtown area. This complex includes Tufts University School of Medicine, Tufts University School of Dental Medicine, the Boston School of Occupational Therapy, the Francis Stern School of Nutrition, the Tufts-New England Medical Center Hospitals, and other affiliated hospitals. At a meeting held in March 1972 at the Countway Library, it was decided that Tufts would service all educational institutions within the area east of Route 495 (a circumferential highway on a radius of approximately 20 miles west of Boston) to one-half mile from the Countway Library.

The "Memorandum of Understanding" represents a contract between NLM and the participating library. The main points of this agreement may be summarized as follows:

NML will provide:

1. access to its data base at hours specified by NLM;

2. training for the person in the participating library who will be responsible for MEDLINE service;
3. updated information concerning changes in the system;
4. on-call assistance to the participating library if trouble is encountered in accessing the system.[6]

The participating library agrees to provide:

1. on-line bibliographic services to users as specified in "Exhibit A";
2. personnel to operate the system (these persons must go to NLM or another qualified institution for training);
3. salaries and other expenses to these persons while they are being trained;
4. indexes and other tools needed to carry out MEDLINE operations;
5. terminal for accessing the system, plus telephone costs;
6. "periodic progress reports, statistical reports, evaluative studies, and copies of products and publications derived from the use of the system."[7]

The "Memorandum of Understanding" has to be approved by the director of the Regional Medical Library and by NLM's associate director for library operations.[8]

The "Memorandum of Understanding" for Tufts was completed in March 1972, approved by the NLM in April,[9] the senior reference librarian was sent to NLM for a three-week training session beginning May 22, 1972, and the MEDLINE system became operational at Tufts in June 1972.

OBJECTIVES

The major objective of the Tufts Medical and Dental Library's MEDLINE service is to provide on-line bibliographic information to the students and staff of the institution, along with the provision of this service to other designated institutions in Massachusetts. In addition to this specific objective is the all-inclusive one of better patient care—which sometimes takes the form of emergency medical information. Even when speed is not of the essence, the ease with which citations may be retrieved in the computer system, as compared to manual methods, should contribute to more thorough literature searches. Since each citation is tagged under many more headings than can be found in *Index Medicus*, the computer search provides more entry points than are available in a manual search. The system is designed to permit the compilation of statistics on types of search requests.

THE COMPUTER

NLM is using a developmental approach with respect to MEDLINE, and the system frequently undergoes changes. In December 1971 NLM "replaced its IBM 360/50 computer and direct access storage devices (2314's) with an IBM 370/155 and faster and larger direct access storage devices (3330's)."[10] Late in 1972 the user could be connected either to the computer at NLM or to one at the Systems Development Corporation in California, depending upon the time of day and upon the number of simultaneous users. A recent issue of the *Medical Library Association News* gives the following information about the expansion of services and a new location for the data base:

> On the NLM computer the saturation point for simultaneous users of MEDLINE is 50. Late in 1972 the AIM-TWX data base at the Systems Development Corporation in Santa Monica was replaced by the MED-LINE data base, which allowed 25 additional ports for five hours each week day. In turn, the MEDLINE data base at SCD will soon be replaced by one at the State University of New York at Albany as soon as contract negotiations are completed. It is anticipated that the SUNY computer will provide 40 ports for nine hours each week day which, with NLM's 50 ports, will make possible a total of 90 simultaneous users.[11]

The SUNY Biomedical Communication Network went into operation in 1968. In the summer of 1971, its IBM 360/50 was replaced by the larger IBM 370/155 and IBM 3330 Direct Access storage.[12] The SUNY backup computer became operational for MEDLINE in March, 1973. The data base for MEDLINE is identical in both systems.

The computers are accessed through an arrangement with Tymshare, Inc., which supplies most of the network. This is backed up with Western Union Datacom and American Telephone and Telegraph Company leased lines.[13] NLM bears the expense of the use of the Tymshare and backup networks.

The terminal chosen by Tufts to access the system is a Texas Instruments No. 725 teletypewriter-compatible terminal, which is part of the "Silent 700" series. "Silent electronic printing is achieved with the use of a dot matrix on a monolithic solid-state printhead that moves across the page."[14] The ink is transferred to special heat-sensitive paper—which means that there are no separate keys for each individual letter, as there are on a typewriter or teletypewriter. The model 725 operates at half-duplex or full-duplex mode at 10, 15, or 30 characters/second. It also has a built-in acoustic coupler. The terminal weighs 35 pounds and is therefore considered to be portable and has its own carrying case. Because it is quiet, this type of terminal does not require a separate room and can be used in the library without disturbing the patrons.

THE SYSTEM

The computer file for MEDLINE consists of citations of articles indexed for *Index Medicus*. Each article is given as many headings as needed. The indexers complete an "indexed citation form" for each article; in addition to the usual bibliographic citations, such as author and title, this form permits up to 21 subject headings, plus "check tags," such as age and animal experiments. The indexers select subject headings from MeSH (*Medical Subject Headings*).[15]

The search programs for MEDLINE are named ELHILL. In January 1973 a new version of the MEDLINE programs, ELHILL IIC, was installed.[16] The December 1972 issue of *National Library of Medicine News* contained an announcement that read in part:

New on-line services planned or already available on the network [Tymshare], in addition to MEDLINE, are:

1. SDILINE—current month of *Index Medicus* on-line (available).
2. CATLINE—monograph cataloging information on-line (January 1973).
3. SERLINE—serial locator file on-line to locate any of 6,000 serial titles in 100 medical libraries (February 1973).
4. COMPFILE—the remainder of the MEDLARS file (2,200 journals), for on-line searching and off-line printing of the bibliography.
5. The Office of Education's ERIC file is available on the network for MEDLINE users.
6. TOXICON—toxicology information on-line (available).
7. National Technical Information Service (NTIS) data base and Chemical Abstracts (Condensates) to be available on-line in January 1973.

Items 5, 6, and 7 are commercially available services.[17]

In this case study, only MEDLINE and SDILINE, both of which are constantly used at Tufts, will be discussed. For a time, Tufts used ERIC, but discontinued when a charge for the service was imposed.

When a new user comes to the library and wants to learn to use the computer an appointment is scheduled for him or her and one hour is allowed for the orientation period. First, the user fills out a "MEDLINE Search Request." Although the form states: "This form should only be used when you cannot visit a MEDLINE center," each patron is asked to fill out a search request for each search, so that use statistics may be compiled. In particular, the responses regarding "Purpose of Search" are useful in compiling statistical summaries of use. The section entitled, "Detailed Statement of Requirements," which asks for terms NOT to be included, is very important to the search formulation. In the MEDLINE program, the subject headings are linked together by the Boolean logic elements, AND, OR and AND NOT. Because articles are indexed by check tags, it is important to state what is not to be included. For example, the data base includes citations of many' articles in foreign languages. If a person wants articles only in English, the phrase, "AND NOT FOREIGN" must be added to the search statement.

The request for "Few, very relevant articles," also has direct application to the terms in the data base. Each article is given several search terms. These are distinguished as being "IM" (a subject heading printed "in" *Index Medicus*) or "NIM" (a subject heading "not in" *Index Medicus*, but is stored in the computer for retrieval). "IM" represents the basic points of the article indexed, and "NIM" represents subjects discussed in the article, but not necessarily the point of the article.

If a patron checks that he or she wishes only a "Few, very relevant articles," an asterisk is placed *before* the search statement, and only citations of articles printed in *Index Medicus* are retrieved.

Having completed the search request, the patron may either learn to use the terminal or have the library conduct the search for him or her. A librarian will help the patron who wishes to learn to use the terminal to formulate a search statement.

The subject headings in the data base must, of necessity, come from a pre-constructed vocabulary. The main headings (MH) are taken from *Medical Subject Headings* (MeSH), which are divided into broad categories. For example, the first four categories are: A = Anatomical Terms; B = Organisms; C = Diseases; D = Chemicals and Drugs. Each term in MeSH is given a letter designating the category plus a number that further qualifies the term within the category. For example, the heading BLOOD is given four numbers— A7.15.; A7.60.21; A10 66.16; A12.13.18—while the term "BLOOD CELLS" is given the number A11.10.[18]

Unlike many subject indexes, MeSH uses very specific terms, and a searcher should look for the heading under the most specific term first, rather than under a general term (i.e., BLOOD CELLS rather than BLOOD). These main headings may be linked up with subheadings, but certain subheadings go with only certain categories. For example, while a person who wants to find out the treatment of disease (category C) must use TH, the truncated (shortened) term for the subheading "therapy," the person who wants to find out the use of a drug (category D) cannot use the term for therapy, but must use TU, the truncated term for "therapeutic use." [19]

In Boolean logic AND is more limiting than OR. If one were searching for COMPUTERS AND PROGRAMMED INSTRUCTION AND NOT FOREIGN, the computer would retrieve only articles that were indexed under both COMPUTERS and PROGRAMMED INSTRUCTION. If COMPUTERS OR PROGRAMMED INSTRUCTION were used, the computer would retrieve articles indexed under *either* heading.

Age in search terms should also be clearly understood. The check tags for adults are broken down into ADULT (ages 19–44); MIDDLE AGE (ages 45–64); and AGED (ages 65 plus). It should be noted that a search statement cannot occupy more than one line.

Before trying to enter a search into the computer, the user is given a demonstration of the terminal's use, so that he or she can see the resulting printout. Before the equipment is turned on, the new user is asked to familiarize him- or herself with the keyboard of the terminal, especially the keys needed for accessing the system. When the user feels ready, he or she turns on the terminal, dials the local Tymshare number, and places the telephone receiver in the acoustic coupler. After the procedure for logging-in is completed, the computer issues a greeting and statement of the most recent month of *Index Medicus* that has been put into the system and asks if the user wishes the NEW-USER OR EXPERIENCED-USER FORMAT. If the user is receiving help in the use of the computer, he or she need not ask for the NEW-USER FORMAT—which prints out, in great detail, instructions for using the system. If the user asks for the EXPERIENCED-USER FORMAT, the computer asks: "SS 1/C?"—which means Search Statement 1 or Command. In this instance, the user would put in the search statement he or she has formulated. The computer would respond with the number of citations, or postings—i.e., PSTG (36).

The MEDLINE service has become so popular that users are now instructed to ask for only 25 citations on-line. If more are needed, the subject is put into the system under the off-line print instructions, and the results are mailed from NLM to the participating library. In asking for results on-line, the user may ask for a simple "PRT" or a "PRT FULL" search result. In giving the "print" command, the user must specify the number of citations desired, such as "PRT 25." Since the program cannot be stopped, the computer stops after every five citations and asks whether the user wants to continue.

At the end of the search, there is a special "STOP" procedure.

The foregoing steps do not, of course, indicate the sophisticated search procedures that are possible when using the MEDLINE interactive program.

The SDILINE program, covering the current month of *Index Medicus*, is used for the library's current awareness service. The library has on file the names of 26 persons for whom 67 subject headings are searched. A printout is sent to each user, who checks off the articles that he or she is interested in and sends the printout back. If the article is in a journal owned by the library, a xerographic copy is made and sent to the user. If not, an interlibrary loan request is made.

In addition to the bibliographic services, there is a "Tymshare news file" that gives news about the system, such as the operating status of the system and a list of dates that citations are entered into the system.

COSTS

MEDLINE went into operation in October of 1971. Negotiations between Tufts and NLM lasted four months, from February to June 1972. Assuming that planning for the MEDLINE installation of Tufts began in November 1971, the planning period lasted about seven months. If the librarian and his staff spent varying percentages of their time with the planning, the salary costs plus costs for supplies and postage might range from $800 to $1,500 for the seven-month period. These figures are conjectural, however.

It cost the Tufts Library $450 to send the senior reference librarian to NLM for three weeks for training. If the $450 training charge is added to the above estimate, the total estimated developmental costs for the MED-LINE installation would range from $1,250 to $1,950.

Cost Per Search

Any costs that might result from the search, such as the increase in inter-library loan or in photocopying, have been omitted in developing the cost per search. Stationery supplies and postage have also been omitteed because most searches are done for persons affiliated with Tufts, and they either pick up the printouts, or the printouts are sent to them by interdepartmental mail. No attempt was made to determine what percentage of the envelope supply is used for mailing search results.

Because the statistics of the number of searches are provided monthly, the charges for MEDLINE have been figured on a monthly basis (see Table 1).

The reference librarian has trained other members of the staff in the use of MEDLINE, and at present three staff members—the senior reference librarian, the cataloger, and the new staff member—spend varying percentages of their time with MEDLINE. Because Boston is a "node city" for Tymshare, Inc., the telephone service is billed at the local downtown Boston business rate. When the reference librarian went for training in May 1972 NLM gave her the supporting indexes and other documental aids for conducting searches free of charge. These are updated annually for about $48.

Table 1
MONTHLY CHARGES RELATING TO MEDLINE

Item	Amount	
Salaries	$730.00	
Terminal Rental	118.75	
Telephone	88.00	($75–$100, avg.)
Paper for Terminal	12.00	(2 rolls/mo.)
Documentation Aids	4.00	($48 ÷ 12)
	Total $952.75	

The number of searches conducted each month at Tufts has increased tremendously: from 55 searches in June 1972 to 936 in March 1973. The computer printout of statistics relative to MEDLINE searches became available as of October 1972. Table 2 gives these statistics for October, November, and December 1972, and February and March 1973 (January is unavailable). March has been considered separately in obtaining the average number of searches because there is such a jump between the figures for February and March. Also, during March, NLM experienced hardware failure, and it is estimated that 10 percent of the data were lost. The average number of searches done for the October, November, December, and February total was 381 (1,524 ÷ 4). If March is included, the average number of searches goes up to 492 (2,460 ÷ 5).

Table 2
MEDLINE SEARCHES COMPUTER STATISTICS

Month	Searches	Connect Hrs.	Mins./Search
October 1972	219	29.9	8.2
November	236	54.8	14.0
December	564	66.6	7.1
February 1973	505	47.7	5.7
4-month total	1,524	199.0	
March 1973	936	52.0	3.4
5-month total	2,460	251.0	

NLM has instituted* a charge of $6 per connect hour, or $.10 per connect minute. Because of the variation in the number of searches per month, the

*On August 20, 1973.

cost per search has been compiled for four figures: (*a*) the number of searches for October; (*b*) the average number of searches for the four months, October, November, December, and February; (*c*) the average if March is included; (*d*) the number of searches for March alone. Table 3 shows the total cost per search for each number, calculated on the basis of the total monthly charges given in Table 1 plus the connect-hour charge of $.10 per minute.

Table 3
COST PER SEARCH

No. of	(*a*)	(*b*)	(*c*)	(*d*)
Searches:	219	381	492	936
Total mo. charges ($952.75) ÷				
No. of searches $4.35		$2.50	$1.94	$1.02
Connect hr. charges				
(@ 10¢/connect min.) .82		.78	.61	.33
Total cost/search $5.17		$3.28	$2.55	$1.35

OBSERVATIONS

When a user conducts a search, the conversational, interactive characteristics of MEDLINE are very useful. The program has a "HELP" command and a "COMMENT" command. In the "help" sequence, the user is given six questions covering situations that might have caused a problem and is asked to choose one by number. This sequence is designed to be helpful at any point the user may have reached in his or her search. The "COMMENT" command allows the user to send a message to the NLM by means of a special procedure.

The orientation period, as it is conducted at Tufts, helps to eliminate the nervousness most people feel when confronted with an on-line situation for the first time. The new user is not left alone at the terminal. If the reference librarian has to leave, someone else comes to be ready to help the user.

The popularity of MEDLINE at Tufts is shown by the increase in the number of searches. Tufts does not charge for searches for persons affiliated with the school, but makes a $10 charge to unaffiliated persons. If it should become necessary for Tufts to charge its own teaching staff and/or students for searches, the number of searches would probably decrease.

The SDILINE has made the current awareness service much easier. The need to scan the contents of incoming journals and copy down the titles of articles manually is eliminated. Prior to the installation of MEDLINE, the citations were sent to the user on cards. The persons for whom current awareness services are provided seem to pay more attention to the printouts than they did to the cards.

While the MEDLINE service is a very valuable and useful one, it will be many years before it becomes a complete bibliographic service since many sources of medical and scientific literature are not included in *Index Medicus* and are therefore not covered in MEDLINE.

A major problem with MEDLINE is its use of a preconstructed vocabulary. The user must search with MEDLINE terminology. This difficulty is partially offset by the fact that the program provides multiple avenues for getting at information and offers assistance in formulating a search while one is on-line. By means of its explanatory sequences, MEDLINE attempts to serve the untrained user, but because the system is somewhat complicated, most users will require the services of a trained and experienced searcher to fully exploit MEDLINE's capabilities. Even for the new user, however, MEDLINE searching is faster and easier than poring through volumes of *Index Medicus*. The system, of course, has many more commands and computer responses than are indicated in this study.

The ever increasing use of the MEDLINE system at Tufts demonstrates that users will work through difficulties of the man-machine interface and the frustration of handling a preconstructed vocabulary if the retrieval of citations is fast, accurate, and free of charge.

NOTES

1. National Library of Medicine, *Fact Sheet*, May 1972.

2. Harold Bloomquist, "MEDLINE," *The Francis A. Countway Library of Medicine Newsletter and List of Recent Acquisitions*, January 1973, p. 1.

3. U.S., Department of Health, Education, and Welfare, National Library of Medicine, *MEDLINE Network Participation Procedure Manual* (Washington, D.C.: Government Printing Office, 1972).

4. Ibid., sec. III.

5. "Exhibit A," which accompanied the "Memorandum of Understanding Between Tufts University and The National Library of Medicine (NLM)," March 1972.

6. "Memorandum of Understanding Between Tufts University and The National Library of Medicine (NLM)," March 1972, p. 1.

7. Ibid., p. 2.

8. *MEDLINE Network Participation Procedure Manual*, secs. IV, V.

9. Confirming letter of approval was sent to the dean of Tufts University School of Medicine by the associate director for library operations, National Library of Medicine, on April 25, 1972.

10. Barbara Sternick, "IBM 370/155 Performance," *Library Network/MEDLARS Technical Bulletin*, June 1972, p. 2.

11. "News from the MLA/NLM Liaison Committee," *Medical Library Association News*, February 1973, p. 9.

12. "SUNY Biomedical Communication Network," *Network Newsletter*, 5 (April 1972), 2.

13. "MEDLINE Communications Network," *Library Network/MEDLARS Technical Bulletin*, June 1972, p. 8.

14. *Silent 700 Electronic Data Terminals Model 725 Series Operating Instructions*, Manual No. 954762-9701 (rev. ed.; Houston, Tex.: Texas Instruments, Inc., 1972), sec. 1–2.

15. U.S. Department of Health, Education and Welfare, National Library of Medicine, *MEDLARS Training Program: MEDLINE Training Syllabus* (Washington, D.C.: Government Printing Office, 1972) p. 53.

16. Barbara L. Greehey and Leonard J. Bahlman, "New Capabilities in MEDLINE," *Library Network/MEDLARS Technical Bulletin*, March 1973, p. 11.

17. "Board of Regents Meets," *National Library of Medicine News*, December 1972, p. 5.

18. U.S. Department of Health, Education, and Welfare, National Library of Medicine, *Medical Subject Headings Alphabetic List* (Washington, D.C.: Government Printing Office, 1973), p. 81.

19. U.S. Department of Health, Education, and Welfare, National Library of Medicine, *Index Medicus Subheadings* (Washington, D.C.: Government Printing Office, 1972).

ACKNOWLEDGMENTS

The assistance of Rosemary G. Kelley in the preparation of this case study is acknowledged with appreciation. Thanks are also extended to Edward P. Leavitt and Margaret K. Young, of the Tufts Medical and Dental Library, and Marcia Ford, systems librarian of the Francis A. Countway Library of Medicine, for providing information and assistance.

Computerized Library Acquisition Systems

Most libraries continue to utilize manual acquisitions systems because their rate of collection building has not put excessive pressure on the acquisitions operation or because the complexity of the acquisitions process prevents an inexpensive transfer of the process from manual to computer control. Of the 1366 library computer applications reported by 506 libraries in the 1971 LARC survey, 215, or about 16 percent, were projects dealing with acquisitions. Of the 215, 107 were full systems, 40 were fund accounting, 28 were book ordering, 11 were acquisitions listings, and the remaining 33 were systems dealing with special aspects of the acquisitions operation.[1]

While the library profession has not yet established precise definitions or parameters for those functions and operations that should fall under the "acquisitions" heading, many libraries regard book ordering, fund accounting, and on-order/in-process files as major functions of an acquisitions system. Occasionally, the selection operation is included in an automated acquisitions system—as in the automated generation of lists or cards from the Library of Congress MARC (Machine-Readable Cataloging) tapes for distribution to faculty, staff, or patrons for selection purposes. Occasionally, certain essential acquisitions operations are automated, sometimes only in part: the verification of bibliographic data supplied by the requester, or the searching of the requested item in standard bibliographies, or national or union catalogs, etc.

The currently operational automated acquisitions systems perform a wide variety of functions, with substantial differences between systems. Among the money-control functions handled by automated systems are fund encumbering and liquidating, budgetary control, accounting records, payment of invoices, and various financial reports. To control the ordering of library materials, automated systems can place orders, update orders, cancel orders, place reorders, deal with additional copies of desired items, and do automatic claiming. These services are among those provided by the Dartmouth College acquisitions system (see chapter 20). These services were also provided by the M.I.T. acquisitions system until events beyond the library's control induced its termination (see chapter 18).

Sometimes bibliographic data is input from on-line MARC records or sometimes information is entered on-line and combined with order information to create a purchase order. The University of Massachusetts acquisitions system makes skillful use of on-line computer capabilities (see chapter 16). Other systems may produce tape for teleprocessing orders. Some systems can maintain vendor lists. The computer can verify order input, prepare on-order lists in various arrangements, books received lists, in-process lists, and accession or newly cataloged lists. The last item represents a merging of some acquisitions and cataloging functions in a single system. The Northeastern University acquisitions system prevents duplicate orders by checking for matches of new orders with orders listed in the computer in-process file (see chapter 15).

Some systems permit the analysis of acquisitions by subject or classification scheme. Some systems generate standing orders, lists of out-of-print materials wanted, or desiderata lists. Some systems prepare Library of Congress card orders, although the wider use of MARC tapes and augmented MARC data bases (e.g., the Ohio College Library Center data base and the network drawing upon this base) will probably reduce the quantity of orders for printed cards that are sent directly to the Library of Congress in the future.

Some systems give detailed control over the movement of materials from department to department in technical services, occasionally by means of punched cards, another indication of mergers of acquisitions and cataloging functions in a single division under automated systems control. Some systems search Library of Congress card numbers for purchase requests against the Library of Congress card numbers of books on order or in process. This search eliminates duplicates and permits the system to escape from the substantial time and expense of manual bibliographic searching. Some systems permit search of the on-order/in-process files by order number, author, title, or Library of Congress card number. The better systems provide adequate avenues of access to their files.

Some librarians, mindful of a need to be responsive to users, have developed systems that produce notices to patrons of order placing, of materials receipt, and of final order processing and cataloging. Such progress reports might well be incorporated in a greater number of automated acquisitions systems.

Some automated acquisitions systems were initiated in the hope of achieving a single data capture for new library materials that could be utilized for the cataloging, circulation, and dissemination of these materials. This hope has not generally materialized because of the different formats and types of data required in these different library operations. Because of the complexity of each of these operations, it is profoundly difficult to achieve a "total system" system.

The possibility of interlibrary communication and cooperation has often been advanced as a reason for library automation projects. However, since standardization—the rallying cry of many computer-oriented professionals—in system design, data collection, terminology, and operation has not been achieved, the movement toward interlibrary activity has been slow and spotty. Some gains and some losses are usually found in such network operations.

Even as in circulation systems, where a certain volume of activity causes manual systems to begin to break down, even so in acquisitions systems, a certain volume of activity tends to go beyond the capacity of card files or traditional accounting techniques to control. When the on-order/in-process file has a steady state of over 30,000 items, and often before that point, errors and delays that clog the system are more and more likely to occur. The automated system offers speed and accuracy at this level of activity that are very difficult to maintain in a manual system. In addition, the automated system offers immediacy of access to totals of funds encumbered and expended that permits better management control, especially toward the end of fiscal periods. Automated systems are also capable of easily and quickly generating many more useful and varied statistical reports than a manual system could provide. The Columbia University Libraries acquisitions system provides sophisticated fiscal and in-process products and control (see chapter 17).

Librarians charged with managing technical services operations are very much aware of the economic and physical problems with which they must deal. While automated procedures may assist them in processing vast quantities of library materials and the information needed to control the processing of these materials, thus far these automated procedures have been developed through trouble-filled pioneering efforts by each library. While some libraries have derived insights and benefits from earlier efforts at other libraries, many library automation efforts have been original and unassisted. Today, automated library acquisitions systems have been developed that are complete, with hardware and software fully operational, ready to perform upon delivery to the library. These turn-key systems, some of which are skillfully designed, offer libraries the opportunity to use the computer without the excessive developmental costs that have been inescapable thus far. Certainly the sacrifice of minor "custom" features in individual library systems will be a small price to pay for the savings to be found in ready-to-go computer systems specifically designed for library housekeeping operations, such as the group of functions, book order, fund encumbering, and on-order/in-process files, etc., usually included under the heading "acquisitions." The Cleveland Public Library acquisitions system utilizes a remarkably efficient and inexpensive minicomputer to perform fiscal and book-order services and supervision (see chapter 19). A substantial increase in the number of automated acquisitions systems, not only in universities, but in larger public libraries, is to be expected in the next decade.

NOTE

1. Frank S. Patrinostro, *A Survey of Automated Activities in the Libraries of the United States*, vol. 1 (Tempe, Ariz.: LARC Association, 1971), p. 4.

15.
Northeastern University Automated Acquisition System

• •

ENVIRONMENT

Northeastern University is the largest private university in the United States. About 43,000 students receive instruction from a teaching staff of 2,000. A commuter-oriented school in an urban setting, the university is a leader in the field of the Co-operative Plan of Education, in which a student alternates a quarter of school with a quarter of work, preferably in the same line as the student's major.

The library has holdings of 300,000 volumes and adds 25,000 each year. The library's annual income is $1,200,000, of which almost $375,000 is expended for books, serials, and other library materials. The monthly circulation from the general collection is 7,500. The library employs 25 professional librarians, 35 supportive personnel, 14 Co-operative Plan students, 107 part-time employees, or a total of 181 employees.

Besides the main library, there are also three on-campus divisional libraries, one divisional library at the suburban campus, and four small off-campus collections for specialized use.

OBJECTIVES

Toward the end of 1966, the Acquisitions Department of Dodge Library, the main library at Northeastern, realized that it was increasingly inundated with paper work. The library was growing at a rapid rate and paper work had reached the point where not only was a substantial amount of professionals' time taken up with clerical duties, but more employees were needed to perform clerical tasks. A decline in service to clientele, especially faculty, was noted. As a means of alleviating this situation, the automation of parts of the Acquisitions Department was considered.

A systems analysis of the existing manual acquisitions system was conducted from January through July 1967 by Albert Donley, associate director of the Northeastern University libraries. This analysis included consideration of the existing system—what it was doing, what it was not doing, and what it should be doing. From this study evolved a set of objectives that the automated system would seek to meet: (1) to improve the acquisitions operation, from selection through ordering, processing, and acquisitions (acquisitions, in this case, meaning that an item had been received, accessioned, stamped, plated, cataloged, and shelved); (2) to generate purchase orders without a great deal of typing; (3) to establish a data file that would be useful for management purposes.

Following a thorough literature search and examination of a number of computerized acquisitions systems, the library staff undertook to design an automated acquisitions system that could be made operational within the following constraints: (1) available money; (2) configuration of Northeastern University computers; (3) availablity of programmers and systems analysts; (4) the university's plans for changing computer configurations; (5) the computers' capacity to handle bibliographic data; (6) limitations on data input.

THE COMPUTER

The Dodge Library acquisitions system is now utilizing the university's IBM 360/25. The system uses disks as the primary storage medium and magnetic tapes as the back-up storage medium. Three tapes are used alternately in a rotating fashion. A cumulative acquisitions tape for the year is also maintained.

The system utilizes the university's IBM 519 reproducer, IBM 559 interpreter, and IBM 407 accounting machine, which is used as a printer and a decollator.

The library rents four IBM 029 keypunch machines, three of which have 64-character keyboards and one of which has a 48-character keyboard. The library also rents one IBM 087 collator and one IBM 082 sorter.

The university's Administrative Computer Services Department does the programming for the library. The programming language used is COBOL.

The following six programs are currently in use:

1. Op-update-em

This program adds a new record, deletes an existing record, or changes an existing record that is part of the "on order, in process, orders complete master file-processing information list" (hereafter referred to as OPCMF-PIL). The disks and the magnetic tape are updated nightly, Monday through Thursday. On Friday night they are updated and a printout of the entire file is made. A "change list," also printed out nightly, Monday through Friday, includes all valid changes in the status of an order.

2. Monthly Acquisitions

This program produces a monthly acquisitions disk file (separate from the OPCMF-PIL). It also generates an acquisitions printout by class and by author, plus an error listing that includes input cards that are invalid for one or more of several reasons, such as mispunched cards, duplicate cards, or cards with missing information, incorrect codes, etc. This program, in addition, merges acquisitions for the month by main entry with a cumulative acquisitions tape that is comprised of monthly acquisitions accumulated for each fiscal year. Four months of acquisitions are kept on four separate disks. Each month new acquisitions are placed on the oldest disk. If, for example, December, January, February, and March materials were kept on disks 1, 2, 3, and 4, respectively, when the April acquisitions were entered, the December entries would be erased and replaced on disk 1 by the April items. This program is run the last day of each month.

3. Op-update-md

This program deletes all records representing acquisitions accumulated during the month from the OPCMF-PIL. It is run monthly after the Monthly Acquisitions Program is run.

4. On-Approval Selections
5. Firm Selections

Although these are two separate programs, they may be described together because the only difference between them is that there is no location code for the On-Approval Selections program. These programs match selection cards, which have been punched from selection slips, on the first 14 columns of the author-title field against a disk, which is temporarily created by merging, by main entry, the OPCMF-PIL with the four monthly acquisitions disk files. The resulting printout is made up of the following two lists: (1) all selection cards submitted that do not match entries on the temporary disk; (2) all selection cards that have matched entries on the disk, plus the entries that have been matched. These programs are run every Monday evening.

6. Print

This program creates the "process information list" (PIL) that lists in one alphabet by *apparent* main entry all items that are on order, in processing, or have been cataloged within the past month.

These six programs deal only with orders for monographs and original orders for continuations that are placed by Selections or by Reserve departments. The purpose of these programs is to eliminate unintentional duplication of orders.

THE SYSTEM

The automated acquisitions system became operational, on a very limited scale, during October 1967. It was initially designed to operate on the university's IBM 1620 and 1410, plus an IBM 407 accounting machine as a printer, a sorter for filing, a collator for matching, and a keypunch machine for card production.

In September 1968 the library's computer time was shifted to the university's second computer, a CDC 3300. Difficulties arose from lack of sufficient tape drives and greater equipment failure or down time. Permission for the library to use the new IBM 360/20 was denied. In the spring of 1970, the IBM 360/20 was modified to an IBM 360/25. The library was given access to this computer and new programs were written and adjustments in routines were made.

The system has been changed as new needs have arisen and better techniques have been devised. The numeric subpriority codes have been phased out and a new alphabetic code has been substituted. This new code allows greater specificity in routing and greater ease in identifying reasons for ordering. Changes and adjustments requiring rewriting of programs have been made continually, and the system, which continues to evolve, now performs the following functions: (1) allows manipulation of data for selection, ordering, receiving, and acquisition; (2) monitors selection for management purposes; (3) records what has been ordered; (4) controls the acquisitions function by identifying the status of each title from selection through acquisition.

The system deals with two major sources of books. One, referred to as "Firm Orders," consists of books the library has ordered either through a jobber or directly from a publisher; the other, referred to as the "On-Approval Plan," consists of about 300 books that arrive in weekly shipments from Richard Abel and Company, Newton, Massachusetts. These shipments include all U.S. and Canadian books that have been published over a selected period of time and that fit the needs of the Northeastern University library as determined by the library and Richard Abel. The books in this approval plan are displayed in a room to which faculty and staff members come to select items they feel should be purchased; unwanted items are simply returned.

The system is designed so that data from each book selection slip is transferred to a single 80-column punched card. Discussions with two university systems programmers resulted in the design of a new, 3-1/2-by-7-1/2-inch, selection slip that more closely related to the punched card format. The punched card, used both in manual files and as computer systems input, is employed for selection, ordering, processing, and acquisitions. More specifically, it is employed for the following functions: (1) to purge files—whatever has not been received and, therefore, needs to be claimed or cancelled; (2) to search titles—to determine whether a title has been ordered or received and, if received, what its status is in the system; (3) to avoid duplicating orders; (4) to permit the librarian to select and list orders on the basis of one or a combination of the following factors: (*a*) the library for which a title was ordered, (*b*) the department of the university that ordered a title, (*c*) the departments that have participated most actively in the selection of items for purchase, or (*d*) the department of the library that has ordered a title for reference, reserve, etc.

The system is a mixture of manual and computer operations. Initial searching and verification of a work requested on a selection slip is done manually, then a keypunched selection card is prepared from the selection slip. The first 14 characters of the selection card are computer-compared with the master file by means of the On-Approval or Firm programs. Lists of potential matches, based on the 14-character comparison, are generated. A manual search through the match list is made to determine which titles are, in fact, real matches. All selections that do not match are ordered. Purchase orders are then typed manually—except for items ordered from Eastern Book Co. that are listed by means of an IBM 407 and attached to the purchase order—and the order code is punched on the selection card. Then, utilizing the computer, orders are added to the OPCMF-PIL file by means of the OP-UPDATE-EM program.

Following the computer run, the selection cards are returned to the Machine Systems Department in the library, and cards are manually filed in the "on-order" file in the Processing Department. Upon receipt of an item, the punched card is pulled from the on-order file and inserted in the book. The book and the card are assigned the same accession number. The card is then sent to the Machine Systems Department where a received code is punched in the card.

The accumulated punched cards are sent to Administrative Computer Services for computer updating of the OPCMF-PIL file by means of the OP-UPDATE-EM program. The cards are then returned to the Machine Systems Department and filed in the "in-process" file in the Processing Department. When books are fully processed (classified, cataloged, plated, etc.), their cards are pulled from the in-process file and their classification numbers are written on the punched cards. They are sent to the Machine Systems Department, where a code indicating that the order has been completed is punched, and then to Administrative Computer Services, where the OPCMF-PIL disk file is updated by means of the OP-UPDATE-EM program.

In addition, a set of acquisitions decklet cards are punched and held by the Machine Systems Department until the end of the month when they are sent to Administrative Computer Services to be computer-entered by means of the Monthly Acquisitions program and the Cumulative Acquisitions program. Following the running of these programs, the OP-UPDATE-MD program is run to delete all records representing acquisitions accumulated during the month from the OPCMF-PIL disk file.

In this acquisitions system there are six shifts from manual to computer operations each month. Considerable transportation of cards from the library to Administrative Computer Services is involved.

COSTS

The library costs for searching, ordering, selecting, invoicing, receiving, and processing about 600 titles (including firm orders, standing orders, and books received on approval) amount to about $140 per week.

The library cost for the rental of four IBM 029 keypunches, an IBM 087 collator, and an IBM 082 sorter total about $24 per week.

The library cost for keypunching, verifying, sorting, collating, printing (on a 407 printer), reproducing, interpreting, and decollating are about $208 per week.

For a total cost to the library of about $372 per week, an average of 600 titles per week are processed at a cost of about $.62 per title. This computation does not include any costs of Administrative Computer Services. which runs the computer programs for this system, because they are not charged to the library. These costs total about $419 per week. If all costs of processing about 600 titles per week are included, the unit cost is approximately $1.32.

OBSERVATIONS

The partially automated acquisitions system at Northeastern University has been slow in developing, occasioned by the fairly rapid turnover in programmers and systems personnel. Each time a new programmer was hired, the programs for the library were changed because the new programmer interpreted the library's needs differently from his predecessor. Changes in the programs were therefore not as much the result of debugging efforts, as the result of different interpretations of needs.

Another reason for this system's slow development is that the Machine Systems Department was not established in the library until 1970. After it was set up, better coordination of the various machine systems in the library and the computer operations at Administrative Computer Services was achieved.

One of the major problems in the acquisitions system is human error. Many opportunities for errors occur in this system. For example, the author/ title entry must be spelled perfectly, especially the first 14 columns of this field, and the main entry must be exactly like the one used for previous orders for the same item, or the On-Approval program or the Firm-Orders program will not report a match. As a result, a duplicate copy of the item may be ordered.

In addition to perfect spelling and identical entry, each item that is selected must be keypunched exactly. If a card is mispunched, particularly in the first 14 columns of the author/title field, the computer programs will not report a match. Standards for abbreviations must be followed with great precision. Because there are, potentially, 80 chances for mispunching a card, keypunching must be very carefully done to forestall problems in the system.

Human errors also produce difficulties in the Processing Department where separate on-order and in-process files are maintained. The punched card for each title is filed alphabetically by main entry in the on-order file. This card is pulled when the book arrives. A packing slip, accompanying the book, usually indicates the order number. If there is an intentional duplicate order for different libraries within the university system, care must be taken to check the order number on the punched card against that on the packing slip because both orders will carry the same author and title information. A similar problem may arise with the same author of different titles or the same author and title, but different editions. Some care is required to correctly pull these cards from the on-order file. Since the department is staffed principally by Northeastern students and is supervised at most three and one-half hours per day, the margin for error is not small.

Until the spring of 1973, the computer comparison of selection cards and the master file was based on the first ten characters of the records. This procedure produced an excessive number of potential matches, often running as high as 80 percent and resulting in printed lists running to 30 pages. Each of these potential matches required a human evaluation. Some matches were, of course, intentional duplicate orders. Most matches on the first ten columns were not, however, found to be actual duplicates. The library staff conducted an investigation to determine the optimum algorithm for matching to reduce the number of false matches. It was decided that comparing the first 14 characters would provide maximum effectiveness. The new matching algorithm has reduced the match list by 80 percent, a very few items requiring human evaluation.

In conjunction with this effort to achieve a better searching strategy, the staff found that a one-week shipment schedule would reduce by about three or four weeks the time between the publication of a book and the shelving of the book for use at Northeastern. This change from biweekly to weekly shipments eliminated excessive batching of materials that had delayed processing.

In this acquisitions system, the shelving of new books is not coordinated with the filing of catalog cards. New books may therefore be placed on the shelves before cards are placed in the catalog. These books will be listed on the OPCMF-PIL disk file until the OP-UPDATE-MD program is run, at which time the books will be listed on the "cumulative acquisitions" list. The matching of new selections punched cards is done against the OPCMF-PIL disk file and four previous "monthly acquisitions" lists. If, as continues to happen, catalog cards for titles already on the shelves are not filed within four months of the OP-UPDATE-MD program that is run for these titles, then the computer will not pick up the title match for these books if they are again requested for purchase. In short, there is no record that the library owns these books, except in the accession book, which book cannot be checked unless catalog cards and a shelflist card are in their proper places in their respective files.

This acquisition system has not developed a claims program, one of the purposes for which the punched cards were designed. Many orders, placed three years ago, are still considered open, and most of them have never been claimed. When the library removed from its records (disk, card, and on-order) all orders placed before June 31, 1969, it did not notify 75 percent of the publishers and jobbers through whom these orders were placed. Some of these orders have arrived, necessitating the punching of new cards and the addition of these titles to the OPCMF-PIL records.

Although there are obviously some problems with this system, the OPCMF-PIL disk file and the cumulative acquisitions list are proving useful in preliminary searching procedures. When a title is selected for purchase, these lists are the first items consulted after verification. Without these files much time would be expended tracking down titles already ordered, but not yet cataloged. The system has come close to reaching most of its objectives, namely, to allow manipulation of data for selection, ordering, receiving, and acquisition; to keep records of selection for management purposes; to monitor what has been ordered, and to control the acquisitions operation by maintaining records of the status of each title from ordering through acquisition.

However, the system does not handle periodicals and serials and does not provide fiscal control. Neither are statistical control and statistics generation part of the automated procedures. Only some of the data in the system are used for management purposes. Since the system functions primarily as a list maker, and since the lists are used only for routine decision making, the computer's potential is not exploited. If there are deficiencies in a manual system, the mere automating of the system will not accomplish significant improvement. The deficiencies must be corrected or eliminated. While some "patching" of the system is taking place, small adjustments will not make this system genuinely successful. A complete systems analysis and substantial changes in system operation are needed.

On the other hand, it is probably true that without the partially automated system the difficulties confronting the Acquisitions Department would be worse. The system permits searches by main entry by computer to eliminate unwanted duplicate purchases. It produces better records than were available in the old manual system. In addition, it renders its modest services for a cost that the library is willing to pay.

ACKNOWLEDGMENTS

Most of the information for this case study was obtained during interviews, in April 1972, with Thomas H. Cahalan, assistant librarian for acquisitions; Albert Donley, associate director of libraries, and Sandra Folkins, machine systems supervisor, Northeastern University. Their cooperation and the assistance of Marilyn T. Pope and Robert Bruen in the preparation of this case study are acknowledged with appreciation..

16.
University of Massachusetts Automated Acquisition System

ENVIRONMENT

The University of Massachusetts, a public institution, offers programs of undergraduate and graduate study for more than 20,000 students at its Amherst campus. A 28-story central library building was recently constructed and occupied during the summer of 1973. The new building is designed to house 2,225,000 volumes and seat 3,000 readers. The library's holdings include about 1,075,000 books, periodicals, and government documents, and 190,000 microforms.[1] During 1970–71, 115,345 books, periodical volumes, and government documents and 38,160 microforms were added to the collection. The library staff included 45 librarians, 2.5 additional professional staff members, and 102 clerical staff members. Expenditures for the year were $3,459,192.[2]

OBJECTIVES

Following a careful consideration of the library's technical services operations, the library administration concluded that automation, rather than additional people, would be the best way to meet the problems imposed by a higher rate of acquisitions. This conclusion was based on the administration's awareness of its own needs and of the university's available computer resources. A detailed study was not conducted.

The basic objective of the library staff was to design and implement a system that would be efficient, effective, inexpensive, and easy to use. Specific objectives were (1) to provide rapid responses to inquiries, (2) to enable operators to enter order information into the system quickly and accurately, (3) to present self-explanatory displays and instructions for operators, and (4) to reduce the amount of operator intervention or keystroking for each transaction. The designers endeavored to provide a system that would afford better control over outstanding orders, claiming, and book-fund accounts.

Specific capabilities sought in the system were: (1) to place and update orders; (2) to receive materials; (3) to do automatic claiming; (4) to furnish on-line maintenance of vendor lists; (5) to verify input; (6) to print various reports (such as notices to patrons when orders are placed) and various statistical reports and summaries. Access to individual orders was to be provided via author, title, or Library of Congress card number.

THE COMPUTER

The library's Acquisitions Department has on-line access using four IBM 2260 display terminals to the Administrative Center's IBM 370/145 through a data-communications Data Processing network. The system also uses one IBM 2314 direct-access storage facility disk pack. The IBM 2260 visual display terminals are capable of displaying up to 12 lines of data, and each line has a capacity of 40 characters.

FASTER BASIC (filing and source data entry technique for easier retrieval), an IBM Type III programming language, is used for on-line applications; COBOL is employed for batch-processing operations.

The on-line files utilized in this system are (1) a vendor name and address file, (2) an order status file, and (3) order cross-references files, arranged by author, title, and Library of Congress card number. These files are also used with the batch-processing COBOL programs. In this acquisitions system, variable-length data, such as author, title, publisher, notes, etc., are handled in fixed-length records.

THE SYSTEM

The acquisition system, launched in 1969, took less than one year to design and implement: less than 12 months elapsed between the original feasibility study in 1968 and the fully operational system. As a matter of fact, in June 1969 the library began placing all orders for monographs through the "book order and selection system" (BOS). Several months later, BOS also began to process serial orders. Currently it processes all orders placed by the library, producing the order slips sent to vendors, maintaining the file of material on order, processing both receiving and invoicing information, and producing claims for items not received.[3]

Before an order request arrives in the Monographic or Serials Acquisition department to be placed on BOS, the Bibliography Division (which has overall responsibility for collection building) adds the number of copies needed and special instructions regarding the processing of material when it is received, such as to show an item to a staff member as soon as it is received. In addition, two codes are assigned: (1) a fund code, based on the subject matter of the material; (2) a priority code, based on the urgency of the need for the material.

In this system, approximately 35 percent of all orders originate from MARC tapes, 35 percent from foreign bibliographies, and 30 percent from brochures, flyers, and requests submitted by faculty, staff and students. The orders that do not originate from MARC tapes are searched conventionally for Library of Congress cataloging. When found they are checked for correct bibliographic information and the Library of Congress card number is noted.

Before orders are placed, vendor numbers, from the 6,200 vendors included in the vendor file, are assigned from a printout of vendors that the system generates weekly. If a desired vendor is not found in this list, the system assigns a number to the vendor when the staff enters this new data into the on-line vendor file through an IBM 2260 display terminal. When necessary, changes in the vendor's record, such as of an address or claim code, are also made through the terminal.

After a vendor number has been assigned, the terminal operator can enter order information into the system. Since the cathode-ray-tube (CRT) displays a mask to be filled in, no special coding forms are necessary. If a mistake is made in keying in a particular field, the error is immediately communicated to the operator by the system. When the operator corrects the error and the system determines that all information is complete for an order, a mask for the next order is displayed. The new mask includes the order number assigned by the system to the item just ordered and the name of the vendor just used.

Selection card/worksheets are used to keypunch cards containing order and cataloging information. Each day the order/catalog cards are read into the computer and matched against the current MARC tapes. The computer automatically edits the data, prints a listing of edit errors, checks the order-status disk for any duplicate orders, checks the vendor disk for validity of vendors, and assigns order numbers.

Each morning, the Order departments receive three products as a result of the previous day's computer processing. The first is a batch of purchase orders in vendor-name sequence, ready to be sent to the vendors. Each purchase order comes in two parts: (*a*) the order slip itself, to be retained by the vendor, and (*b*) a packing slip, to be returned to the library when the material is sent.

The second product is a batch of duplicate order slips, arranged by main entry, to be filed in the card catalog. This is the only place where a hard-copy record of an order is on file in the library. As these slips are filed, a final manual check is made for duplicate orders. If a duplicate is found, the order is cancelled through the IBM 2260 terminal, and the printed purchase order is not mailed. The third product of the nightly processing run is a batch of requester notices for items requested by faculty or staff members of the university who indicated that they want to be notified when the library orders the item. Requesters enter their employee numbers on the request forms sent to the library. The BOS system converts this number into a name and campus address that is printed at the bottom of the requester notice.

The computer also retains a record of the order on the processing disk file, and transfers complete cataloging data to the bibliographic tape file. The bibliographic file will be used later, when the ordered item has been received, to produce a complete set of catalog cards.

Within five working days after the receipt of the item, the computer will generate a complete set of catalog cards and punched cards with spine-label data. The catalog cards are produced in proper filing sequence for each of four groups: author/title, subject, shelflist, and branch library.

One of the checks the system must make is to verify that all essential data items are present when it attempts to format a set of cards. The system prints a daily report of errors or missing data elements. Until the necessary changes are made, the cards will not be printed, but the system will keep including the item in the daily error report. Once cataloging copy for a title has been entered into the system, the data are retained in the master bibliographic file. If another set of cards is needed at any time, they can be produced on demand. In May 1970, sometime after the initial implementation of the BOS system, a precataloging system was interfaced with the BOS system. However, the precataloging system is currently being phased out because of the high number of unnecessary sets of catalog cards that have been produced. At the present time about 65 items per month (or about 2 percent of the orders processed) are precataloged. This precataloging is limited to non-MARC titles for which Library of Congress copy is available from microfiche.[4]

Sometimes when ordered materials are received at the library, the packing slip portion of the original order form is not returned by the vendor. In such cases, the operator may use a computer program, LBØ6, to key in the author's name and receive a display of all titles by that author that are currently on order, with BOS order numbers for each. To search the file the system uses a four-character alpha-numeric code generated by the FASTER program. Although this program sometimes displays material unrelated to what was requested, it retrieves what is asked for very quickly.

When the order number for the material just received has been retrieved, the operator takes a printout of the order to accompany the book and can use another computer program, LBØ5, to enter invoice information into the BOS system. The invoice number and date are entered on the top line. On following lines are entered the order number of each item on the invoice and the invoice price of each item. The BOS system checks this information to be sure it is valid. It makes sure, for example, that the material has not been received previously or that the order has not been cancelled. It also displays a code which alerts the receiver that a particular order was updated since the order was placed and that the complete order should be looked up for detailed information. The books are sent on to be processed as are the invoices.

The order-status file is continuously updated as the need arises. Changes in status may include a receipt, a cancellation, a claim, or a reorder. The claiming process, an essential part of the work of an acquisitions department, is often difficult to manage in a manual system. The computerized BOS system has simplified this process by assigning a claim period to all orders at the time they are placed and by automatically generating a claim for the item if it has not arrived by the end of the period. Claim periods are 12 weeks for North America, 18 weeks for Europe and South America, and 24 weeks for the Middle and Far East. The number of outstanding orders ranges between 15,000 and 25,000 items. Although the claim is usually handled automatically according to the vendor to which an order has been assigned, this normal claim period may be overridden if necessary. Once a week the system generates two different types of claim formats: one type for monographic items, a second type for serials. At the same time, the system prints out a report of the number of claims generated and a report describing claims processed for items that have previously been claimed. The latter report gives statistics on the number of first, second, third, and fourth claims generated for the week and statistics on the number of claims generated for each priority category. Thus it alerts the staff to particular orders which may require attention.

When responses to these claims are received from vendors, the display terminals are used to update the on-line order file. Using codes that represent different kinds of reports received from vendors, the operator adds the vendor's answer to the order file. The vendor's response may cause the library to cancel an order, or to cancel and reorder from another vendor, so the operator may need to change the status code at this time. When it is necessary to change the status code, report code, claim code, or the vendor number, the operator uses program LBØ3. The operator depresses the new-line key to bring the cursor (a tiny light on the display screen indicating where any keyed information will be entered) to the line that must be changed and enters the update information. If the system determines that the information has been entered incorrectly, the operator is notified immediately. Once the operator corrects the error, all data for that item are displayed. The BOS system allows the staff to enter information into the order file not only in code, but in natural language as well.

In addition to maintaining the order file, BOS provides management with essential financial information. On a regular basis, it prints a report showing, both by type of material and by fund code, how funds have been encumbered. It also reports, by both type of material and fund code, the extent to which funds have been spent for materials received.

The system has such a substantial array of functions and printouts that it might prove helpful to summarize them here.

By means of the 2260 display terminal, an operator can perform the following on-line functions:

1. Enter new orders.
2. Change or update pending orders to record vendor's reports, including cancellations, if necessary.
3. Update orders to report receipt of monographs.
4. Search orders by order number, author, title, or Library of Congress card number.
5. Enter, update, or display vendor data.

By means of separate batch-processing computer runs the following printouts are generated automatically:

1. Purchase orders.
2. Public catalog slips for orders placed.
3. Notices to requesters of orders placed.
4. Claim notices for overdue orders.
5. Statistical reports for management, such as orders placed and received by time period and category, and estimated fiscal commitments.
6. Maintenance and history file listings, cross-referenced by author, title, and Library of Congress card number.

COSTS

The acquisitions system processed 47,000 orders during the academic year 1970–71 and 37,000 orders during 1971–72, or an average of 42,000 items processed annually in this two-year period.

Table 1
COST OF THE ACQUISITIONS SYSTEM—1971–72

Item	Amount
Acquisitions personnel (5)	$ 43,500
Search section personnel (7)	42,000
Computer (70 hr./yr.)	7,000
Terminals (4 @ $1,500/yr.)	6,000
Disk (1)	3,600
MARC (shared cost)	200
Supplies	4,700
Total	$107,000

Since approximately one-third of all searches are duplicates, the unit cost for searching processed orders is about $.75. On the basis of 42,000 average annual orders, the unit cost for acquisition of an item, including searching cost, is $2.55. For this figure the system provides not only control over ordering and receiving, but management information, fund control and fiscal reports, and useful input for cataloging, much of which is full cataloging data. In fact, the figure should be lower since a portion of the above personnel costs should be assigned to cataloging rather than to acquisitions, but the precise amount has not been determined.

OBSERVATIONS

The automated acquisitions system permits the determination of the status of an order from the day it is placed, readily answers inquiries about outstanding orders, automatically claims overdue orders, and eliminates extensive manual files. It has reduced the manual filing required to control library acquisitions. It has increased the efficiency of acquisition operations. It has contributed to better library management by providing statistical and financial reports that were not available previously. The system has not only resulted in a reduction in acquisitions staff, but it has enabled the library to process orders for library materials in less time and space. One terminal operator can enter up to 300 orders per day. The system has eliminated backlogs of materials to be processed.

A systems manager and four programmer/analysts are a part of the library staff. The systems manager is responsible for the design and implementation of the system. He is available to make any changes or modifications in the system that may be desired. To date, apart from the precataloging program, the changes have been minimal.

Most staff members feel that the programming for the system has been successful. Efforts have been made to counteract any dehumanizing effect of the computer. Masks for inputting data are simple rather than complex. Order and receipt operators do not need extensive training to operate the terminals. The printed outputs of the system, including public catalog slips, are legible and easily understood. The more extensive use of MARC tapes and the phase-out of the precataloging program have improved the system. The system maintains accurate computer files that are accessible by order number, author, title, or Library of Congress card number. In addition, the system prints out, when needed, vendor lists, purchase orders, requester notices, claims, and statistical and fund reports.

One of the major benefits of a computerized system for a library process, such as acquisitions, cataloging, or circulation, is that it forces the tightening and regularizing of the flow of records and materials. The system demands a higher level of accuracy at input and is therefore able to produce improved outputs. In addition, the accuracy of computer counting and calculating inspires management and staff confidence. The speed of computer operations tends to forestall delays and backlogs. The capacity of the computer to handle clerical routines that humans find boring and tedious fosters better staff morale. All of these benefits have been realized in the University of Massachusetts system.

The system, especially in view of its contribution toward savings in cataloging costs, is surprisingly economical to operate. It provides library management with a flexibility and efficiency that should characterize library computerization efforts.

The rise and fall of the precataloging process is proof, once again, that experience alone reveals what libraries really need from computer systems. Of course, needs may change, or come and go, and systems must be able to adapt to these developments. The University of Massachusetts system, fortunately, was able to reduce the precataloging operation with a minimum of effort and expense.

In its use of MARC tapes for selection of library materials, this system is making intelligent use of an expensive resource. When one looks back on the history of the MARC development, one can't help being disconcerted by the fact that the tapes were first distributed to a few large libraries, not in response to a felt need, but rather with the invitation, or challenge, to try to think of something to do with them. Most libraries found the tapes were expensive to run, contained extraneous data, and required them to do substantial programming before they could get at the data. The University of Massachusetts utilization of MARC records has been unusually direct and economical. Of course, the OCLC networking approach tends to spread MARC costs across a wider base, but some libraries have not been able to achieve a viable interface with the network. Whether the University of Massachusetts will participate in the OCLC-NELINET network will depend on costs. During 1972 NELINET advised the University of Massachusetts that it would cost $55,000 to join the network. The university library performed the work that NELINET would have done for it for one-sixth of that figure. It is, therefore, unlikely that the library will participate in this venture.

This system has experienced characteristic patterns of staff reaction to computer systems across time. Initially the staff responded to the computer system with apprehension. Of course, initial system problems, such as downtime, scheduling difficulties, and slow-response times, did little to assuage such apprehension. However, the built-in system-checking and verification routines helped the staff to begin to rely on the system and relieved staff fears that they might commit major errors. Gradually, the staff came to trust the system and now uses it with ease and confidence. In particular, staff gained confidence in using codes, instead of messages, to deal with changes in outstanding orders. In addition, the staff appreciates being relieved of tedious manual file maintenance. Management has responded to quicker access to information on outstanding orders than was available in the manual system, as well as to more timely statistical and fiscal data, by running a tauter and better controlled acquisitions operation. The computer system is now an integral, accepted, and valued part of the Acquisitions Department.

NOTES

1. IBM, *Online Library Acquisition System at the University of Massachusetts—Application Brief* (New York: International Business Machines Corporation Data Processing Division, June 1972).

2. U.S. Department of Health, Education and Welfare, *Library Statistics of Colleges and Universities, Institutional Data, Part A, Fall 1971, Basic Information on Collections, Staff and Expenditures* (Washington, D.C.: Government Printing Office, 1972), 70, 116.

3. Kennedy, James H. and James S. Sokoloski, "Man-Machine Considerations of an Operational On-line University Library Acquisition System" in *Proceedings of the American Society for Information Science*, 7 (1970), 65–67.

4. Interview with Janet Uden, Monographic Acquisitions Department, University of Massachusetts, Amherst, Mass., April 1973.

ACKNOWLEDGMENTS

The assistance of Marjorie C. Resnic in the preparation of this case study is acknowledged with appreciation. Thanks are also extended to Richard Talbot, director of libraries, to Janet Uden, acting head of monographic acquisitions, and to James Sokoloski, library systems manager, University of Massachusetts, for their assistance and cooperation.

17.
Columbia University
Automated Acquisition System

· ·

ENVIRONMENT

The Columbia University libraries, comprised of about 4,500,000 volumes, serve an enrolled population of over 16,000 undergraduate and graduate students and a research and faculty population of around 5,000 persons. About 17,000 individuals use the library each day. The university is located in upper Manhattan.

The libraries operate on a budget of over $5,000,000, plus $1,000,000 for overhead. The annual book budget is about $1,500,000. The libraries employ anout 155 professional librarians and 300 clerical and other personnel. One centralized acquisitions operation, which functions within the Technical Services Division, processes anout 135,000 volumes each year, of which about 65,000 are discrete titles. The libraries hold approximately 100,000 serial titles and subscribe to 55,000 current serials each year. About 50 percent of these come through the central Technical Services Division and are centrally checked in. The other 50 percent are sent directly to departmental libraries. There are printed union lists of serials for the science and medical divisions.

The libraries maintain a union catalog of more than 6 million cards. The main catalog is split into author/title and subject catalogs. The Library of Congress classification scheme is used for all classification. The Library of Congress cataloging data cover about 80 percent of current English-language acquisitions and about 60 percent of foreign and non-Roman-alphabet items.

The Technical Services Department provides acquisitions and cataloging service for about 40 separate departmental or divisional libraries, varying in size from 30,000 to 3 million volumes. Since there are 11 separate Science Department libraries, there is heavy duplication of materials and much multiple-copy acquisition.

OBJECTIVES

In 1964 the Columbia University libraries' management decided to begin experiments with computers. After exploring ways to initiate, organize, and fund such an effort, a new staff office, the Systems Office, was created and given the responsibility for carrying out a systematic description and analysis of all library activities, initiating and coordinating all automation projects within the library system, and launching a program of education for the library staff in the areas of systems analysis and automation. In order to ensure that the objectives and responsibilities of the monograph acquisition section were understood by the automation project personnel, the Systems Office staff formulated the following list of acquisitions objectives:

1. To be responsible, through cooperation among selection officers, for the overall development of the collection;
2. To be aware of current and retrospective library materials which are available in subjects served by the libraries;
3. To select those materials which, within budget limitations, are judged to be most valuable for present and future research and instructional activities of the university;
4. To obtain materials selected as quickly and inexpensively as practicable;
5. To prevent undesired duplication;
6. To maintain process control and temporary bibliographic control over items on order or received until formal bibliographic control is achieved;
7. To assemble and transmit such bibliographic and control data as are useful for cataloging;
8. To assist in providing the information necessary for fiscal control;
9. To solicit and receive gift materials and use them as productively as possible;
10. To dispose of unwanted material in the most effective ways;
11. To coordiante and centralize, as much as is practical and desirable, the procedures necissary to accomplish the above objectives.

Next, in accord with these 11 objectives of the Acquisitions Division, the Systems Office formulated the following project objectives:

1. To design, program, and test a generalized computer-based system

to increase the overall processing efficiency of monograph acquisitions by

(a) using fully the inquiry, maintenance, and retrieval capabilities of a computerized file;
(b) reducing duplicate searching and ordering by early input and rapid display of order information;
(c) allowing for system flexibility and growth; and
(d) anticipating and accommodating the needs of other areas of library processing (e.g., cataloging) to achieve eventually an integrated technical processing system.

2. To maintain process control and temporary bibliographical control over orders and books until formal bibliographical control is achieved by

(a) building a centralized, magnetic data store to which there is decentralized access via on-line terminals, and/or printed lists;
(b) identifying the process status for each item in the system;
(c) increasing communications between the Acquisitions Division and other units in the library system; and
(d) providing information to management by the automatic accumulation of production statistics and precise and up-to-date material processing and budget information.

3. To increase and improve service to patrons and librarians by

(a) consolidating and centralizing procedures into fewer functional paths;
(b) reducing processing steps and time throughout the acquisitions process;
(c) speeding the flow of material from the time of receipt to shelving by eliminating categories of clerical work necessary under the manual system; and
(d) providing more and better communications with various users of the system.

In accord with these project objectives, between 1964 and 1966 the staff conducted experiments with various aspects of the library system, such as monograph acquisitions, monograph cataloging, circulation, and reserve-book processing. Between 1966 and 1968 the staff designed a modular acquisitions system to be implemented in two major stages. The first stage, consisting of the Encode I and Fiscal modules of the integrated system, was developed and implemented between 1968 and the third quarter of 1969. The second stage, involving the Encode II and In-Process modules, was implemented in the last quarter of 1971.

In the design, development, and implementation of this system, the systems staff members have displayed notable fidelity to the objectives of the Acquisitions Division and to their own project goals.

THE COMPUTER

The automated acquisitions system makes use of the centralized computer facility at the university. The computer, an IBM 360/91, coupled with a 75, is one of the most powerful in the world. It uses the IBM Operating System (OS). It has 2,500,000 bytes of core. The computer, while it has remarkable research capabilities, has a small output capacity and is therefore not well suited for library-type operations.

Input for the acquisitions system is prepared on an IBM magnetic tape/ Selectric typewriter, Model 5, and a Digidata, System 30, converter. Output for the system is produced on a 1403 line printer, with a TN train, all in upper case.

Programs for the acquisitions system are written in PL/1, Version 5.

The Systems Office senior staff members meet regularly with the Computer Center staff to coordinate their activities. There are three systems analysts and two programmers in the Systems Office.

THE SYSTEM

The Acquisitions Division, in processing about 65,000 orders annually and in spending close to $1 million against 300 separate funds, devotes more than 55 percent of the personnel budget and 45 percent of the book budget exclusively to the ordering and processing of monographic materials. As this large and complex acquisitions operation was analyzed by the Systems Office staff, certain logically related functions were identified. The preorder functions included selection, order searching, and preparing and processing order requests. The order-generation functions involved the preparation and dispersing of forms. The functions of (1) file creation, (2) updating, (3) reporting, and (4) processing are essential not only for orders, but for fiscal control as well. Exception routine functions are necessary to deal with special problems in processing. The analysis by the Systems Office staff revealed three levels of data flow, namely, (1) process control, or the flow of order data and the processing status of each order through the system; (2) fiscal data flow, or the encumbering of funds, paying of invoices and reporting of fund status, and (3) bibliographic data flow, or the assembling, verifying, storing, and transferring of bibliographic data needed in the cataloging process, such as Library of Congress proofslips, Title II cards, and Library of Congress Machine-Readable Cataloging (MARC) data.

Having identified the various functions, levels, and kinds of data flow in the acquisitions operations, the Systems Office staff first developed a Fiscal module, with two major programs, Checkwrite and Weekly/Monthly Fiscal. The Fiscal module creates and maintains separate files for encumbering, recording, and summarizing expenditures against various library funds; writes checks to pay for monographic and serial materials; creates machine-readable data to be used as input to the university controller's system, and creates periodic reports reflecting the current status of all library book funds.

The first major program, Checkwrite, processes dealer invoices for payment, performing such functions as currency conversion or summarizing of expenditures by fund; writes checks to pay dealer invoices; edits and verifies the checks that are written, creates printed records and reports for use by the library and the university controller, and creates machine-readable input to update library and university accounts.

In the daily fiscal processing, invoices that have been approved for payment are received in batches from the acquisitions office. Invoices from domestic and foreign dealers are separated and filed alphabetically by dealer. If more than one invoice is received from a dealer, all of that dealer's invoices (up to five) are batched and paid by one check.

Within each batch, all payments made from the same library fund on a single invoice are totaled. Foreign currencies are converted to U.S. dollar amounts. An adding machine tape is made totaling each invoice; a second tape is made totaling all invoices from one dealer for the check amount. Totals are verified, dealer name and address are reviewed for completeness, and dealer invoice numbers, if any, are indicated.

Checks are assembled in groups of five and an adding machine tape of the five check amounts is made. The total of this tape, which is attached to the batch, is compared after machine processing with the "check summary statement" produced by the computer.

Data from the invoices are transcribed by a typist onto a blank check form using a cassette typewriter. This operation also creates a cassette containing such data elements as check number, check amount, payee name, fund numbers, and amounts, for input to the Checkwrite program. After every fifth check is typed, the total for the five check amounts is typed. The computer verifies check amounts against itemized fund amounts and, as a further control, compares the five individual check amounts against the total of the five typed checks.

After the typed checks have been proofread and corrections have been made (which may include errors made the previous day and detected in the computer run), the information on the cassette is transferred to nine-track magnetic tape and submitted for computer processing each evening. Checks and invoices are held until the computer output is received. Each morning the computer-produced check summary statement is matched with the original checks. Original dealer invoices are attached to an account voucher and filed in a paid invoice file by check number. If a copy of the invoice is to be returned to the dealer, it is attached to the check. Checks are sent to the university controller's office for signing and mailing. Incorrect checks, which are rejected by the computer, are compared with an "error message listing," and necessary corrections are typed to be submitted with new input at the end of the day.

In the Checkwrite program, checks are typed manually, check summary statements and error lists are printed by the computer, and an error file for checks that could not be processed and check data and other transactions that are input into the "daily fiscal update file" are produced on magnetic tape.

The other major program, the Weekly/Monthly Fiscal program, maintains a record of all transactions occurring against the libraries' funds, and records the balance for each fund. This program, on each weekly run, writes a new fiscal file with update information and prints a "trial balance report." At the end of the month, the program writes a new fiscal file with month-end balances and outstanding encumbrances held over from the previous month. It also prints a monthly trial balance report, a statement of encumbrances, a report of dropped encumbrances, a detailed expenditure statement, and error messages.

The Systems Office staff next developed an Encode module in two successive versions. Encode I produced computer-printed order records that were filed in existing manual files. Encode II, which has superseded Encode I, replaced the manual files with a comprehensive computer file and computer-produced in-process lists. Encode II was developed in conjunction with an In-Process module, which begins with order placement, controls the flow of orders through acquisitions and cataloging, and ends when formal bibliographic control is achieved, or when catalog cards are filed in the public catalog.

Since the final module, MARCSRCH, which accepts machine-readable data from the Encode II module to search the cumulative MARC files and produce cataloging copy worksheets, is more concerned with cataloging than acquisitions, this module is not described in detail in this case study.

Materials currently input in the Encode II module include all monographic and monographic series material in all Roman alphabet languages, as well as transliterated Cyrillic languages. Microforms, maps, and speech records are included, but serial publications are not. The system integrates materials received, whether through purchase, blanket or standing order, gift, exchange, deposit, or cooperative acquisitions programs. As order data are input, a computer record is created that integrates bibliographic, processing, and fiscal data. Individual records are identified by a unique six-digit control number that is assigned before input. All data elements are assigned two-digit Library of Congress MARC compatible tags by the input typist while keying the record. Order typing is done daily and batched for computer processing each evening.

The Encode II program prints daily all purchase orders and other order forms, all claim forms and cancellation notices to dealers, notifications to departmental libraries and the National Program for Acquisitions and Cataloging at the Library of Congress, and a variety of lists, such as a sequential numeric listing of all new orders input; a duplicate orders list; a daily cumulative in-process list (IPL) by title, which contains all new orders input and all records that have been changed in processing status since the last weekly printing of a master IPL.

For each new order, three forms, a "material update" (MatUp), a "cataloging update" (CatUp), and a "fiscal update" (FisUp), are filed in a "manual sequence file" (MSF). The MSF, in order-number sequence, contains all original documents and update forms associated with each order.

Selected order data, formatted and automatically sent to a MARC search file by the Encode II program, search for matching MARC cataloging copy and remain in the file until a match is made. A substantial percentage of orders (about 60 percent of English-language titles) are matched by MARC records, thereby eliminating a large amount of original cataloging, as well as much manual searching and re-searching.

The in-process file contains a record for all orders and material accessioned by the library, as well as a record of various processing steps, such as notations of when material is received, when orders are cancelled or deleted, when titles are sent to cataloging backlog, or when cataloging is completed.

The Encode II program also automatically sends book-fund-encumbrance information to the Fiscal module.

The processing status of all individual monographic items received in the liberty and going through technical processing, reflected in the in-process file and list, is maintained on a current basis by the inputting of update information. The update forms, MatUp, CatUp, and FisUp, are taken from MSF and manually matched to the material and invoices received for each order. These forms travel with the material and, as successive processing steps are completed, are annotated with an update code and returned to a central point for keying into the computer in-process file.

The in-process program automatically reviews the in-process file on a continuing basis for all orders that are overdue and require claiming. All potential claims are printed out on a report list for management review before being printed onto mailing forms. Other reports are printed periodically, including subsets of the in-process file by various categories, and a comprehensive statistical summary of in-process file activity.

On a *daily* basis, the ENCODII processing program of the Encode II module will produce an "in-process list/daily supplement;" purchase orders (including regular, confirming, or prepaid), gift and exchange information, Mat-Up, CatUp, and FisUp forms, a "permanent order list," a list reflecting duplicate orders in the in-process file, cancellation notices and mailing labels, claim forms and mailing labels, OP (out-of-print) quotation requests, and claim decision forms.

On a *weekly* basis, the Master processing program of the Encode II module will produce a claim list and an in-process list/weekly master, which, as the name indicates, is a cumulative list of all order records in the in-process file incorporating the week's new input.

On a *biweekly*, or *on-demand* basis, departmental in-process lists are produced. On a *quarterly* basis, a list of cancelled orders is generated. Processing statistics are printed in various tabulations on demand. A number of special listings are also prepared on request.

The system, which has been fully operational since the latter part of 1971, was implemented with few difficulties, considering its magnitude, and has experienced little system disruption from computer downtime. It is now solidly operational.

COSTS

Costs of this computerized acquisitions system, except for those for development, are based on the Columbia University Computer Center's new pricing algorithm. The costs of the Fiscal and In-Process modules have been computed separately. In the Fiscal module the natural unit for consideration is a check; however, for the sake of clarity, since input and output both involve a summary for every batch of five checks, the unit is defined as a record, and a record is a check plus one-fifth of the cost of a batch summary statement. The development costs of the Fiscal module appear in Table 1.

Table 1
FISCAL MODULE DEVELOPMENT COSTS

Salaries (not including fringe or overhead)	$12,488.00
Computer costs (@ $300/hr.)	543.00
Total	$13,031.00
Five-year prorated annual cost	$2,606.00
Cost per record (17,400 records/yr.)	$ .14

The input cost per record is $.47, based on twelve months of operating experience from April 1970 to March 1971 and including keying, input device, and processor costs. The operating cost per record, based on the same period of time, is $.09. Based on an annual volume of 17,400 records, the total cost for development, input, and operating in the Fiscal module is $.70 per record. The development costs of the Encode II module appear in Table 2.

Table 2
ENCODE II MODULE'S DEVELOPMENT COSTS

Salaries (including fringe and overhead)		$16,500.00
Computer costs (testing)		5,000.00
Supplies		200.00
	Total	$21,700.00
Five-year prorated annual cost		$ 4,340.00
Cost per record (30,000 records/year)		$ .14

The input cost per entry is $.36, based on a daily volume of 250 records and 200 updates for 20 working days a month and a seven-hour working day, and allowing for an average of three updates per order record. The operating cost is $.30 per record for processing, based on typical processing of 30,000 records in the in-process file, with an average of three updates per order record and an average retention in the master in-process file of eight months. Based on a volume of 30,000 records, the unit cost per order record for development, input, and processing costs in the Encode II module is $.80.

In the Fiscal module, the unit cost per fiscal record was found to be $.70. Since there are approximately 5.2 orders per fiscal record, the per order record cost is $.13. Adding together the Encode II module unit cost of $.80 and the Fiscal module cost of $.13 per order record, the combined cost per order record in the acquisitions system is $.93.

The Systems Office staff recommends that these cost figures be viewed with some reservation. The operating experience with the computerized system has not been long enough to permit the collection of meaningful average records. For this reason, further cost studies are contemplated.

OBSERVATIONS

An evaluation of this automated acquisitions system conducted in 1971 revealed several major advantages. The most significant was its ability to handle a greater number of records in the available space. The manual outstanding order file, a card file holding between 100,000 and 150,000 items, had grown to an unwieldy size. Types of materials that could not be included in the manual file, such as gift and exchange requests and receipts or transliterated Cyrillic alphabet materials, are now listed in the computer file.

The manual file was weeded once a year, and all cards for materials received before a given date were discarded. In view of the substantial disparity in cataloging times for various materials, some cards remained in the file long after the materials had been cataloged, while other cards were removed while the materials were being held in a cataloging backlog. The computer listing not only indicates the date of receipt; it also indicates which materials are assigned to the cataloging backlog. Entries remain in the computer file for a period of time after cataloging is completed to allow for the printing and filing of catalog cards, and then the entries are dropped automatically. The computer file therefore reflects more accurately the status of in-process materials.

Subsets of the in-process list, by division or individual library, are readily produced, thereby making information on outstanding orders available to units other than central acquisitions. Selected statistical and fiscal data are also distributed to various library units.

This computer system checks daily and weekly for duplicated order records. However, in the present system there is a slightly longer turnaround time to get an order into the in-process file. If two order requests for the same title are being processed at the same time, it is possible that both orders will be placed. Searching to prevent duplication must be conducted in additional locations. Except for the time immediately after a master run, new orders have to be searched in both the master in-process list and the cumulative supplement.

However, the initial increase of order duplication under the computer system has been reduced not only by an automatic daily and weekly programmed review for order duplication, but by the use of cross-references and author entries for nondistinctive title in the in-process list, by the inclusion of gift and exchange receipts, monographic series volumes, documents, backlogged titles, etc., as well as by greater staff familiarity with the in-process list and supplementary files and listings. In addition, since the in-process list is arranged by title rather than by main entry, the detection of duplication orders has been made easier.

The computer in-process file contains full bibliographic data, but the printed in-process file does not. While occasionally the searching staff will have to consult the "permanent order list" (POL) for the full bibliographic entry, experience discloses that only 3 percent of the total in-process-file searching requires reference to more complete bibliographic information. The Systems Office staff does not plan to provide on-line access to the in-process file.

In the manual system, reports from dealers, claims, correspondence, etc., were recorded on the back of the order card. In other words, a complete, historical record of the order was maintained on the order card. In the computer system, only the most recent updating of the order record appears. Although the full record is maintained in the master file in the computer, there is no convenient way to retrieve this information. For most orders, the history of the order is not necessary. When difficulties with an order arise, a search of the computer-produced permanent order list, the claims lists, or the cancellation lists will usually uncover a sufficient audit trail to resolve the problem.

Because this batch-mode computer system has a built-in time delay from input to output, certain types of transactions, such as on-demand check payments, immediate cancellation of orders, and rush orders, have to fall into line within the job stream with all other transactions for normal computer processing. Manual procedures have, however, been devised to process special transactions and to deal with special situations. Of course, after manual processing, information regarding the manual transactions must be input into the computer system for the system to regain in-process control.

While the manual card files have inherently greater flexibility than machine-based files, the computer files have taken over many clerical tasks and services and have provided new services that were not practicable under the manual system. The ability of the Encode II module to encumber appropriate book funds automatically has resulted in a considerable saving in time over the old system. Also, since orders are searched against the cumulated MARC tapes, if a match is found, cataloging information is immediately made available, often before the material itself is received. The regularly scheduled generation of a claiming list provides a continual, systematic review of the entire order file. While this has increased dealer correspondence, it has also resulted in some materials being more promptly acquired.

When a new computer system is being installed, it is vital that appropriate orientation and training be given to all library personnel who will be affected by the new system. More extensive and formalized instruction for the operating staff would probably have smoothed out the shift from the manual to the computer system.

The clerical load in the data control or input section proved to be both heavier than expected and more variable in flow, with sharper peak and slump periods, than was anticipated. Since user departments relied on daily products from the automated system, and a backlog of input was not only undesirable but destructive to system integrity, it was necessary to organize the staffing pattern between input sections so that personnel could be shifted to maintain a continuous flow throughout the system.

The system's advantages are (1) that it handles a large volume of orders in relatively little space; (2) that it maintains in-process control from the time an order is placed until the material is cataloged and on the shelf; (3) that it disseminates information to divisions and individual libraries by means of lists and reports; (4) that it generates selective information and statistics as required; (5) that it sharply reduces manual filing time; (6) that it automatically reviews the master file for claiming, automatically encumbers book funds, and automatically searches against the MARC cumulative file, and (7) that it provides greater standardization, enhanced quality control, and better interfacing between technical processing units.

Because of the range of acquisitions, the volume of orders being processed, and the complexities of fiscal procedures, a sophisticated control system was required. The system can handle up to 325 different book funds and 200 dealers. The automated acquisitions system for the Columbia University Libraries has been designed, developed, implemented, costed, and evaluated in a very orderly and forthright manner. It has achieved increased consistency and standardization in forms, processes, and reports. It has provided services that were not provided in the manual system, such as checkwriting, fund reporting, MARC data searching, and status reporting for all materials in-process. These additional functions have added to the overall cost of the system. They have also enhanced the system's efficiency of and the quality of its service. While the costs of such additional features are included in the system costs of less than $1.00 per order record, the increased efficiency and quality of service can only be evaluated on a qualitative level. The system has been well received by the library staff, as it should have been. It is an excellent system.

ACKNOWLEDGMENTS

This case study is based on information obtained during an on-site visit to the Columbia University Libraries in March 1972; interviews with Jerome Yavarkovsky, assistant to the director (Systems) and Heike Kordish, head of the systems office, and the following reports prepared under grants from the U.S. National Science Foundation, Office of Science Information Service, Special Projects Program (NSF-GN-694):

Paul J. Fasana, *Automation Efforts at the Columbia University Libraries.* pt. 1, January 1970.
Paul J. Fasana and Heike C. Kordish, *The Columbia University Libraries Integrated Technical Services System, Part II: Acquisitions, Introduction.* August 1970.
Paul J. Fasana and others, *The Columbia University Libraries Integrated Technical Services System, Part II: Acquisitions, FISCAL Module,* September 1971.
——, *The Columbia University Libraries Integrated Technical Services System, Part II: Acquisitions, ENCODE II/IN PROCESS.* July 1972.

Mr. Yavarkovsky's and Ms. Kordish's helpful cooperation in the preparation of this case study are acknowledged with appreciation.

18.
M.I.T. Libraries
Automated Acquisition System

· ·

ENVIRONMENT

The Massachusetts Institute of Technology libraries consist of 14 branch libraries and some 28 reading rooms that serve an academic community of approximately 19,935. This figure includes 7,717 students; 7,304 staff, of which 3,081 are academic staff; approximately 3,081 academic staff spouses; approximately 1,200 special users with library privileges, and about 450 Wellesley College students who are exchange students at M.I.T. The libraries in 1973 had holdings of 1,463,000 volumes (including approximately 160,000 bound periodicals), plus subscriptions to 17,000 current journals and serials. The total budget for the M.I.T. libraries for 1972–73 was $2,582,000, of which $653,000 was for materials (books, serials, and journals) and binding. The libraries circulate outside of room use about 370,000 items per year and employ 57 professional librarians, 144 nonprofessionals and 22 students in full-time equivalency.

OBJECTIVES

In 1958 M.I.T. pioneered in the field of library automation with the creation of a serials listing produced by punched cards. In 1962 Technical Information Project (TIP), originally funded by the National Science Foundation, was started as a three-phase research-and-development project to study the feasibility of, design, and develop an automatic retrieval system of bibliographic data from 21 physics journals. The objectives of the Technical Information Project were:

To provide a test-bed facility to evaluate search strategy, learn from direct experience what contribution modern technology can make in solving the problem of scientific exchange and to localize those areas in information process where technological improvements were most likely to succeed.[1]

A resident systems staff has been at the M.I.T. libraries since 1963. It consists of a director, one to three systems designers, three to nine programmers, and up to 20 supporting personnel members. This staff has been engaged primarily in government-sponsored research, rather than library applications, and the size of its staff has varied in accordance with level of funding. A number of research experiments involving on-line cataloging, bibliographic indexing, and information retrieval, related to the M.I.T. libraries, but not directly part of its automation aims, have been conducted by the systems staff.

From 1962 to 1965, Dr. M. M. Kessler supervised the development of a multipurpose text-handling system providing on-line retrieval with full Boolean logic, code conversion, editing, formatting, sorting, and calculating. Only two major library applications systems have been developed and implemented for the libraries: an automated catalog for serials and journals, and the acquisitions system described here.

In 1965 the automation of serials began and was in complete service by 1967 via the CTSS (compatible time-sharing system) in operation at M.I.T.'s Information Processing Center (IPC).

In the first stage of the automated TIP system, a purified serials disk file was produced from punched cards, data were translated by computers into upper and lower case, file keys were generated for main entry, typesetting was controlled, and validity checks were established. Since the purification of data was essential, individual libraries were asked to review entries. Fifteen hundred errors were corrected manually, and the computer reported 2,000 more. A sort program was written in accord with the *ALA Filing Rules*. In the second stage of the automated TIP system, acquisitions and accounting control for monographs and serials was made fully operational in 1969. Testing and utilization of the new system occurred simultaneously. It took six months to write and debug the TIP automated acquisitions programs.

One of the central concerns in the development of the TIP automated monograph acquisitions system was fiscal. Special attention was given to cost analysis. A major objective of TIP was to design and implement a system that reflected an awareness of cost factors. Recognized methods of analysis were to be employed in ascertaining costs. A subsidiary objective in the development of this system was to build great flexibility into it so that advantage could be taken of any computer configuration or any cost savings that might be, or become, available.

THE COMPUTER

The library's automated monograph acquisitions system utilizes only part of the CTSS at the Information Processing Center.[2] The system was first implemented on an IBM 7094 computer during the years 1968–70, and was operated until 1972. The IBM 7094 was sold in July 1973. Prior to that date, most applications were transferred to other computers at the university's Information Processing Center. The IBM 370/165 was one of those computers. Concurrently, a reimplementation of the acquisitions system was begun late in 1971 for this new machine. Internally, the reimplementation represented a complete reprogramming and some refinements in design. However, as of July 1973, efforts to reactivate the system have been discontinued.

Input for the acquisitions system was prepared on two Friden 2303 Flexowriter paper tape punches. A third machine was available for backup purposes. An operator of this machine could punch at speeds up to 15 characters per second. The Flexowriters produced both paper tape and a printout. There were three IBM 2741 communications terminals, each with dataphones.

A Mohawk Data Sciences (MDS) 6400 data converter was used to read the paper tape and convert it to magnetic tape for use by the computer. A full week's output of two typists typing full time—nearly 1/2 million characters—took less than one hour to convert.[3]

Programs written for the acquisitions system were in MAD and FAP. The major applications programs unique to the acquisitions system were: (1) "Validation," which processed the input transactions and tested for accuracy in form and content; (2) "Updating," which updated new transactions against the master file and produced a new master file, budgetary records, and several other files; (3) "Log formatting," which reformatted the master file for printing; (4) "Budgeting," which recorded all financial transactions and adjusted accounts.

A number of minor programs for formatting other reports, keeping statistics, maintenance, and backup were also unique to the system. System utility programs supplied by IBM were used for editing and printing. Applications programs unique to the acquisitions system drew heavily upon a set of generalized text-handling programs developed for this and other purposes at M.I.T. These basic programs underlay other information retrieval functions in the library as well.

THE SYSTEM

In this system, all acquisitions input, preparation, updating, and output were performed in a central Acquisitions Department in M.I.T. libraries. Library staff members at all 14 M.I.T. libraries selected their own material and generated their own orders, which were forwarded to this central acquisitions department. Since the libraries had their own subject specialists, the staff at Hayden Library did no presearching, but accepted orders as received.

Each month, over 2,000 orders were initiated by the various divisional libraries and reading rooms. By volume, over 80 percent of these orders were placed by the five major divisional libraries. About 90 percent of the orders placed were eventually received. The rest remained as outstanding orders or were cancelled. Over 90 percent of the orders were for monographs. The rest were for serials, journals, and other material. Most monograph orders were for single copies of a single-volume work. Monograph orders were sent directly to publishers or to dealers; journal orders were usually sent to a subscription agency. In any given month hundreds of vendors were involved. There were over 300 internal accounts and funds from which purchases could be made. When an order was placed, the estimated price was posted as a commitment against a designated fund and account. The dollar volume of such commitments averaged about $25,000 per month. The average purchase price of individual monographs was about $12. Many special cases had to be accommodated, such as deposit accounts, gifts, exchanges, and foreign currency conversions. Although the Comptroller's Department issued checks covering the library's expenditures, the M.I.T. libraries controlled placement of orders, processing receipts, checking invoices, cataloging, as well as budgetary and other administrative functions.

The acquisitions system was comprised of nine major functional operations: (1) input, (2) editing, (3) encumbering, (4) validation, (5) updating, (6) log production, (7) budgeting, (8) statistical, and (9) housekeeping. These operations formed natural breaking points in the regular processing of the acquisitions system and each could be run asynchronously. The nine operations are further broken down into the following 44 processing steps.

Input

1. *Input preparation.* In the acquisitions department, copies of orders and invoices were routed to an input area where forms that reported on receipts, cancellations, claims, desiderata, cataloging, and corrections were prepared. These input forms were put into batches, each batch typically consisting of 25 or so similar transactions of a single date.

2. *Input typing.* The input typists punched the batches of transactions on Friden flexowriters. These machines simultaneously produced paper tape and printed copies of all the transactions. Each typist made up a daily report indicating the total volume of each kind of transaction typed. The output of this step thus consisted of the paper tape, a printed copy, and a summary report.

3. *Paper tape packaging.* At the end of each week the paper tapes produced during the week were wound onto teletype reels, given an identifying name, and sent to the Information Processing Center with a shipping list attached.

4. *Paper tape conversion.* Information Processing Center personnel converted all the tapes for one week onto a single reel of magnetic tape, using a Mohawk Data Sciences 6400 data converter. Then they returned both the paper tapes and the shipping list with a notation indicating how many characters in length each paper tape was.

5. *Input tape loading.* This step involved conversion from the Friden paper tape code structure to EBCDIC, an internal code recognized by IBM machines.

6. *Input proof copy printing.* A printout of the entire file was made, using an upper-and-lower-case print train. This printout was used during the editing phase (see below).

7. *Input traffic summary.* A summary report of the daily input typing reports was prepared manually each week to show the total volume of transactions typed. This information was sent back to the acquisitions department for cross-checking purposes.

Editing

8. *Scanning.* A program read the input and printed out the first line and last ten lines of each file and the label line for each batch in the input. This printout gave a general assurance of data integrity and was used in the proofreading step.

9. *Proofreading.* A proofreader marked an abbreviated list produced by the scan program, using standard proofreading symbols. Errors noted on the Flexowriter copy were transcribed along with any other errors noted during a quick visual check of the proof.

10. *Editing.* Utilizing an IBM 2741 console, all errors noted in the proofreading step were corrected.

11. *Edited proof printing.* Another printout was then made of the file, which reflected the changes made during editing. These edited proofs were placed into binders and used as reference copies during later steps.

Encumbering

12. *Order posting.* Order information was posted to one of the nearly 300 different accounts. A "postings" file resulted, giving for each named account the number of items, and the total dollar amounts, posted against that account.

13. *Posting sorting.* The postings were sorted into order by library, account, fund, and type.

14. *Posting editing.* Since the above procedures were performed on unvalidated data, some erroneous accounts occasionally resulted. These incorrect postings were resolved by intervention, using the editing program to change the postings to their proper accounts.

15. *Posting printing.* The resulting file was then printed, and the printout was submitted to the library accounting department for use in projecting the rate of expenditure on each account.

Validation

16. *Validation.* The month's input text was processed by a very rigorous validating program. This program detected errors in input format and content. Over 100 separate tests were made, ranging from such very simple checks as, "Is the type code M,S, or J?" (to indicate monograph, serial, or journal) to such fairly sophisticated checks of consistency as the plausibility of starting and ending dates for subscriptions, the legitimacy of the account name, and accuracy of invoice totals. Conversion from foreign currencies was also done at this stage, according to a table updated from information supplied by a local bank. The validation program produced a file consisting of all transactions that successfully passed the validation tests; an error file consisting of transactions that failed, together with a detailed explanation of the reason for failure; and a traffic report indicating how many transactions of each kind were read and how many were written into each output file.

17. *Validation error printing.* The error output file from the validation step was printed on a high-speed printer.

18. *Validation error proofreading.* The reason for each error was noted, and using standard proofreading marks, the invalid data were corrected.

19. *Validation error editing.* Using the above corrected proof, the error file was edited with the on-line editing program. The error file was created in a format that could be reread by the validation program.

20. *Revalidation.* The corrected error files were again submitted to the validation program. This process could theoretically repeat itself indefinitely. In fact, any errors still resulting after one revalidation were usually postponed for input to the next month's run.

Updating

21. *Transaction sorting.* The entire month's validated data were sorted by order number, type of transaction, and transaction date. A separate transaction file was created for each library.

22. *Updating.* On a library-by-library basis, the transaction file was matched against the master file of all outstanding orders. Each transaction, as a rule, caused information in the master record to be changed. Six output files were created by this run: (1) a newly updated file; (2) a history file of all master records that action has been completed on; (3) a reject file consisting of transactions that were inconsistent; (4) a budgetary records file; (5) a statistical summary file, and (6) a transactions summary file. An update report was also printed by this program, indicating the total number of transactions processed by type of transaction, and a count of the number of records in the input master file, the new master file, the history file, the reject file, and the budgetary record file.

23. *Reject file printing.* The rejected transactions, together with an explanation for each rejected transaction were printed on a high-speed printer.

24. *Reject file proofreading.* The Acquisitions Department staff inspected the reject file and marked appropriate actions. This procedure was more complicated than validation error proofreading (step 18). It frequently involved reference to the master file for troubleshooting.

25. *Reject file correction.* The reject file was corrected using the on-line editing program.

26. *Reject file revalidation.* The reject file was put aside to be revalidated as part of the next month's input.

Log Production

27. *Acquisitions log formatting.* The new master file was formatted into a printed log that displayed important elements of the file, one item per line. As part of this same process a secondary file consisting of purchase order number, main entry, title, author, and call number (if there were one) was created and used to produce the reference log.

28. *Acquisitions log printing.* The formatted acquisitions log, arranged by purchase order number, was printed on three-ply paper. One copy was sent to the acquisitions department, one was sent to the divisional library, and one was filed with the operations personnel.

29. *Reference log sorting.* The secondary file, created during the acquisitions log formatting step (27), was sorted by main entry for each library and formatted for printing.

30. *Reference log printing.* The reference log was printed and distributed in a fashion similar to the "acquisitions log" and acted as a cross-reference to it, readily allowing the user to ascertain the purchase order number if the main entry were known.

Budgeting

31. *Budgetary record sorting.* The budgetary records file, produced by the updating step (22) and consisting of information concerning each master record for which any changes having fiscal implications had occurred, was sorted by library and budgetary group. For the most part this file reflected fiscal information for new orders and invoice payments. These records were then sorted into order by account name.

32. *Budgeting.* The budget master file, which reflected the current status of all accounts, and the sorted budgetary records were read by the budgeting program, which updated the budget master and wrote a new file, containing invoice details (discussed later). A "deposits master file," which was also read and updated during this step, contained record keeping for accounts relating to deposits with government agencies and professional societies. Finally, a budget report was produced by this program, accounting for the total number of items processed and the dollar volume.

33. *Budget report formatting.* The new budget master was formatted for printing in three different forms: (1) the "complete financial statement," for use by the library administration; (2) the "librarian's financial statement," for use by the divisional librarians; (3) the "invoice financial statement," for comparison with monthly statements from the comptroller's office.

34. *Budget report printing.* These files were then printed and distributed to the appropriate persons.

35. *Invoice detail sorting.* The invoice details produced by step 32 were sorted (1) by vendor and order number for one report, (2) by budgetary group for another, and (3) by deposit vendor for a third report.

36. *Payment.* The budgetary group detail information was formatted into a report and a set of punch cards. The punch cards were sent to the comptroller's office and formed the basis on which individual accounts were debited or credited. The vendor and deposit groups were put in separate reports.

37. *Comptroller's report printing.* The information formatted by the payment step was printed on three-ply paper and distributed to the library administration, the Acquisitions Department, and/or the comptroller.

Statistics

38. *Statistical.* The statistical summary records produced during updating (step 22) were summarized and formatted into a report. This report showed cumulative statistics on such things as books ordered, by course number; volumes received, by form (book, microfiche, etc.), and successful transactions through the system, by type of transaction (order, invoice, etc.) within library.

39. *Statistical record printing.* The statistical records were printed and dis-

tributed to the library administration for use in its annual report and for projective purposes.

40. *Transaction record analysis.* The transaction records file produced in the updating step (22) was analyzed to provide information on the time lag between transaction steps and the number of items waiting to be processed at each step in the Acquisitions Department.

41. *Transactions analysis printing.* Reports derived from the transaction analysis were printed for use by the systems analysts and the library administration.

Housekeeping

42. *Table maintenance.* Established procedures allowed for editing and modification of the important cumulative tables used in the system. The system had the ability to add new accounts, alter the amounts allocated for any account, establish new deposit accounts, and change foreign currency conversion rates.

43. *Backup.* Methods were provided for writing backup copies of the master files, history files, budgetary records, transaction updates, and transaction records. In this process, a printout of all holdings in the backup archive was produced.

44. *Direct editing.* A set of programs for administrative editing of the master files was provided for emergency intervention and patching of data destroyed by system mishap. This set of programs was used only by authorized personnel and was not part of the regular operating system.

In the libraries' preparation of input, the original source document and natural language, not coding forms, were used to maintain a flexible system. The staff did not input or process data that the computer could generate or manipulate itself. A seven-part order form was prepared by the divisional libraries. Parts 1 and 2 were retained by the divisional library (part 1 was placed in the card catalog of that library until the material was received). Parts 3–7 went to the Acquisitions Department for distribution. Parts 3 and 4 went to the vendor (part 3 included shipping instructions; part 4 was to be returned with the material). Part 5 went into the Institute Library Catalog, a union catalog located in the Humanities Library. Part 6 was for the shelflisting. Part 7 was used for the input to the system and then returned to the Technical Services Department until material was received or other action had to be taken. The form had a preprinted six-digit order number with spaces designated for various accounting functions. Obvious abbreviations (in natural language) were used, and computer tags appeared in red on part 7, a manila copy. When the Acquisitions Department received its copies (parts 3–7), is designated the vendor, added special instructions when necessary, and mailed parts 3 and 4. When a sizable number of orders had been completed, the manila copies (part 7) were sent to the input typist who typed the fields shown in red. The results of that typing were a paper tape and a hard copy. When either part of the order or the whole order was received, the manila form (part 7) was marked accordingly by the Technical Services Department clerk and then sent back to the input typist.

When invoices were received, the clerk in Technical Services checked them for order numbers and circled important data in red. These invoices were then sent to the input typist who added appropriate information to the record.

Cataloging was done by the Technical Services Department Cataloging Division staff who, after completing catalog cards, sent the input typist a form that included the order number, the number of volumes, and the call number. Less frequent transactions, such as cancellations, desiderata, deletions, claim reports, etc., were handled in a manner similar to that used for receipts. Corrections and accounting transactions, such as budget allocations, were similar to those for cataloging.

Since the TIP system had been designed to utilize the most economical equipment available at any given time, it was very flexible and used a variety of hardware. With code conversion routines, there was little problem of incompatibility. As input was keypunched, about 125 items per day, on paper tape by a Friden 2303 Flexowriter paper tape machine, the tapes were wound on reels and put into a box to be collected by a courier who took them to the Information Processing Center. A total of 30 tapes per month were sent to IPC for acquisitions runs. Each box was marked "FORD-1," etc., to indicate Friden, order, and the number of the tape, and the date was indicated. The high cost of computer time necessitated this accumulation, and the information was only kept on-line and input during one week of the month—the seven-day period that began the seventeenth of the month. Editing was done during this week of on-line use. Difficult to do on tape, error correction was readily done through any of three IBM 2741 communications terminals. By using a "foreground initiated background" (FIB) procedure, the console operator could indicate the day and time at which a program was to be processed. The operator could select times when the fees for the computer to run the program would be lowest.

Files were arranged by order number in master files until the ordered material was on the shelf, cards were in the catalog, and bills were paid. Records then were moved to a history file. Financial and statistical data were kept in a budget file, arranged by fiscal year. Updating routines, to supply data and information not available on input, included order routines to: (1) create filing keys, (2) determine claim categories, (3) calculate processing target dates, (4) identify number of volumes to be billed and cataloged, and (5) indicate the form of materials. Invoice routines included (1) comparing estimates and actual prices; (2) reporting errors; (3) checking the number billed against the number ordered and received, to charge funds, to maintain accounts, to convert foreign currency; (4) balancing invoices, to establish account categories, and (5) matching vendors. Other routines utilized similar programs and files.

At TIP, input printouts were made by the Friden Flexowriter 2303, the IBM 2741, or the IBM 360. Output reports were produced by the IBM 360. There were six main reports. The acquisition log, arranged by order number, was sent *in toto* to the Technical Services Department. Each library received pertinent sections once a month. Since a complete listing of all file information was too expensive and too complex for full presentation, the log was a selection of the fields that best showed the current status of an order. Order number, main entry, fund, account, type, vendor, price estimation, invoice number, actual price, date ordered, invoice date, report of claim, date received, data cataloged, and RICTW were included. This last heading referred to "receipts, invoices, claims, cataloging, and warnings." Any item in this category with an asterisk appeared on an action list. Originally, 60 days were allowed before claiming, but this period was extended. By providing divisional libraries with essential information, the acquisition logs reduced the number of telephone calls to the Technical Services Department by 75 percent and simplified interlibrary communications.

A reference list, arranged by main entry, was produced by the computer when the acquisition log was compiled. The list contained author, title, call number for cataloged material, and cross-references for volumes received as part of a series. A "new title list" as well as an "action list" were prepared regularly. The action list included overdue items, and functioned as a special errors list, e.g., an actual bill that was 20 percent different from an estimated one was listed on the action list. For payment of bills, a "comptroller's report" was generated. "Budget reports," for each of the account categories, indicated appropriation, committed funds, amount paid, and balances, Individual libraries received an abridged version of the budget report. When a bill was received, the computer added the invoices and subtracted from the estimated column. The balance equaled the credits and allocations minus the commitments and voids. The "monthly deposit fund report" enabled the billing to be distributed among the libraries receiving materials. The system also prepared statistical reports at various intervals. TIP kept the most complete records, since individual libraries and the comptroller only needed to know what funds had been committed and what bills needed to be paid during the fiscal year.

This system made no attempt to do computerized bibliographic searching for the acquisitions operation. The computer's role in this M.I.T. system was, therefore, an administrative and managerial one, beginning after the final book selection was made and the first order form was filled out.[5]

COSTS

Operation

The automated acquisitions system handled about 125 items per day, or about 30,000 titles per year. During the six-month period, July 1–December 31, 1972, the system handled:

12,174	orders
11,308	standard receipts
1,020	monographic series receipts
14,896	invoices
9,711	cataloging
6,060	claims
1,203	cancellations
309	desiderata
3,337	corrections

While 30,000 items were ordered annually, only 12,174, were processed in the last six months of 1972 because two of those six months were during summer recess, which was a slower time for library purchasing.

With input costs of $.078/title, processing costs of $.028, and storage costs of $.02 per outstanding order, the average cost for these operations was $.126 per item. To run the acquisitions program each month took six hours of computer time, for which the libraries were charged $2,400. This figure included all computer-related costs, such as tape conversion, editing, validation, updating, budget, and printing. The annual cost for a total of 72 hours of computer processing was $28,800. There were 13 people (other than the employees of divisional libraries or reading rooms) involved in this operation. Since the system designer was no longer involved in the operation, she was omitted from this appraisal of the system. These 13 people included the head of acquisitions (¼ time), a technical services head (½ time), an invoice clerk (¼ time), eight general clerks (¼ time), and two Flexowriter operators (full time), whose salaries for time devoted to this system totaled about $33,000 annually. It is estimated that the preparation of reports costs about $440 per year.

These expenditures total $66,020, making the unit cost per monograph acquired about $2.20.

Some other costs cannot be well documented, but deserve mention. The system placed a burden on the Acquisitions Department in the form of rerouting order slips, preparation of forms, and especially, checking on validation errors and update rejects. This probably amounted to about one full-time clerical equivalent (about $6,000). A small amount of management time for these functions was also involved. Further, when mishaps occurred, a systems specialist was called in for troubleshooting. This may have amounted to one-quarter of a full-time person (about $5,000).

OBSERVATIONS

M.I.T.'s automated monograph acquisitions system provided service for M.I.T.'s 14 libraries. It processed about 30,000 items per year at a cost of about $2.20 per title. The system was in part a hybrid on-line system, utilizing the CTSS (compatible time-sharing system), in part a batch-processing system, and in part a manual operation. Since the system used routine code conversion programs, it was able to minimize any problems of compatibility.

Because its major goal was to be as economical as possible, the system, which had great flexibility, utilized whatever facilities were available, for the lowest cost.

One positive cost advantage of the computer system was that it enabled the library to conduct a rapid and accurate retrospective search of orders that resulted in the cancelling of 12,000 outstanding orders, thereby freeing a substantial and much needed sum of money. In addition, the computer's reconciliation of manual and machine records enabled the library to remove undetected orders from expensive computer storage.

Another economy achieved by the system was the elimination of a seven-part processing form for temporary shelflists, on-order cards for a union catalog, routing slips, and notices to the *National Union Catalog*. In addition, some manual files were eliminated.

The system had reduced the average time between selection and acquisition of new books It brought simplification and order into both computer and manual operations. The acquisition logs and reference lists replaced some order cards and processing forms. Although not always timely, the reports generated by the system provided all libraries with information on the status of orders, with fiscal summaries, and with statistical tables for management control. There were these notable limitations in the system, however:

1. The system was not well documented, especially with regard to costs.

In addition, although statements of design goals were available, there is no statement of library administrative goals in developing the system.

2. The system did not make a successful transition from the systems development phase to regular operation in the Acquisitions Department. This failure may have been caused by design complexity, by inadequate training in the acquisitions department, by administrative oversight, or by inadequate funding.

3. Although the system was designed to give special listings, such as lists of orders unfilled for over one year, this feature was not exploited. Moreover, some of the regular printouts and listings were not needed or were not consistently used by the acquisitions staff.

4. The character of the system as a passive recorder of events, rather than an active participator, caused considerable clerical effort to be expended within the Acquisitions Department on tasks for which the computerized system could easily have been utilized, given better system design.

5. The once-a-month distribution of information to divisional librarians was not timely enough for their needs.

One of the dominant cost factors inhibiting optimum operation of this computerized system was the expense of on-line storage. Although information was put on disk when first introduced into the system, it was immediately transferred to magnetic tape files. When this information was to be updated, the FIB request (foreground initiated background, used for routine runs without communicating) had the tapes reloaded onto disk. Regularly printed outputs substituted for on-line access, but in order to make this attempt at cost reduction worthwhile, the time between printouts had to be relatively long. With this time delay, the printouts lost the value of currency. It should also be noted that converting magnetic tape to disk for special demands and then back again was expensive and negated some of the saving obtained from magnetic tape storage. At the present time, however, these limitations do not constitute the major problem of the M.I.T. system. Its major problem is that it has no funds with which to operate at all. The funds by which this system had been operating were not part of the libraries' budget, but were carried on the budget of the Computer Center. The funds were cut off in September 1972, and the automated acquisitions system has not been run since then. Acquisitions work is being carried on manually. For a time, all records were sent to the input typist, who created tapes. It was expected that when funds were restored, this information could be transferred to disks and run in order to update and reactivate the computerized system.

A further complication is that the computer used by Project MAC and TIP was recently replaced by a Honeywell 6180 (which uses Honeywell tape drives). This change in hardware would require changes in software. Efforts to make these changes in software have been discontinued. The director of libraries has decided not to make any further efforts to reactivate the computer acquisitions system.

These developments at M.I.T. point up two vital facts of life for librarians.

First, librarians must not allow systems to be dependent on funding that is beyond their management and control. When money for essential links in the flow of library activities can be cut off by external decisions, the library has lost control of its own house. Users of libraries may be disinclined to believe that the library has been victimized. Rather, they will be likely to assume the library is badly managed, even if this is not so.

Second, librarians must not allow their operations to be dependent on equipment that is beyond their control. The frequent changes in computers at M.I.T. and the costly reprogramming these changes have forced on the libraries have delayed the implementation of an economical and efficient acquisitions system. Continuity is paramount in library operations. Librarians are well advised not to become dependent on computer centers that may not only be relatively indifferent to library needs and requirements, but often have goals that require equipment not well suited to handle library requirements. Computers designed for research requirements are often not best suited for library housekeeping chores. Computer centers are happy to have libraries assume the responsibility of underwriting some of their often extravagant costs, but they seldom feel any reciprocal responsibility for seeing that library systems are not subjected to excessive changes. For libraries, having a computerized system for one of its major operations is rather like having a baby. One cannot be a little bit computerized any more than one can be a little bit pregnant.

Libraries are well advised not to be seduced by the glamor of computers until they are sure they have long-term access to the funds to support the costly and demanding little devices.

NOTES

1. M. M. Kessler, "The MIT Technical Information Project," *Physics Today,* 18 (March 1965), 28.
2. P. A. Crisman, ed., *The Compatible Time Sharing System, A Programmer's Guide* (2nd ed.; Cambridge: M.I.T. Press, 1965).
3. W. D. Mathews, "Some Facts about the Acquisitions System" (10-page memo regarding implementation of the library acquisitions system on the 370/165).
4. Much of the information contained in this case study was obtained from Patricia M. Sheehan,

"A Cost-Responsive Acquisitions System," American Society for Information Sciences *Proceedings*, 8 (1971), 311–319.

ACKNOWLEDGMENTS

The assistance of Susan D. Jacobson, Sandy Lane, and Leona Mathews in the preparation of this case study is acknowledged with appreciation. Information for this study came from interviews at M.I.T. with Leo Ryan, operations manager, and Mr. Corcoran, computer operator at the Information Processing Center; Robert Hadlock, head of the Technical Services Department, and Patricia Sheehan and William D. Mathews, of the Technical Information Program, and thanks are also extended to them for their helpful cooperation.

19.
Cleveland Public Library
Automated Acquisition System

• •

ENVIRONMENT

Cleveland Public Library has holdings of about 3,750,000 volumes and an annual budget of over $8,000,000, and it circulates over 4 million items per year. It disburses annually almost $600,000 for books, $114,000 for periodicals, $55,300 for audiovisual materials, and $44,400 for bound periodicals. The library has 14 subject departments, 36 branches, and two bookmobiles, and it services 28 hospital libraries, ten institutional libraries, 20 fire stations, and two general stations, or a total of more than 112 library agencies.

In the early 1960s, the library installed an IBM batch-processing acquisitions system to assist in the handling of a very large volume of book ordering activity.

OBJECTIVES

In 1969, after about five years of experience with the batch-processing system, the library staff decided to reevaluate its decision to utilize a batch-processing procedure for the library's acquisitions operation. The staff members considered further demands that they might need to place on their computer system. They then compared the ability of their existing computer system with the ability of a proposed on-line minicomputer system to meet these demands. Among the demands considered were:

1. Many of the major processes within the library, such as book ordering, book processing, cataloging, and fiscal control, are continuous

in nature. Therefore, the system should be capable of servicing these functions on a continuous basis, rather than on a once-a-week or once-a-day basis, as was the case with the batch-processing computer system.

2. The various processing functions are physically distributed within the library complex. The computer system should reflect this distribution and not force a concentration of data processing at a single physical location, as was the case with the batch-processing computer system.

3. The use of a computer system within the library should not require a costly data processing department, with analysts, programmers, machine operators, etc., as was the case with the batch-processing computer system. The library was having difficulty in obtaining and keeping the data processing talent that was necessary to solve its routine, but complex information problems. The library administration found that talented data processing personnel are expensive, and that these people prefer to work in challenging environments where there are a large array of new and intriguing problems. The library's need was for a reliable, workhorse system that would deal with repetitive housekeeping chores.

5. Since the library was operating under a limited budget, the administration and staff felt that the allocation of funds within the budget should be focused on maximum service to the user community. Therefore, any computer system should offer tangible benefits, both by direct cost savings and by contributing to better quality service offered by the library. The system should reduce data processing costs, both machine and personnel, produce better management tools, and provide greater flexibility in library operations. These objectives were not being achieved with the batch-processing system.

6. The library needed a computer system that was modular and would allow the staff to implement individual systems, as needed, in a planned, step-by-step fashion. The staff did not want to be trapped by the myth that it should buy a larger computer than it now needed to avoid the alleged costly conversion to larger equipment in the near future. The staff also felt that the alleged upward compatibility of some computer systems might be a myth, as some libraries had discovered when they moved from one generation of IBM equipment to another and were forced to emulate or reprogram in order to use the larger models.

Following a cost comparison of several large computer systems and a proposed minicomputer system, the staff concluded that the proposed minicomputer system offered a better system at a lower cost than any large computer system. The lower hardware cost allowed a change in emphasis in system design. Instead of one large system, individual systems could be made available to carry out particular tasks or groups of tasks on a dedicated on-line basis. Data entries or requests for information could be serviced by the dedicated systems immediately. No waiting for batch-processing times, in order to make use of the computer facility, would be required.

The small size of a minicomputer system, coupled with its freedom from environmental constraints, such as air-conditioning or extra power, would allow complete data processing units, each roughly the size of an office desk, to be placed in the operating departments rather than in a separate computer center. These small units, complete with direct-access storage, would form an expandable data processing system. Communication with the system in a user-oriented, conversational mode would allow it to be used by library personnel without formal computer training.

With reference to the staffing of a new computer system, the staff concluded that it should concentrate on the overall planning of its information needs, and contract out for the design, programming, and installation of any computer system. Preferably, each system would be acquired as a total package, including the equipment and the programming. The staff's acceptance would be based on the ability of the system supplied to carry out the defined tasks. In this way, the staff would be able to enjoy the benefits of modern data processing equipment and techniques without the burden of staffing and maintaining an expensive in-house data processing department or of exhorbitant development costs.

The staff selected as its first objective the conversion from its IBM batch-processing system to a minicomputer system of its book acquisitions, payroll, and service to the Braille and Talking Book Department processes. The staff felt that this approach would bring immediate cost benefits, build an acquisitions file as a byproduct, and supply a major component of the input required for an accounting system. If, later, an accounts payable for nonbook materials system were added, the staff would be able to implement a complete accounting and budgeting system. Also, as the acquisitions file grew, it could be used as the starting point for a circulation control system. On the basis of all these considerations, the library staff decided to move forward to its first objective, the conversion to a minicomputer system of its payroll, book acquisitions and processing, and service to the Braille and Talking Book Department.

THE COMPUTER

On May 22, 1971, the Cleveland Public Library secured authorization from the Board of Trustees for the purchase of two LIBS Model 100 computer systems with a LIBS 103 fast printer attached, preprogrammed and ready to run, to be delivered as operational units to the library by Computer Library Services, Inc., (CLSI) of Wellesley, Massachusetts. One LIBS 100 system was installed in the Order Department in February 1972, and one was installed in the Accounting Department on March 17, 1972. At the time of delivery, the implemented applications included a book-ordering and accounts-payable system, a payroll system, and a system to serve the Braille and Talking Book Department.

The library had been using an IBM 360/20 computer and peripheral equipment. This IBM system was phased out, in August 1972, after parallel runs on the CLSI LIBS 100 systems.

The LIBS 100 basic configuration consists of a central processor, with a 16,192-character memory, and a direct memory access channel of 1 million characters per second; two moving-head, removable-cartridge disk drives, with a capacity of 4 million characters per cartridge and an average access time of 70 milliseconds; a split-platen printer; a keyboard including a full alpha-numeric set in typewriter configuration, a numeric set in adding-machine configuration, and a set of special function keys; and an operator "instruction panel" with lights under program control and a 9 by 4 matrix of messages for the operator. In addition, as noted above, the installation at Cleveland Public Library has an LIBS 103 fast printer.

The support software consists of a disk operating system (DOS) and an interpreter. The DOS uses variable-length, indexed-sequential files and maintains an inventory of available file space. It creates a virtual memory (disk storage is treated as an extension of core memory) of up to 128,000 characters environment for FLIRT (file language in real time) programs, which are executed interpretively.

The LIBS 100 is designed for direct input of new data and the updating of data, and it is conversational, allowing the user immediate access to information stored in the system. All data files are maintained continuously as new data are entered. Because all data are entered directly, the operations normally associated with other data processing systems, such as keypunching and verifying, are eliminated.

THE SYSTEM

The Cleveland Public Library book acquisition system consists of four major, interrelated subsystems as follows.

Order. This subsystem accepts order requests, captures agency fund information for book distribution and management control, automatically creates and maintains purchase orders, prints orders, computes and prints pay-in-advance checks, and compiles order summaries.

Receipt. This subsystem receives, processes, and distributes books. It deals with the accumulated requests for a title on a particular order, collects financial information for the "financial management" subsystem on all books being kept by the library, processes any books to be returned, requests and accepts call number information, charges agencies for books being kept, prints book labels, proves invoices, and generates an accounts-payable record. It also reports the shipment of books to the various agencies.

Financial Management. This subsystem processes transactions created by the "order" and "receipt" subsystems and accepts adjustments to vendor accounts. The transactions generated by the order and receipt subsystems are pay-in-advance checks, regular checks to pay invoices, agency financial data, and credit/debit memorandums for adjustment of invoice amounts or return-of-materials notices. To assure the accounting integrity of the data, all charges to vendor accounts are made by creating a separate transaction, rather than by modifying an existing transaction.

Claim. This subsystem monitors overdue orders, generates vendor claim and/or cancel notices, allows extension or cancellation of individual items, and generates agency cancellation reports.

The information in the book acquisition system is organized into the following set of files:

Book Information File. Contains such information as title, author, list price, and classification; it also indicates whether or not a book is on order.

Order Information File. Contains detailed status information about the books on order and in processing, as well as the agencies expecting copies, etc.

Vendor Account File. Contains financial information relating to vendor accounts.

Publisher File. Contains information about publishers and the assignment of publishers to vendors.

Agency File. Contains agency-fund statistics and budget information.

In addition, the system contains special purpose support files. In general, the system's support programs for file maintenance may be used to add, delete, change, rename, or list information stored by the system. As a safeguard, the system will not permit the operator to change or delete data needed for system integrity. For example, a vendor may not be deleted if there are any outstanding financial transactions for it.

Because certain elements of book information are not frequently referred to after the book has been processed, this information is periodically placed on historic file, from which it may be recalled when needed. In addition, some titles are simply deleted from the files. These may include out-of-print books, books rejected in book selection after one year, and books weeded from the collection. A list of deleted titles is printed as they are removed.

In addition to the listing capabilities provided by the file maintenance support programs and the reporting capabilities provided by the report programs, this system has a powerful facility for producing abbreviated reports. These short reports include book order status, vendor financial status, vendor order status, and vendor's publishers.

When a book is entered into the library's automated acquisitions system, an author/title book key is created. A normal nine-character book key consists of the first three letters of the author's surname and the first letters of the first four words of the title, and two uniqueness digits that are system-generated. Standard adaptations are made if the title has fewer than four words or if the work is entered under title. If the book has been ordered before, the author and title on file are printed so the operator can check whether there is an exact match. The operator enters the number of copies required, the agency ordering the book, the fund to be charged, and whether the work is for reference or circulation, and whether it is adult or juvenile.

If the book is not on file, the system asks the operator for new title information. This includes author(s), full title, publisher code number, year of publication, edition, Library of Congress card number (if available), call number (if available), and estimated list price, size, language, volume, etc. The operator may also indicate whether payment is to be made in advance and whether the order is rush.

Works from various publishers are normally obtained from preselected jobbers or vendors. The vendor may, of course, also be the publisher. If desired, the operator may select an alternate vendor when a title is ordered.

For each new title, a form is produced containing all information entered about the book. This allows cataloging or bibliographic work to be done before the book is received.

Orders to vendors are produced when and as required. The order print routine allows the operator to print either all accumulated orders or rush orders, or to select only orders that contain more than a certain number of items. The number is selected by the operator. This feature allows large orders to be dispatched, for example, once per day, and orders to vendors with only a few items, once per week. When orders are produced, a summary is also printed for management information.

Books received from vendors are checked against the vendor's invoice, and any shortages or damaged volumes are noted on the invoice. The operator then enters the order number and may either proceed through the invoice sequentially or call individual titles by means of the book key. The system then prints the author and title and quantity ordered on the printer. For each item, the operator enters the number of volumes received, the number damaged and category of damage, if necessary, and the list price, discount, net price, or end-of-line amount, as required. This procedure permits flexibility in dealing with a variety of vendor invoicing procedures.

If the call number exists in the file at the time of receipt, labels are printed immediately for the spine, pocket, and book card. These are placed in the books, which then go to final physical processing.

If a call number is not recorded in the file, a form is produced showing all available information about the book. This form is sent, with the book, to the Cataloging Department. When this form is returned with the call number, the operator enters the number, and the book labels are printed.

If a shipment contains fewer copies of a particular item than were ordered, the system will allocate the copies in accordance with library policy.

At the conclusion of processing each invoice, the system checks the invoice total. The system also has an end-of-invoicing routine to deal with postage, shipping charges, and sales tax. Any changes in the invoice caused by the receipt of damaged books, shortages, incorrect extensions, inclusion of sales tax, etc., will result in a credit memo. A copy of this memo may be sent, together with damaged books if any, to the vendor. A second copy may be sent together with the payment check.

Payments can be made as and when required. For any orders requiring payment in advance, checks are printed to accompany orders. Checks are also printed by the system to pay invoices from each vendor, less any credit, as detailed on the credit memos.

If books are not received from the vendor after a specified time period from the order date (normally 90 days), notification is sent to the vendor, requesting delivery of the books or a cause-of-delay memo. If no response is received during the claim period (normally 60 days), the item is automatically cancelled and the vendor is so notified. A list of these cancelled items is produced and sent to each library agency, to allow reordering if desired.

The time period for sending notification can be set for the system and changed as required. The system time period is overridden by an entry in the vendor record showing that a different time, usually longer, should be allowed for this vendor. This is particularly useful for foreign vendors.

Shipping notices, produced weekly for each agency, list all books for which book labels have been printed.

A variety of reports is produced by the system, including:

Shipping Report (items to agencies)—weekly.

Agency Financial Summary Report (expenditure of allocated funds)—monthly.

Agency Cancellation Report (items cancelled)—monthly.

Vendor-Publisher List (list of all publishers, about 4,000, with 5-digit publisher code)—about monthly.

Vendor Statistics Report (vendor performance report)—annually.

Received-But-Not-Cataloged Report (in cataloging more than n-days)—on demand.

In Binding-More-Than-n-Days Report—on demand.

Direct inquiry in a conversational mode will answer such questions as: Is a title currently on order? With which vendor is the order placed? Which agency ordered the title? When was it ordered? Which departments or branches have this title for circulation or reference? What is the LC card number for this title? What is the call number?

This system, which has been operational at Cleveland Public Library since June 1972, processes an average of 10,000 items per month, or about 120,000 items per year, including books, films, records, filmstrips, some continuations, and microforms, but no periodicals. The system does, however, handle fund accounting of periodicals for agencies by putting in negative appropriations. The order system is currently operating for 65 hours per week, or one and one-half shifts, with three operators, two of whom were drawn from existing Acquisitions Department personnel.

COSTS

In October 1972 the library prepared a comparison of costs of the former IBM installation and the CLSI minicomputer system for payroll, order and book processing, and the services to the Braille and Talking Book Department. For this comparison, 1972 figures were used for salary, rental, service, and all other costs. No attempt was made to estimate any increases that may occur during the next several years, since it was considered likely that changes in the economy would be reflected about equally in either system.

Table 1
ANNUAL COSTS—IBM

Equipment rental, including service	$52,980	
Data Processing Dept. salaries (10 staff members)	63,405	
Fringe benefits @ 11%	6,975	
Total	$123,360	
5-year projection		$616,800

To arrive at a cost comparison, each installation's costs were projected for a five-year period. The resulting cost for the IBM system is $616,800. The comparative cost for the CLSI system included the initial system cost, $112,560, as well as a five-year projection of continuing annual costs, $32,412, for a total of $274,620.

The differential in costs over a five-year period was projected as $342,180 in favor of the CLSI system.

Costs for the CLSI order system have also been calculated (see Table 3).

Table 2
CLSI COSTS

Initial costs		
Purchase of 2 computers with application pkg.	$108,560	
Library for the Blind program	4,000	
Total		$112,560

Annual costs		
Service contract	$ 4,680	
Data Processing Dept. salaries (2 staff members)	20,623	
Fringe benefits @ 11%	2,269	
Order & Accounting Dept salaries (with upgrading 5 clerks)	4,360	
Fringe benefits @ 11%	480	
Total	$32,412	
5-year projection of annual costs		$162,060
TOTAL initial costs plus 5-year projection		$274,620

Table 3
ANNUAL COSTS—CLSI ORDER SYSTEM

3 operators @ $5,400	$16,200	
Data processing ($^1/_2$ of Data Processing Dept. time)	10,311	
Order Dept., asst. head ($^1/_2$ of time)	4,500	
Supervisor ($^1/_4$ of time)	5,000	
Fringe benefits (11% of above)	3,961	
Total staff costs		$39,972
Supplies		2,500
Maintenance contract on LIBS 100		2,340
LIBS 100 ($^1/_5$ of purchase price)		10,856
Total annual order system costs		$55,668

Since the system processes 120,000 items per year, the unit cost is about $.46 for ordering, receiving, paying, labeling, agency accounting, and providing management information. The former IBM system cost over $.50 per item and wrote no checks, printed no labels, and provided no management information.

OBSERVATIONS

Before converting to the minicomputer system, the Cleveland Public Library had had experience with some early tabulating equipment, with an IBM 1401 (1965–68) and with an IBM 360/20 (1968–72). The staff's interest was not therefore, in whether or not to automate some of its operations, but rather which system would provide the best services at the least cost to the library. The primary objective of the staff in 1971 was to escape from a batch-processing system, with a separate data processing department and a separate order department, and the many problems that had sprung from split responsibilities. It wanted to establish an on-line, in-house, individual-department system that was responsive to the library's real needs. The staff wanted to get away from the massive generation of reports and listings that were of little value for management purposes, and to gain instead truly useful management information, such as answers to control questions: What items are delayed? Where are items located? What funds are encumbered? What funds are expended? etc. The present minicomputer system is enabling the staff to keep track of the flow of materials and dollars at a reasonable price.

The conversion of the system was not without problems and some adverse publicity. With hindsight, it is easy to recognize that the old IBM system should have overlapped the new system until all orders on the old system had been cleared. The decision to reenter all outstanding orders in the new LIBS 100 system almost submerged it before it was fully operational. A six months' overlap would have been adequate to avoid system tieups and would have cost about $62,000. This expenditure might have been difficult to justify, but would have preserved better relations with staff, public, and trustees during the conversion period.

The staff chose to buy rather than lease its new computer equipment because this option is likely to prove more economical in the long run. While some businesses may lease computer equipment for tax advantages, such tax considerations were not involved in the staff's decision.

The new system has reduced the time between a book purchase request and receipt of the item from 22 to 16 weeks. The system was still slightly behind from the problems of the conversion from the IBM system in the spring of 1973, but it was catching up and expected to have the delivery time down to 11 weeks in the summer of 1973. Further reductions in time will require some modification in the selection process. The rush-order capabilities of the LIBS 100 system are such that orders can be in the mail in 15 minutes or less.

The new system has had less than 5 percent downtime, has required very little on-site maintenance, and has been very quickly repaired. Since the library has purchased two LIBS 100s, it has its own backup equipment for its systems. One machine is in the Order Department and one is in the Accounting Department, both of which are on the same floor. The LIBS 100s may be used interchangeably. Both machines have never been down at the same time. This minicomputer system enables the library staff to provide continuous service for its book ordering and processing operations. The system maintains continuous fiscal control. It provides management control information on demand. Separate LIBS 100s are available in the Order Department and in the Accounting Department, where they are conveniently accessible. The staff has been relieved of the problems and expense of running a separate data processing department. A reduction in unit processing costs has demonstrated the economy of the minicomputer system. At the same time, the system has provided better management information and greater flexibility in library operations. The system should be adequate for the library's projected needs for the next five years. The system has been made successfully operational with minimal training and orientation of library personnel. The library staff is moving easily to a complete accounting and budgeting system.

Computer systems such as the Cleveland Public Library's offer any library with an annual budget in excess of $500,000 an opportunity to achieve total control over its own responsibilities, operations, and expenditures. It may be leased for an annual amount approximately equivalent to the salaries of two clerks. It offers such a library a viable and low-cost escape from subservience to central computer centers that may have policies or procedures inimical to the library's needs or best interests. The on-line, in-house computer, fully programmed and ready to operate with the turn of a key, is worthy of active consideration by a number of libraries that have been beset by computerization problems in the past decade.

ACKNOWLEDGMENTS

Thanks are extended to James M. O'Brien, director of technical services, Cleveland Public Library, and to Dennis Beaumont, Béla Hatvany, and Mimi Cummings of Computer Library Services, Inc., for providing information and assistance in the preparation of this case study.

20.
Dartmouth College
Automated Acquisition System
• •

ENVIRONMENT

Dartmouth College, a private, nonsectarian liberal arts college, was chartered in 1769 by King George III. It enrolled only men for over 200 years, becoming a coeducational college in the fall of 1972. It now has almost 4,000 students, a very small percentage of whom are women. It recently adopted the Dartmouth Plan of year-round on-and-off-campus study. The institution is in the process of becoming a small university, with a number of strong graduate programs. It has a 10-1 student-faculty ratio.

The Dartmouth College library operates on a budget of close to $2 million. Annual expenditures for library materials are over $500,000 and comprise about 28 percent of the budget. The library now holds approximately 1,100,000 volumes. The millionth book was cataloged in 1970, and the collection is growing at a rate of more than 30,000 volumes per year.

The units of the Dartmouth College library include Baker Library (the main library) and seven branch libraries. All orders (regular orders, new standing orders, blanket orders, items from approval plans) and gifts are handled by the acquisitions department of Baker Library.

OBJECTIVES

Since the cost of input/output equipment was not a concern in the design of an automated acquisitions system, because a variety of input/output components was available, the question of economic feasibility was not paramount in the system design. The objectives of the computer-based operation were mainly (1) to alleviate the problem of ever-growing manual files; (2) to eliminate, as much as possible, clerical tasks of a repetitive nature; (3) to provide the staff, as well as the user, with immediate answers to various inquiries about the status of books on order or in process; (4) to improve the processing of books by reducing delays in cataloging, and (5) to permit a better fiscal control by accurate and current adjustment of fund accounting.[1]

The system was designed so that it could be easily integrated into a total system of library operations. Within this total-system concept, the automation of some aspects of the Serials Department operations has already taken place.

THE COMPUTER

Dartmouth College enjoys a privileged situation in computational facilities due to the presence on campus of the Dartmouth Time Sharing System initially developed by Professors John G. Kemeny (now president of the college) and Thomas G. Kurtz of the Department of Mathematics. The Kiewit Computational Center at the college houses a complex of interconnected electronic digital computing equipment manufactured by the General Electric Company:

1. The components include:
   (a) Two central processors (Honeywell GE-635).
   (b) Core storage units with a memory capacity of 160,000 words.
   (c) Mass storage units including a magnetic drum storage unit of 768,000 words and 16 disk storage units of 4.6 million words each.
2. Each device can transmit 60,000 words/second.
3. The input-output devices include six magnetic tape drives with a speed of 10,000 words/second, and:
   (a) one line printer (1,200 lines/minute);
   (b) one card reader (1,000 cards/minute);
   (c) one card punch (100 cards/minute);
   (d) one console typewriter (15 characters/second).
4. The telecommunication equipment includes two Datanet-30s, which can handle more than 165 terminals of all kinds (e.g., medium-speed printers, cathode-ray-tube, teletypewriter, punched tape).[2]
5. The hardware of the library's acquisitions and cataloging sections includes:
   (a) two cathode-ray-tube terminals;
   (b) two model 33 teletypewriters;
   (c) one medium-speed printer.

The above elements all operate via voice-grade telephone lines connected to the Kiewit Computational Center.

The programming language is BASIC (beginner's all-purpose symbolic instruction code), which was originally developed at Dartmouth. All automated records of the Acquisitions Department are stored on magnetic tapes for permanent retention as a backup in case of a major loss of storage files at Kiewit.

THE SYSTEM

In the early 1970s the administration of the Dartmouth College library began the study of an automation program for various library departments.[3] By December, 1971, the automation of the acquisitions and processing departments was ready for test operation. After a four-month run in parallel with the former manual system, the automated on-line, real-time system became fully operation in April 1972, when manual operations were discontinued.

All systems design, development, and implementation was accomplished by Donald L. Saporito, chief of automation services. He was assisted by two part-time student programmers. The design takes full advantage of the particular conditions offered by the Kiewit Computational Center at Dartmouth College. Its most striking feature is perhaps the ease of operation of the overall system, which was conceived to enable an employee with little or no training in computer data processing to interact with the system. Enough flexibility is built in to permit modifications of system characteristics as needs arise.

The system operates basically on two major sets of files: the "in-process files" and the "vendor files," both of which are divided into random-access string character and random-access numeric files. The in-process and vendor files both have on-line access and can be updated through various subprograms.

A diagram representative of the structure of the files is set forth in Figure 1.

The main operations of the Orders Processing Department can be broken down as follows: (1) selection; (2) new orders, searching; (3) ordering; (4) updating (including any modification of the status of an order, such as claiming, cancelling, etc.); (5) receiving and processing; (6) funds accounting; (7) cataloging.

Selection

To insure continuity in the character and quality of the collection of the Dartmouth College library, selection is carried out by several selection officers, specialists in their respective fields of selection and by branch librarians. No provision has been made for use of the MARC records as a selection tool, although one could envision this possibility. New orders must be approved by

Figure 1
ON-LINE REAL-TIME ACQUISITIONS PROCESSING [4]

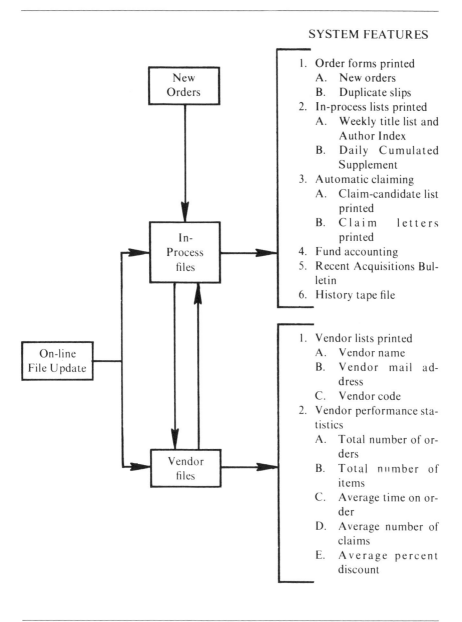

SYSTEM FEATURES

1. Order forms printed
   A. New orders
   B. Duplicate slips
2. In-process lists printed
   A. Weekly title list and Author Index
   B. Daily Cumulated Supplement
3. Automatic claiming
   A. Claim-candidate list printed
   B. Claim letters printed
4. Fund accounting
5. Recent Acquisitions Bulletin
6. History tape file

1. Vendor lists printed
   A. Vendor name
   B. Vendor mail address
   C. Vendor code
2. Vendor performance statistics
   A. Total number of orders
   B. Total number of items
   C. Average time on order
   D. Average number of claims
   E. Average percent discount

the respective selection officers, who provide all of the bibliographic information they have available.

New Orders, Searching

The requisition forms to input regular orders, new standing orders, and new serial subscriptions have been designed to minimize errors at the input stage. These forms include variable and fixed fields for entering data. Each data field must be prefixed with an identifying tag at the input stage. The tags are mnemonic in nature and have been printed in place on the requisition forms. String character fields may vary in length from zero to a preset maximum. Tags, field names and lengths are listed in Table 1.

Table 1 — LISTING OF DATA FIELDS

Tag	Field	Max. No. Characters in Field	Comments
OR	Order No	8	
DO	Date Ord	8	Unique for each order, program assigned.
DX	Date Exp	8	
DD	Date To Del	8	
NO	No. Copies	2	
VC	Vendor Code	4	
FU	Fund	4	
LP	List Price	7	
NP	Net Pr	7	
AU	Author		Author-Title-Edition have been assigned a
TI	Title		maximum combined length of 175 characters.
ED	Edition		
PL	Place		Place-Publisher-Pub Date have been assigned
PU	Publisher		a maximum combined length of 46 characters.
PD	Pub Date		
SE	Series	100	
VN	Vend Name	20	Supplied from vendor files when VC is entered.
VO	Vols	3	
MO	Mon. Code	2	
PP	Prepaid	1	
IS	ISBN	13	
LC	LC Card No	12	
AP	Appr. By	4	
BI	Bibl. Source	50	
CH	Charge	15	
CO	Comments	100	

Table 1 (cont.)

Tag	Field	Characters	Comments
CA	Cat For	15	
DU	Dup For	15	
SC	Serial Code	1	
RE	Requested By	10	
HF	Hold For	15	
RU	Rush	1	
CN	Call No	30	
SR	Searcher	4	
	Trans. Hist.	800	Accessed by command "HIST."
Vendor Tags			
VC	Vendor Code	4	Staff-assigned four-letter mnemonic code.
CL	Claim Int.(Number)		Set automatically to 90; may be reset at will.
#O	# Orders (Tot)		
#I	# Items (tot)		
#C	# Claims (tot)		
#D	#Days/Ord (Av)		
%D	%Disc. (Av)		
VN	Vend Name	20	
CU	Cust Acc. No.	18	
MA	Mail Addr.	250	5 lines max., each with 50 characters, max.

Searching procedures are not intended to provide bibliographic information beyond reasonable identification of the request and avoidance of duplication. For this purpose the main catalog (an author-title alphabetic catalog) and the in-process list (see below) are scanned. A vendor is assigned to the order. All order forms are then sent to the automation department.

Ordering

New orders are input daily through a program called LINPUT. Field tags are typed as they appear on the order form along with the data they represent. Numbers for new orders are generated automatically by the system. They include two digits for the year and five more digits in a chronological sequence. Though the whole system operates basically on two files, a third file, the "new order file," is used as a separate temporary file to input new orders. All data concerning new orders are stored in this file until the program has scanned them for errors. An edit sheet with flagged errors is generated as new orders are merged with the in-process file. Errors detected subsequently are corrected on-line through use of a program called UPDATE. By means of a series of subprograms the vendor code input with new orders is checked against the vendor code in the vendor files, the orders are sorted by vendor, and a teletype-format file is generated that contains all orders and vendors with their mailing addresses. The file is then used to print the orders with the vendors' addresses on specially formatted slips. Order forms are printed in the library facilities on a 240-line-per-minute line printer. The orders are mailed without proofreading, and all parts of the form are sent to the vendor. No manual file of order slips is maintained in the library; the vendor is requested to return two parts of the order form for the library's use in processing and invoicing.

Updating

The system has been designed as a synoptic data bank, so that all data stored on-line can be accessed and displayed to present a fully updated history on any transaction. Various subprograms enable the operators to update any transaction, and, at the same time, allow other inquirers to call for the display of data without danger of alteration of the files.

When the program UPDATE is called, several data fields are displayed. These include the order number, the order date or the date of receipt, the status of the order, the vendor code and name, the number of copies, the approval and the charge. Twenty-five other data fields can be displayed by special commands. To input any new data or to alter previous data, the operator simply types in the two-letter tag followed by the correct data. The corrected order is then formatted on the face of the screen. All the fields, covering the complete history of the transaction, can be displayed.

Reports from vendors are also entered through the UPDATE program. Special commands can generate specific actions, such as deletion and cancellation, with immediate or delayed effects.

A similar program to UPDATE is VUPDATE, which operates on the vendor files. This program allows full display of the information stored for any vendor, gives access to various fields for change of data and allows insertion of new vendors into the files.

The program BOOK allows staff to inquire about the status of any book listed in the in-process list. It gives a full history of the current status of the transaction and is used for display only.

Inquiries can also be answered by scanning the in-process list, which is produced weekly. Each entry on the list consists of title, author, publisher, place and date of publication, the order number, the date of the current status and the status of the order (e.g., on-order, pending, in-process), catalog number (if already processed), cancelled, or other. The list is sorted by title, and an author index is provided. A cumulative supplement is printed daily. Any book cataloged is deleted from the in-process list four weeks after it has reached the shelves. After one year of operation, the in-process list currently includes slightly over 13,000 items.

The system has been designed to generate automatic claiming for every item not received or not reported within the "claim interval." The claim interval is unique for each vendor in the vendor files and has been assigned on the basis of such factors as the vendor's past performance and geographical location. A second claiming procedure is initiated after a calculated period of time. Should it be deemed necessary to postpone the claim, a subprogram called CLAIMSUP can be called, and the claiming date changed by typing the order number of the item in question. This subprogram operates on a list of candidates for claiming that is generated weekly.

Receiving and Processing

As books arrive they are checked to ascertain that the vendor has returned the order control slips. Any missing slips can be generated as duplicate slips by use of the program for printing order slips.

Titles of books received are searched on the OCLC system. If a record is found, the call number is entered on the order control slip; cataloging cards are ordered through the OCLC system with any modification required by the Dartmouth College library (e.g., code for branch libraries); and the book is sent for processing. Books with LC numbers are set apart to be searched for LC cataloging. Books for which original cataloging is required are kept together. Any original cataloging record is later entered into the OCLC system.

The programs INVOICE and CALLNUMBER are then called in order to enter check-in information. The date received is automatically generated by the system when the order number of an item is called through INVOICE or CALLNUMBER. Other information, such as the fund charge and the net price, are entered. If an item is to be sent to the bindery, that information is entered here. The data input through these programs are merged with the in-process files at the end of the day.

Receipt of standing orders is not controlled by the system. Any item received on a standing order or blanket order is entered into the system at receipt by calling for a new order number through the program LINPUT. The same procedures for error scanning is followed and slips are produced. After all new data have been properly entered into the system, the book is cataloged by the usual procedure.

Funds Accounting

Funds are debited at the receipt of an item and are monitored by the system. A weekly report is generated showing the amount spent and the current balance in each fund. Provision has been made in the program UPDATE to enter any amount to be prepaid. Should an error have been made on the charge distribution, the subprograms FUNDEBIT and FUNDCRED allow modification of the state of any fund. A third program, FUNDLOOK, allows on-line display only of various data concerning budgets of each selection officer. The current debit and credit, with the dates of the last credit and debit entries, can be displayed.

Cataloging

The Dartmouth College Library has participated in the on-line OCLC cataloging system since 1971. This operation has considerably decreased the amount of time required to catalog a book. The scanning of MARC records is carried out as a book is received. Of the 37,962 volumes added to the collection for the year 1971–72, over half, or 20,255 new titles were cataloged by means of Library of Congress cataloging data.

At the present time, approximately two-thirds of the books received are being cataloged and shelved within six months of receipt, one-third of the latter within three months. For comparison, only one-third of the books received had been shelved within six months of the date of receipt with use of previous cataloging procedures.

Background Programs

As mentioned earlier, new data are merged daily with the in-process files. This step is carried out by a background program. Various other tasks are also performed: ORSCAN and STSCAN printouts for the scanning of errors in the input of orders; claim and cancellation letters requested by operators through the program UPDATE, and the daily SUPPLEMENT of the in-process list.

The weekly background program performs the same tasks as the daily one. It produces, in addition, a weekly in-process list (printed at the Kiewit Computation Center), as well as a claim list, which is a compilation of all candidates for claim letters of the previous week. Four weeks after cataloging has been recorded, the program removes through INGARB all orders processed or cancelled and writes them onto a history tape. It produces a weekly list of items cataloged during the week. This weekly list is used as a checklist for receipt and control of OCLC cards.

FUNDPRINT, which is run monthly, is a full report on the current status of all funds and of the budgets of the selection officers.

A third background program is run at the discretion of the acquisitions staff, usually at quarterly intervals. This program performs the following operations: (1) through VENDGARB is removes all deleted vendors from the vendor files; (2) through VENLIST it produces a full vendor list arranged by vendor code; (3) through VENMAIL it produces a full vendor list arranged by vendor name and also produces lists of vendors (abbreviated), one arranged by vendor code and another by vendor name.[5]

COSTS

A perusal of the literature concerning cost analysis of library services uncovered the opinion that it is very difficult to arrive at any definite conclusion regarding the various costs of library operation. This judgment applies equally to the particular case treated here of the cost of processing books. William J. Baumol stated, in "On the Economics of Library Operation, a Mathematica Report," that he "attempted no breakdown of costs on the basis of library function.... Obviously [these data have not been provided] in part because the figures are simply not available; ... the data are unlikely to become available even if substantial effort is devoted to their acquisition."[6] Furthermore, the statement appears in *Annual Review of Information Science and Technology* that "data presented must be interpreted, clarified, adapted by whoever wants to use them, but no manager can expect to find a cost system that he can apply 'as is' to his own operation."[7]

In view of the preceding remark, the present study can in no way pretend to have arrived at an absolute cost figure. Rather, the attempt has been made to present as accurately as possible the parameters considered and to give in each case the source of information. Several assumptions had to be made. In each case they have been made as precise as possible.

Unless one is directly concerned with the management of an operation, it is difficult to be aware of all the economic factors involved. Because certain shortcomings of cost studies are unavoidable, the words of caution quoted above must be kept in mind.

The guidelines followed are those indicated in Hayes and Becker.[8] An analysis has been made of development, installation, and operational costs. The operational costs have been broken down into the following cost categories: (a) equipment, (b) salaries, (c) computer.

Allowances have also been made for administrative expenses and overhead costs. These were calculated on the basis of data appearing in the *Dartmouth College Library Statistical Report 1971–1972.*[9] Administrative expenses (exclusive of salaries) represent roughly 12.5 percent of total salaries for the library as a whole and overhead (building) costs represent about 25 percent of total salaries. In computing the total overhead charge for departmental costs an additional 10 percent of salaries of departmental personnel has been added as an appropriate charge for the salaries of the library administration (five persons), who are assigned to no operational department.

Development Costs

An initial period of six months is assumed for system design and development work. During this period the staff consisted of one professional librarian and two student programmers. The salaries for this staff are based on those indicated for 1969 in *Library Statistics of Colleges and Universities*.[10] Fifteen percent has been added to the salaries in this source to allow for the effects of inflation since 1969. Costs of computer time for the development period were calculated on the assumption that monthly operational costs were 80 percent of present monthly costs.

Installation Costs

No cost allowance has been included for training of personnel, which in fact required many hours of meetings and discussions. However, a normal work load was carried by the personnel during the training period, so that training costs can be considered negligible.

Neither has any allowance been made for specific installation costs. Required labor and material are assumed to be covered by overhead costs.

It should be mentioned that, as is actually the case in the situation studied, considerable space can be saved through automation merely by the elimination of manual files and the reduction of the number of people involved in the operations.

The costs of the parallel operation of automatic and manual systems of four months' duration have been calculated on the basis of monthly operational costs. As in the case of the development costs, the charges to installations were amortized on a five-year basis. There has been no conversion of existing manual files to automated files.

Operational Costs

Equipment. Most equipment is rented. The costs of items that have been purchased (two of the teletypewriters) have been calculated on the basis of a five-year amortization.

The medium-speed printer includes the following components: (1) Bright printer; (2) GTE Novar 5-41 teletypewriter; (3) Telecommunication Dataset.

The costs of the acoustic couplers have been included. Rental costs include the required communication lines. Since the equipment is also used presently for further developmental purposes, the percentage of actual use has been estimated.

Salaries. The salaries included represent those of the personnel directly involved with the processing of data through keyboarding, as well as those involved with the acquisitions department in general. Though the cataloging of books through the OCLC system is directly integrated into the sequence of operations of the acquisitions system, this aspect of processing has been ignored.

The amount of time required for keyboarding is indicated by the number of operators working on the system. Since several operators use the keyboards on a part-time basis, the time is stated in terms of full-time equivalents, as follows:

1. Two full-time employees are required in the acquisitions department. Their functions include: 2
   (a) input of new orders and standing orders;
   (b) correction of errors;
   (c) updating of the order file;
   (d) running of the printing program for mailing orders and for error printouts;
   (e) updating of the fund and vendor files.
2. One half-time operator is required for invoice and call number posting. $^1/_2$
3. One full-time operator does OCLC scanning. 1

   Total $3^1/_2$

Computer Costs. Because of their significance for a system design, the cost figures for machine operation have been broken down into their various components.[11]

Presently the total memory space used for the data files and the programs for the entire system is 1.25 million words. All programs operate within a core limit of 16,000 words.

The most costly operations demanded of the computer are probably the printout of the following items: the daily ORSCAN and STSCAN, the supplement to the in-process list, the claim letters, the order slips, the vendor list, and above all, the weekly printing of the in-process list.

Details of the cost analysis are given in Table 2 and a summary of monthly charges and unit costs in Table 3. For comparison, the corresponding costs for the former manual operation are given in Table 4.

The cost per unit processed by the automated system is $8.75, while that for the manual system is estimated to presently be $5.21. The latter figure is somewhat lower than that indicated in Hayes and Becker for "burdened cost."[12]

In view of these results, the conclusion that automation does not decrease costs initially is verified. However, since growth in the size of the library and in the volume of material to be processed was anticipated, the increasing size of the files was expected to exceed the capacity of a manual system to function effectively. The advantages of an automated system, which would allow substantial growth without impairing the functioning of the system and without substantial increases in operating costs, were compelling enough to trigger the decision to computerize the system, since economic feasibility was not a major factor in the choice.

Table 2

COST ANALYSIS, AUTOMATED SYSTEM,
ACQUISITIONS DEPARTMENT

Developmental Costs

Item	Annual Cost	Total Cost	Monthly Charge
Salary/chief of automation	$11,500	$5,750	$96
Salaries/2 student programmers	4,600 ea.	4,600	77
Computer costs	38,400	19,200	320
Total			$493

Installation Costs

Four months parallel operation	$4,000/mo.	$16,000	$270

Operational Costs

Equipment	Monthly Rental	% Use	Monthly Charge
Bright printer and Nova	$400	50	$200
Tel. Dataset	70	50	35
1 Model 33 TTY	59	75	44
1 Sugarman CRT	80	100	80
1 Beehive CRT	94	100	94
3 Acoustic Couplers	45	100	45
Total			$498

Salaries

Position	Mean Annual Salary	Monthly Charge
Selection, Searching:		
5 Selection Officers	$10,000 (ea.)	$4,167
2 Searchers	6,000	1,000
Automation:		
Chief of Automation	11,500	957
Assistant	10,000	833
Ordering, Updating,		
Receiving,		
Fund Accounting:		
2.5 Employees	5,000	1,040
Others:		
1.5 Supervisors	10,000	1,250
4 Employees	5,000 (ea.)	1,667
1 Student, 40 hrs/week	$2/hr.	333
Total		$11,247

Computer Time and Costs

Computer	Rate	Monthly Average Use	Monthly Charge*
Terminal-Model 33†	1.40/hr.	262 hrs.	$347
Terminal-CRT†	2.55/hr.	270 hrs.	655
Terminal-Line Printer†	5.95/hr.	21 hrs.	118
Foreground CPU sec.	0.04/sec.	8497 sec.	323
Background CPU sec.	0.04/sec.	34,400 sec.	1307
Foreground I/O units	0.00055/un.	429,000 units	223
Background I/O units	0.00055/un.	768,000 units	402
Storage units#	0.35/unit	1,300 units	432
Print lines	0.0005/line	380,000 lines	180
Total			$3987

NOTES: *Actual cost less 5% for other development uses.
        †Terminal charges based on hours of actual connection to computer.
        #One storage unit = 1,000 words.

Table 3

SUMMARY, MONTHLY CHARGES AND UNIT COSTS

Cost Category	Monthly Charge	Unit Cost*
Development Costs	$493	$0.20
Installation Costs	270	0.11
Operational Costs:		
Equipment	498	0.20
Salaries	11,247	4.50
Computer Costs	3,987	1.60
Administrative Costs at		
12.5% of Salaries	1,406	0.56
Overhead at 35% Salaries	3,940	1.58
	Total	$8.75

NOTES: *Unit Cost based on 2,500 units processed per month.

Table 4

COST ANALYSIS, MANUAL SYSTEM,
ACQUISITIONS DEPARTMENT

Item	Mean Annual Salary	Monthly Charge	Unit Cost
Salaries:			
Selection Officers			
+ Supervisor (6)	$10,000 (ea.)	5,000	
3 Searchers	6,000 (ea.)	1,500	
6 Employees	5,000 (ea.)	2,500	
4 Students, 40 hrs./wk.	$2/hr.	1,333	
Total salaries		$10,333	$4.14
Administrative Costs			
at 15% Salaries			0.62
Overhead at 35% Salaries			1.45
		Total	$6.21

OBSERVATIONS

This on-line, real-time acquisitions system has achieved its major objectives. It has eliminated several large manual files; it has eliminated a number of repetitive clerical tasks; it has made available up-to-date information on the status of on-order and in-process books; it has helped to reduce delays in cataloging, and it has provided accurate and current fund accounting.

The availability of the very substantial resources of the Kiewit Computational Center has facilitated the development and successful operation of this system.

The system illustrates what may become an axiom about library computer systems, namely: What a librarian originally thinks he or she wants from a system is not, in fact, what he or she needs. Of course, experience will ultimately reveal the librarian's real needs. Experience with the present system has demonstrated that the need for on-line access varies greatly with the processing status of each particular order. For example, once a book has been checked in on the system and placed in a cataloging backlog to await catalog copy, the need for complete on-line information about the order is sharply reduced. When catalog copy becomes available and the book is removed from the backlog for cataloging, then full on-line information is again desirable. In view of this fact, future plans call for an abbreviated entry to be maintained on-line while an item is in the processing backlog, with the full record stored off-line. These off-line records will be available for overnight retrieval and restoration to full on-line status. This feature is expected to reduce on-line storage requirements by 20 to 25 percent.

Similarly, experience has shown that the amount of on-line storage space for vendor files could be reduced by retaining on-line only those vendors who handle a substantial volume of orders. A master list of all vendors could be established, but only a list of active vendors needs to be retained on-line.

Automation of the acquisitions and processing departments has greatly reduced the space required for files and the time required for manual filing. It has enabled the library to eliminate manual files in the acquisitions department and to discontinue the filing of temporary catalog slips in the public catalog. The system, nevertheless, provides immediate and easy access to information about the current status of books ordered or funds expended.

The cost analysis of the system reveals that the computerized system is more expensive than the library's manual system would be by more than $2.50 per unit processed. Although the system has speeded the processing of new materials and has furnished more rapid and convenient fiscal reports and control, a tauter, less complex system could provide adequate speed and control at a substantially lower cost. While the cost per item processed rises as the size of the library's holdings increases (and explains somewhat the higher processing costs in large libraries), librarians in these big systems must not be complacent when they find their processing costs, either manual or computerized, exceeding the purchase price of library materials. They must make more vigorous efforts to clarify and simplify their operations until they have achieved significant cost reductions. Over a generation ago, Turin demonstrated in the field of logic that any problem that has a solution can be restated so that it can be solved by a simpler technique. Librarians are far from reaching the simplest way of doing things. Much superfluous activity and much unnecessary record keeping can still be eliminated in libraries. Such reduction to the essential will not reduce library service, but will rather lead to more effective utilization of library resources. The cost squeeze on libraries may ultimately prove highly beneficial because it will squeeze extraneous elements from both manual and computerized systems. It would appear that such squeezing would bring benefits to the Dartmouth system.

NOTES

1. William B. Meredith, "Automation in the Dartmouth College Libraries," *Dartmouth College Library Bulletin*, 13 (November 1972), 41.
2. "The Kiewit Computation Center and the Dartmouth Time-Sharing System" (pamphlet).
3. William B. Meredith, pp. 39–44.
4. This diagram was supplied by Donald L. Saporito, chief of automation services, Dartmouth College Library.
5. "DCL Acquisitions System: Manual of Program Operations." Liberal use of information from this source has been made throughout this case study.
6. William J. Baumel, "On the Economics of Library Operation, a Mathematica Report," *Libraries at Large*, ed. Douglas M. Knight (New York: R. R. Bowker, 1969), p. 170.
7. John H. Wilson, Jr., "Costs, Budgeting, and Economics of Information Processing," *Annual Review of Information Science and Technology*, 7, (Washington, D.C.: American Society for Information Science), p. 41.
8. Robert M. Hayes and Joseph Becker, *Handbook of Data Processing for Libraries* (New York: Becker and Hayes/John Wiley, 1970).
9. *The Dartmouth College Library Statistical Report 1971–1972*, p. 9.
10. Bronson Price, *Library Statistics of Colleges and Universities* (Washington, D.C.: U.S. Government Printing Office, June 1970).
11. Donald L. Saporito, chief of automation services, provided the detailed monthly operation figures.
12. Hayes and Becker, p. 102.

ACKNOWLEDGMENTS

The assistance of Monique C. Cleland in the preparation of this case study is acknowledged with appreciation. Thanks are also extended to William B. Meredith, associate director, Library Services, Dartmouth College, and Donald L. Saporito, chief of automation services, Dartmouth College, for providing help and information.

Summary
and Observations

The 20 case studies in this volume describe six circulation, eight serials, and six acquisitions systems. Both batch-process and on-line systems are represented in each category. Most of the systems provide features not available in previous manual operations.

CIRCULATION SYSTEMS

A summary of the six circulation systems is set forth in Table 1.

The Brockton system (1) utilizes machine-readable student ID and book cards, affords no computer-controlled overdue or fine notices, prints weekly circulation reports, and appears to have been launched simply because a cen-

Table 1
CIRCULATION SYSTEMS

Library	Daily Circs.	Computer	Type	Cost/Circ.
1. Brockton	90	Univac 9300	Batch	$ .28
2. Michigan	1,000	IBM 360/67	Batch	.22
3. Harvard	1,000	IBM 360/30	Batch	.56
4. British Columbia	3,000	Honeywell 2000	Batch	.42
5. Eastern Illinois	320	IBM 360/50	On-line	.76
6. Northwestern	1,100	IBM 370/135	On-line	$ .67

tral computer facility was available. The result was a poor match between the library's needs and the system.

The Michigan system (2) uses punched student ID and book cards, includes overdue and fine notices, prints daily, weekly, and periodic reports as desired, and furnishes rapid, accurate, and convenient control of the fast turn-around of closed reserve books. Queuing is held to a minimum. The previous manual system could not handle 1,000 circulations per day as this system does. Circulation statistics provide useful insight for library management. The computer system is well matched to the library's requirements.

The Harvard system (3) requires handwritten charge cards because identification cards are not machine-readable and the library does not use book cards. Materials that are at the bindery, in departmental libraries, out on interlibrary loan, etc., are listed in the computer circulation record. The fact that the system is likely to be replaced in the near future suggests that it has proved less than fully satisfactory.

The British Columbia system (4) handles over 3,000 circulations per day, includes fine, call-in, and overdue notices, prints statistics, and runs analytical programs, for about $.42 per circulation. This system not only handles a scale of activity that would defeat a manual operation, but provides insights for the relocation and acquisition of materials that are in heavy demand. It demonstrates the capacity of a computer system to perform a range of functions beyond the reach of a manual system and to do so for a viable cost.

The Eastern Illinois on-line system (5) permits inquiry of the computer file via a cathode-ray-tube (CRT) display terminal. It prints fine and overdue notices, places holds on circulating materials, and compiles statistics. The system may be overpowered for its present level of circulation activity. Costs per circulation will doubtless drop as the rate of circulation moves closer to 1,000 per day.

The Northwestern on-line library system (6) permits self-service charging with machine-readable identification and book cards, inquiry via an IBM 2740 terminal with printed response, and an on-going inventory of the collection. The emphasis has been on improved service rather than management data or statistics. The added conveniences and services provided by the Eastern Illinois and Northwestern on-line systems naturally cost more than the lesser services of the batch systems.

The unit costs of these six circulation systems show that increases in cost are roughly in proportion to the increases in system features and services.

SERIALS SYSTEMS

A summary of the eight serials systems is set forth in Table 2.

Table 2

SERIALS SYSTEMS

Library	Serials Processed	Computer	Type	Cost
7. Swarthmore	2,200	IBM 1130	Batch	$40/mo.
8. SMCL	4,079	IBM Sys 3	Batch	$51.10/copy
9. San Francisco	10,000	IBM 370/100	Batch	$6/title
10. M.I.T. Lincoln Lab	7,200	IBM 360/67	Batch	$.29/doc.
11. Harvard Business School	2,600	IBM 370/145-155	Batch	$.74/issue
12. A.D. Little	300	IBM 360/40	Batch	$.25/issue
13. Tufts Serials	5,600	Honeywell 200	Batch	$.37/title
14. Tufts Medline	492	IBM 370/155	On-line	$2.55/search

The Swarthmore system (7) prints, by title and by subject, current lists of periodical titles in the science libraries. This uncomplicated system has improved service at very modest cost.

The SMCL system (8) produces 27 copies of a union list of periodical titles and holdings once a year. The libraries involved find it useful.

The San Francisco system (9) publishes 200 book catalogs of periodical holdings: title catalogs, twice a year; subject catalogs, once. The system affords the same level of bibliographic access at branch libraries that once was available only at the main library. The system is well-designed and effective.

The M.I.T. Lincoln Laboratory system (10) not only provides control of classified government documents, but controls acquisitions processing and circulation as well. The system is efficient and is proving very inexpensive for the library. Most of the costs, of course, are paid by nonlibrary departments.

The Harvard Business School system (11) produces lists of periodicals, issues publications regarding the library's serial holdings, and provides control over the handling of serials. The system is reasonably sophisticated and, in consequence, rather expensive.

The ADL routing slip system (12) provides for the distribution of 300 serials issues to 150 employees for less money than was required in the former manual system. It is a tidy and efficient system that will soon take on the task of distributing all periodicals to all employees at ADL. The system's capacity is sufficient to handle the enlarged assignment without change.

The Tufts serials system (13) produces a spiral-bound union list of serials, which is distributed to a number of campus libraries, university departments, and other Boston-area libraries. It affords modest services for a moderate cost.

The Tufts Medline system (14) permits on-line searches of the Medline data base via the State University of New York system. The number of searches has been rising rapidly each month since the system became operational. Costs per search are difficult to establish as the volume of activity has not yet stabilized.

The eight serials systems elude comparisons of either services, features, or costs. Each system stands alone in its uniqueness.

ACQUISITIONS SYSTEMS

A summary of the six acquisitions systems is set forth in Table 3.

The Northeastern system (15) is about half manual and half computerized. The system works reasonably well in preventing duplicate purchases and in recording the in-process status of materials. The system needs further study and improvement.

The University of Massachusetts system (16) is an efficient on-line operation that delivers order and vendor data as well as input for cataloging with dispatch and economy.

The Columbia system (17) is a carefully designed, developed, and implemented system that provides sophisticated records and control for all in-process and fiscal functions of acquisitions. It is operating with efficiency and economy.

The M.I.T. system (18) suffered from frequent changes in computers at the computer center. The system has been terminated not only for lack of funds,

Table 3

ACQUISITIONS SYSTEMS

Library	Ordered/ Week	Computer	Type	Cost
15. Northeastern	600	IBM 360/25	Batch	.62
16. Massachusetts	800	IBM 370/145	On-line Batch	2.55
17. Columbia	1,250	IBM 360/75-91	Batch	.93
18. M.I.T.	600	IBM 7094 IBM 360	Batch	2.20
19. Cleveland	2,400	CCSI LIBS 100	Mini- On-Line	.46
20. Dartmouth	625	Honeywell GE-635	On-line	8.75

but because reprogramming for the latest computer would take more time than the library staff could live with an inoperable system.

The Cleveland system (19), employing a new fully programmed and ready-to-run minicomputer, costs less than the former IBM system. The minicomputer is compact, efficient, accurate, fast, and totally under the library's control. It is also very inexpensive.

The Dartmouth system (20) was designed and implemented to provide on-line access to in-process and vendor files. This on-line capability, while desirable, is very expensive. It should be noted, however, that the cost figure for Dartmouth is a "burdened" cost and includes fringe benefits and overhead. These are not generally included in the cost figures of the other libraries. The system is perceptively designed, is operating successfully, and is providing luxury features for a cost that the library administration is willing to pay.

COSTS

Although unit costs have been given for each of the computer systems described in this book, and although these unit costs have been conscientiously computed in each case, they should not be compared without noting that they were not computed on a standard basis. Each library had a different way of determining how much of the personnel, equipment, and supply costs should be charged to the system. The figure for Dartmouth College (20) is most likely to represent actual costs for an on-line system.

In many of the cases it is not known whether computer system costs are greater than manual system costs because comparative costs are unavailable. In two cases (12 and 19), the costs are lower than in the previous system. In a number of cases (2, 3, 4, 6, 9, 15, 16, 17, 18, 19, and 20), the level of activity required the installation of a computer system regardless of costs. In these cases, the costs of a computer system, while an important consideration, were not considered apart from other essential considerations, such as needs for greater processing control, increased accuracy, better service, more speed, or more adequate feedback.

CONSIDERATIONS

Of course, the choice confronting librarians today is not simply between a manual and a computer system. There are many types and levels of both manual and computer systems. Even as there are libraries of different size, quality, and budget, there are systems with different capacity, capability, and cost. Library systems should match the quality of the library. While manual systems may adequately serve a small library, it is likely that a large and heavily used library will require sophisticated computer systems.

An important consideration in the selection of an appropriate library system is the requisite speed of service. While a businessman could travel a long distance far less expensively than by jet plane, the value of his time usually argues against his traveling on the ground. Those deciding whether or not to computerize a library function should consider the extent to which a computer system will save library patrons' time. The system that provides the best fit between the patron's needs and the library's services should win acceptance by both patrons and librarians. The cheapest operation is seldom, if ever, the best. While libraries should be run in a cost/effective manner, they need not be run in a poverty-stricken fashion.

In only one of the situations that were examined were the librarians desirous of returning to manual systems. In most systems where a suitable match between the library's requirements and the computer system was not achieved, the librarians were more desirous of adjusting the system than abandoning it.

As indicated earlier, minicomputer systems offer substantial economies for libraries with acquisitions of less than 100,000 items (or 30,000 titles) per year. Not only are significant advantages over manual systems in speed, accuracy, and fiscal control achieved, but repetitive manual operations are sharply reduced. In addition, the library retains its autonomy and complete control over the system.

Allen B. Veaner writes that there are three major, practical reasons for automating library functions:

1. To do something less expensively, more accurately, or more rapidly;
2. To do something that can no longer be done effectively in the manual system because of increased complexity or overwhelming volume of operations;
3. To perform some function that cannot now be performed in the manual system—providing always that the administrator actually wants to perform the new service, has the resources to pay for it, and is not endangering the performance of existing services for which there is an established demand.[1]

Librarians with reasons such as these for computerizing a library operation are likely to experience success. If, in their planning, they are able to match the computer system to their requirements, they are very likely to achieve viable systems. They may, in fact, actually get what they pay for, and want what they get.

There is no question that there have been some mismatches between library needs and computer systems in the past. Some of these mismatches are difficult to excuse. However, there have been a very substantial number of genuine successes, some of which have been described in this book. There certainly are sufficient documented successes to refute Ellsworth Mason's assertion that the "computer is not for library use . . . and . . . should be stamped out." As a matter of fact, with the increasing sophistication and seasoning of librarians, the coming decade should see a great many more successful library computer systems.

NOTE

1. Allen B. Veaner, "Major Decision Points in Library Automation," *College and Research Libraries*, 31 (September 1970), 303–304.

Table of Computers Used in Case Studies

Listed here are the systems, computers, and programming language used at each library described. The number in parentheses following the library name is the chapter number.

Library	System	Computer	Language
British Columbia, University of (4)	Circulation	Honeywell 2000 (2)	Cobol
Brockton High School (1)	Circulation	Univac 9300	Cobol
Cleveland Public (19)	Acquisitions	CLSI Libs 100	Flirt
Columbia University (17)	Acquisitions	IBM 360/75-91	PL/1, 5
Dartmouth College (20)	Acquisitions	Honeywell GE-635	Basic
Eastern Illinois University (5)	Circulation	IBM 360/50	PL/1, F
Harvard University, Baker (11)	Serials	IBM 360/145-155	Cobol
Harvard University, Widener (3)	Circulation	IBM 360/30	Autocoder
Little, A.D., Inc. (12)	Serials	IBM 360/40	Cobol
M.I.T. Libraries (18)	Acquisitions	IBM 7094 & 360	MAD, FAP
M.I.T., Lincoln Laboratory (10)	Serials	IBM 360/67	Cobol
Massachusetts, University of (16)	Acquisitions	IBM 370/145	Faster Basic & Cobol
Michigan, University of (2)	Circulation	IBM 360/67	Cobol
Northeastern University (15)	Acquisitions	IBM 360/25	Cobol

Northwestern University (6)	Circulation	IBM 370/135	
San Francisco Public (9)	Serials	IBM 370/100 (2), 360/20	
Southeastern Massachusetts Cooperating Libraries (8)	Serials	IBM System 3	RPG II
Swarthmore (7)	Serials	IBM 1130	Fortran
Tufts University (13)	Serials	Honeywell 200	Cobol D
Tufts Medical and Dental (14)	Serials	IBM 370/155	